THE FOUNDATION OF JOY

THE FOUNDATION OF JOY

Assurance in the Theology of John Flavel

Jeff Strickland

Reformation Heritage Books

Grand Rapids, Michigan

The Foundation of Joy
© 2025 by Jeff Strickland

All rights reserved. No part of this book may be used or reproduced in any manner whatsoever without written permission except in the case of brief quotations embodied in critical articles and reviews. Direct your requests to the publisher at the following addresses:

Reformation Heritage Books
3070 29th St. SE
Grand Rapids, MI 49512
616–977–0889
orders@heritagebooks.org
www.heritagebooks.org

Printed in the United States of America
25 26 27 28 29 30/10 9 8 7 6 5 4 3 2 1

Library of Congress Cataloging-in-Publication Data

Names: Strickland, Jeff (Pastor) author.
Title: The foundation of joy : assurance in the theology of John Flavel / Jeff
    Strickland.
Description: Grand Rapids, Michigan : Reformation Heritage Books, [2025] |
    Includes bibliographical references. | Summary: "An investigation of the
    link between John Flavel's understanding of assurance of salvation and
    joy"— Provided by publisher.
Identifiers: LCCN 2024051892 (print) | LCCN 2024051893 (ebook) |
    ISBN 9798886861617 (paperback) | ISBN 9798886861624 (epub)
Subjects: LCSH: Flavel, John, 1630?-1691. | Puritans—Doctrines—History. |
    Assurance (Theology) | Joy—Religious aspects—Puritans.
Classification: LCC BX9339.F53 S77 2025 (print) | LCC BX9339.F53 (ebook) |
    DDC 230/.59092—dc23/eng/20241219
LC record available at https://lccn.loc.gov/2024051892
LC ebook record available at https://lccn.loc.gov/2024051893

For my wife,
Stephanie
You are such a gift from the Lord,
and this work is the fruit of your steadfast support
and unwavering belief.

For our two little men,
Carson Nolan and Knox William
I pray that you both will know Christ
and His incomparable joy.

Table of Contents

Preface

This work was made possible only due to the faithful and generous help of so many. My doctoral supervisor, Dr. Stephen Yuille, who first introduced me to John Flavel, proved to be a most dependable and valuable guide throughout the entirety of this process. I am truly grateful for his gifts, his time, and his friendship. I am also indebted to the diligent scholars of Flavel who have gone before me—especially Brian Cosby, Adam Embry, Clifford Boone, and Nathan Parker; their research and feedback have been immensely beneficial. Men like Dr. Joel Beeke, Dr. Don Whitney, Dr. Shawn Wright, and many others have shaped both me and this work greatly. Additionally, I cannot imagine completing a work like this one at any institution other than Southern Seminary, which God has used enormously for my good.

Finally, this project has required great sacrifice from my wife, Stephanie, and our two boys. Their love, patience, and encouragement has been exemplary. It is my joy to celebrate this accomplishment with them.

—Jeff Strickland

Chapter 1

Introduction

"Spirituality," as Alister McGrath explains, "is the outworking in real life of a person's religious faith—what a person does with what they believe."[1] In other words, spirituality is the experience of theology in everyday life. At times, it is difficult to ascertain precisely how a particular theological understanding affects the believer's life. In the case of Christian assurance, however, this relationship is abundantly clear. Rare is the believer who, upon personal reflection, does not ask, "Am I really saved?" This is, in one sense, the all-important question of the Christian life. Its answer lies at the foundation of the believer's hope and joy. Uncertainty here generates unrest and distress, while confidence enlivens and supports the soul in the midst of the most trying circumstances.

Given its significance to the Christian life, it is unfortunate that this doctrine has been mired in confusion and controversy throughout much of the church's history.[2] Because of its inextricable relationship

---

1. Alister E. McGrath, *Christian Spirituality: An Introduction* (Oxford: Blackwell, 1999), 2.

2. The varying views on assurance can be divided into three primary categories (with variations within each). The first belongs to the Roman Catholic Church. For all intents and purposes, it denies any normative experience of assurance. This is due, in part, to the belief that salvation may be lost, and that final perseverance is rarely, if ever, guaranteed. The Council of Trent declares, "No one, moreover, as long as he is in this mortal life, ought so far to presume as regards the secret mystery of divine predestination, as to determine for certain that he is assuredly in the number of the predestinate; as if it were true, that he that is justified, either cannot sin any more, or if he does sin, that he ought to promise himself an assured repentance; for except by special revelation, it cannot be known whom God has chosen unto himself." Philip Schaff and David S. Schaff, eds., *The Creeds of Christendom: With a History and*

to other core doctrines, the doctrine of assurance is, in the words of Matthew Pinson, "a handy gauge of one's theological vantage point."[3] He adds, "The way people handle this subject tells a great deal about where they locate themselves on the theological spectrum."[4] It follows, therefore, that this doctrine also proves to be an excellent gauge of one's spirituality. It acts as a signpost, for it reveals one's theological perspective while at the same time displaying what lies at the core of his or her vision of the Christian life. As such, it proves to be an important foundation stone in the study of spirituality.

The evidence of this assertion is on display in the Puritan movement.[5] It is possible to study Puritanism from ecclesiastical, political, and theological vantage points, yet at its center it was primarily "a spiritual movement, passionately concerned with God and godliness."[6] Behind this passion for God and godliness stands the doctrine of

---

Critical Notes (Grand Rapids: Baker, 2007), 2:103. For more on this, see Avery Dulles, *The Assurance of Things Hoped For: A Theology of Christian Faith* (Oxford: Oxford University Press, 1994); and Edward J. Gratsch, ed., *Principles of Catholic Theology: A Synthesis of Dogma and Morals* (New York: Alba House, 1981). The second category belongs to Calvinistic Protestantism. It disagrees with Roman Catholicism, affirming that assurance of salvation is both possible and normative for the Christian. Believing that the Bible teaches that Christians persevere to the end, it sees assurance as one of the great blessings of life in Christ, even though many believers may struggle to experience it. For more on this, see Louis Berkhof, *The Assurance of Faith* (Grand Rapids: Eerdmans, 1939); Robert A. Peterson, *Our Secure Salvation: Preservation and Apostasy* (Phillipsburg, N.J.: P&R, 2009); Joel R. Beeke, *Knowing and Growing in Assurance of Faith* (Fearn, Scotland: Christian Focus, 2017); and Donald S. Whitney, *How Can I Be Sure I'm a Christian? The Satisfying Certainty of Eternal Life* (Colorado Springs: NavPress, 2019). The third category is Arminian Protestantism, which maintains that while assurance of present salvation is standard for a believer, assurance of final salvation is not. Believers can fall away from Christ and thus lose their salvation. For more on this, see Mark A. Noll, "John Wesley and the Doctrine of Assurance," *Bibliotheca Sacra* 132, no. 526 (April 1975): 161–78; Michael Scott Horton and J. Matthew Pinson, eds., *Four Views on Eternal Security* (Grand Rapids: Zondervan, 2002); and I. Howard Marshall, *Kept by the Power of God: A Study of Perseverance and Falling Away* (Minneapolis: Bethany Fellowship, 1974).

3. Horton and Pinson, *Four Views*, 7.

4. Horton and Pinson, *Four Views*, 7.

5. See chapter 2 of this volume.

6. J. I. Packer, *A Quest for Godliness: A Puritan Vision of the Christian Life* (Wheaton, Ill.: Crossway, 1990), 28. See also J. Stephen Yuille, *Puritan Spirituality: The Fear of God in the Affective Theology of George Swinnock* (Eugene, Ore.: Wipf & Stock, 2007), 5–17.

assurance. As R. M. Hawkes notes, "In English Puritan theology, the doctrine of assurance is of abiding importance. Any description of the aims of Puritanism must include…reforming the hearts of men.… [This] internal reformation of the Puritan's pilgrim soul was to seek an assured faith following God's revealed way to himself."[7] The Puritans understood the importance of rightly handling the doctrine of assurance, as evidenced by the significant place it occupies in their thought and practice.[8] A case in point is the seventeenth-century pastor, John Flavel (1630–1691).

This book focuses on Flavel for two chief reasons. The first is the extent to which the doctrine of assurance informs Flavel's spirituality.[9] Not only is this emphasis evident in his teaching and preaching (rarely does he preach or write without some acknowledgment of assurance) but it is also extremely prevalent in his life. As one anonymous biographer observes,

> These things being previously dispatched, he tried himself by the scripture marks of sincerity and regeneration; by this means he attained to a well-grounded assurance, the ravishing comforts of which were many times shed abroad in his soul; this made him a powerful and successful preacher, as one who spoke from his own heart to those of others.[10]

Flavel only preached what he first applied to himself. He powerfully expounded the truths of the gospel as one who had been transformed by them. Because of his experience of the joy of a well-grounded assurance, Flavel labored throughout his ministry to

---

7. R. M. Hawkes, "The Logic of Assurance in English Puritan Theology," *The Westminster Theological Journal* 52, no. 2 (September 1990): 248.

8. For example, see Joel R. Beeke, *Assurance of Faith: Calvin, English Puritanism, and the Dutch Second Reformation*, American University Studies 89 (New York: P. Lang, 1991), 192–93nn8–9.

9. For example, Flavel notes this doctrine throughout his forty-two sermons within *The Fountain of Life*: the introductory epistle; sermons 3, 6, 8, 10, 13, 15, 16, 20, 21, 23, 25, 26, 28, 36, 38, 39, 42. See John Flavel, *The Fountain of Life: A Display of Christ in His Essential and Mediatorial Glory*, in *Works of John Flavel*, vol. 1 (1820; repr., Edinburgh: Banner of Truth Trust, 2015).

10. "The Life of the Late Rev. Mr. John Flavel, Minister of Dartmouth," in *Works of John Flavel* (1820; repr., Edinburgh: Banner of Truth Trust, 2015), 1:xi–xii.

impress upon his flock the need for an experience of assurance of salvation in Christ.

The second reason for choosing Flavel is his relative anonymity. The lack of research into his life and ministry is astounding, especially considering the extent of his influence in his own day. One of his congregants declared,

> I could say much, though not enough, of the excellency of his preaching; of his seasonable, suitable, and spiritual matter; of his plain expositions of scripture, his taking method, his genuine and natural deductions, his convincing arguments, his clear and powerful demonstrations, his heart-searching applications, and his comfortable supports to those that were afflicted in conscience. In short that person must have a very soft head, or a very hard heart, or both, that could sit under his ministry unaffected.[11]

Flavel's influence was not limited to his local congregation. Anthony à Wood (1632–1695), a historian and contemporary, noted that Flavel obtained "more disciples than ever John Owen the Independent, or Richard Baxter the Presbyterian did."[12] Flavel was recognized not only as a preacher but as a writer—one of his biographers and friends, John Galpine (n.d.), noted that he was "famous among the writers of this age."[13] Galpine tells the story of a London bookstore owner in 1673, who encountered a young gentleman in search of playbooks. The owner gave one of Flavel's works to the man. The young man threatened to burn the book and wanted nothing to do with it. Eventually, he took it, and a month later he returned to the store, exclaiming, "Sir, I most heartily thank you for putting this book into my hands; I bless God that moved you to do it, it hath saved my soul; blessed be God that ever I came into your shop."[14] As

---

11. "Life of the Late," 1:vi.

12. Anthony à Wood, *Athenae Oxonienses: An Exact History of All the Writers and Bishops Who Have Had Their Education in the University of Oxford* (New York: Lackington, Hughes, Harding, et al., 1820), 4:323.

13. John Galpine, "A Short Life of John Flavel," in *Flavel, the Quaker, and the Crown: John Flavel, Clement Lake, and Religious Liberty in Seventeenth-Century England* (Cambridge, Mass.: Rhwhym Books, 2000), 13.

14. "Life of the Late," 1:xiv.

the story goes, the young man purchased a hundred of Flavel's books to distribute among the poor.

Flavel's influence was also well documented by his opponents. Edmund Elys (1633–1708), a critic and contemporary, writes, "Sir, I congratulate to you the virtue of your good design for the service of the church, & I hope I shall be able to give you some assistance in it especially in reference to these three enemies of the church whose writings have made so much noise in the world, Dr. Owen, R. Baxter, & John Flavel."[15] Elys was right to speak of "the world" in his critique, for Flavel's ministry was known, not only in England but across the Atlantic in New England. As Increase Mather (1639–1723) explains in the preface to one of Flavel's works: "The worthy author of the discourse emitted herewith, is one whose praise in the gospel is throughout all churches. His other books have made his name precious and famous in *both Englands*."[16]

Flavel's influence not only crossed oceans but spanned generations, as seen in the writings of the two towers of the First Great Awakening, Jonathan Edwards (1703–1758) and George Whitefield (1714–1770). Edwards frequently quotes Flavel in his famous work *Religious Affections*, and Whitefield not only carried Flavel's works on his travels but said that they were "enquired after, and bought up, more and more every day."[17]

Flavel's life and ministry clearly deserve more attention and consideration. The precision of his theological understanding, the illustrative and applicative style of his preaching, and the richness of his deep biblical spirituality should make him as popular today as he was in his own day and in the immediate generations that followed him. This book seeks to contribute to the recovery of this neglected Puritan by delving into the essence of his spirituality—namely, what he perceived to be the joy of assurance.

---

15. Clifford B. Boone, *Puritan Evangelism: Preaching for Conversion in Late Seventeenth Century English Puritanism as Seen in the Works of John Flavel* (London: Paternoster, 2013), 37.

16. Increase Mather, preface to John Flavel, *England's Duty under the Present Gospel Liberty*, in *Works*, 4:16. Italics in the original.

17. George Whitefield, quoted in Iain H. Murray, *The Puritan Hope: Revival and the Interpretation of Prophecy* (Edinburgh: Banner of Truth Trust, 1971), 143.

No Longer Lost, but Lacking

With the resurgence of Puritan studies over the past fifty years, there has been some renewed interest in Flavel. In terms of academic studies, there are five doctoral dissertations. The first was produced by Kwai Chang in 1952. He presents a helpful biographical summary of Flavel's life, ministry, and teaching.[18] As the first academic contribution to this field of study, Chang's thesis represents a solid introduction, but says little about Flavel's spirituality or understanding of assurance. John Thomas produced the second Flavel dissertation in 2007, analyzing Flavel's preaching.[19] Employing James Shaddix's understanding of application, Thomas documents Flavel's use of application in his sermons.[20] While Flavel's preaching is significant to understanding his spirituality, Thomas's analysis is narrow in focus and lends little to this study or to research on Flavel as a whole.

Of far greater significance is the third dissertation, produced by Clifford Boone in 2009. It has been published as *Puritan Evangelism: Preaching for Conversion in Late Seventeenth-Century English Puritanism as seen in the Works of John Flavel.* Boone's research centers on Flavel's evangelistic zeal and seeks to show the relationship between his theological convictions and homiletic style. Boone writes, "Our contention is that within the generally accepted homiletic framework of this tradition the Puritan preacher's understanding of the effectual call was the main factor that influenced the content, arrangement, and presentation of his sermons to the unconverted."[21] After placing his study in the larger context of Flavel's ministry and Puritan preaching, Boone devotes much of his work to explaining Flavel's doctrines of man, sin, and effectual call, and how these directly influenced the content and style of Flavel's preaching. His work provides a helpful overview of Puritan preaching, offers useful insights into Flavel's life and ministry, and establishes the foundation for further study of his

---

18. Kwai Sing Chang, "John Flavel of Dartmouth, 1630–1691" (PhD diss., University of Edinburgh, 1952).

19. John Thomas Jr., "An Analysis of the Use of Application in the Preaching of John Flavel" (PhD diss., New Orleans Baptist Theological Seminary, 2007).

20. Jim Shaddix, *The Passion Driven Sermon: Changing the Way Pastors Preach and Congregations Listen* (Nashville: Broadman & Holman, 2003).

21. Boone, *Puritan Evangelism*, 3.

understanding and practice of theology. Boone's thesis represents an important building block in the study of Flavel but touches very little on his spirituality.

The fourth dissertation, written in 2012, is Brian Cosby's "The Theology of Suffering and Sovereignty as Seen in the Writings and Ministry of John Flavel."[22] Cosby's work presents Flavel's teaching on one of the most critical concerns of the Christian life—namely, the relationship between human suffering and divine sovereignty. Cosby argues two primary theses. First, he asserts, "Flavel quantitatively and pastorally developed the theology of the Westminster Assembly by articulating an understanding of human suffering and divine sovereignty with greater theological precision and pastoral application."[23] Second, he contends, "Flavel believed that human suffering and divine sovereignty are not two unrelated concepts, but rather exist together as theologically coherent realities."[24] Cosby defends these two theses by exploring the theology of suffering and sovereignty first in the great corpus of Puritan thinking, then in Flavel's writing, and finally in Flavel's ministry to the suffering. The result is a clear presentation of a motif that was central to Flavel's life. Cosby's work is of great benefit to the present work. Not only does he demonstrate Flavel's indebtedness to the Westminster divines and John Calvin, he also devotes an entire chapter to Flavel's understanding of the doctrine of assurance, demonstrating its significance in his ministry. This work provides a foundation upon which to build, as well as the rationale for investigating the relationship between Flavel's doctrine of assurance and the pursuit of joy.

The final dissertation was completed by Nathan Parker in 2013: "Proselytisation and Apocalypticism in the British Atlantic World: The Theology of John Flavel."[25] Parker focuses on Flavel's theology of conversion and how it shaped his evangelistic preaching. While there

---

22. Brian H. Cosby, "The Theology of Suffering and Sovereignty as Seen in the Writings and Ministry of John Flavel, ca. 1630–1691" (PhD diss., Australian College of Theology, 2012).

23. Cosby, "Theology of Suffering," 11.

24. Cosby, "Theology of Suffering," 11–12.

25. Nathan Thomas Parker, "Proselytisation and Apocalypticism in the British Atlantic World: The Theology of John Flavel" (PhD diss., Durham University, 2013).

is some overlap with Boone's work, Parker charts a different course in terms of his emphasis. In his work, he interacts with Flavel's doctrine of assurance and its significance for his ministry. He writes, "Flavel perhaps spoke more about assurance than any other facet of Christian salvation."[26] Parker notes the significance of assurance for Flavel's theology and ministry, but he does not explore its centrality to understanding Flavel's spirituality.

In addition to these dissertations, there are several books and theses on Flavel.[27] Of particular significance is Adam Embry's book, *Keeper of the Great Seal of Heaven*, which explores Flavel's understanding of the sealing of the Holy Spirit in detail.[28] "This book," writes Embry, "specifically examines John Flavel's (1627–1691) view of sealing of the Spirit, that is, assurance of salvation, in relation to his life and writings."[29] He describes Flavel's view of the Holy Spirit, specifically His work of sealing. Embry concludes with a brief discussion of the impact of Flavel's thought on future generations, especially those within the evangelical movement. Embry helpfully shows the connection between Flavel's doctrine of the Spirit and his understanding of assurance. His work, along with Cosby's, provides the most in-depth look into Flavel's conception of assurance. Embry's focus, however, is especially on Flavel's notion of the sealing of the Spirit and how it relates to the idea of the immediate witness of the Holy Spirit as expressed by certain Puritan

---

26. Parker, "Proselytisation," 132n387.

27. For example, see Stephen Yuille, *The Inner Sanctum of Puritan Piety: John Flavel's Doctrine of Mystical Union with Christ* (Grand Rapids: Reformation Heritage Books, 2007); Brian H. Cosby, *John Flavel: Puritan Life and Thought in Stuart England* (Lanham, Md.: Lexington Books, 2014); Brian H. Cosby, *Suffering and Sovereignty: John Flavel and the Puritans on Afflictive Providence* (Grand Rapids: Reformation Heritage Books, 2012); and Adam Embry, *An Honest, Well-Experienced Heart: The Piety of John Flavel*, Profiles in Reformed Spirituality (Grand Rapids: Reformation Heritage Books, 2012). Additionally, two Master's theses have been completed on Flavel in recent years: Lewis James Greenwood Allen, "The Theologian as Pastor: The Life, Times and Ministry of John Flavel" (ThM thesis, Westminster Theological Seminary, 2014); Douglas McCallum, "The Christology of John Flavel" (ThM thesis, Westminster Theological Seminary, 2017).

28. Adam Embry, *Keeper of the Great Seal of Heaven: Sealing of the Spirit in the Life and Thought of John Flavel* (Grand Rapids: Reformation Heritage Books, 2011).

29. Embry, *Keeper*, 1.

writers.[30] Thus, Embry provides little discussion of how assurance connects to Flavel's spirituality or understanding of joy.

Flavel's Heart: His Spirituality

Though John Flavel is no longer the "lost Puritan," there is still much of this faithful pastor's life and theology to bring to light.[31] This book seeks to contribute to a fuller understanding of Flavel by considering an area largely ignored—his spirituality. Here, one is able to see into the very heart of Flavel and his ministry. The main goal of this work, then, is to demonstrate the link between Flavel's understanding of the doctrine of assurance and the pursuit of joy. The aim is to see that joy is the hallmark of his spirituality, and that such joy is to a great extent informed by his understanding of what it means to be assured of salvation in Christ. This is captured in the title of this work, which will unpack Flavel's understanding of the doctrine of assurance, and then demonstrate its essence in the pursuit of joy and its expression in looking to Jesus, discerning the Spirit, obeying the law, carrying the cross, and keeping the heart. While the use of *essence* is not to imply *only*—there are other aspects to his joy and spirituality—it is to contend that the joy of assurance is central to Flavel's spirituality.

Flavel's Joy: A Seeker Not a Stealer

The chief concern of this present work is to discuss and display John Flavel's spirituality, especially his emphasis on the connection between joy and assurance. It should be noted, however, that this book does

---

30. Embry, at time, seems to place Flavel in this "immediate witness" camp. For instance, Embry describes Flavel's view of the immediate witness as similar to Sibbes's and Goodwin's, and then quotes Goodwin, stating that the "sealing of the Holy Spirit is an *immediate* assurance by a heavenly and divine light of a divine authority, which the Holy Ghost sheddeth in a man's heart." Embry, *Keeper*, 85. Though Embry qualifies that Flavel does not understand the sealing of the Holy Spirit as only an immediate witness, such a distinction is not always clear. While Flavel, only at certain points in his life, does allow for an immediate witness of the Spirit to assurance, he very rarely makes any appeal to this type of experience and overwhelmingly speaks of sealing and assurance in a way that aligns with the dominant Puritan understanding recorded in the Westminster Confession of Faith (WCF).

31. See Brian H. Cosby, "John Flavel: The Lost Puritan," *Puritan Reformed Journal* 3, no. 1 (January 2011): 113–32.

provide a valuable example of how some Puritan pastors handled assurance. Flavel strongly held, as this book will demonstrate, that a thoroughly biblical pursuit of assurance would lead to a rich and robust joy in Christ. Flavel was intent to seek the joy of his people, not steal from it. Such a desire, as Jean Williams asserts, might seem out of place with how Flavel's contemporaries and current scholarship have understood the Puritan endeavor for assurance. She writes, "For the Puritans were aware that self-examination could lead to pastoral problems for those with a natural tendency to introspection and self-doubt. Contemporaries accused Puritan piety of causing melancholy, and modern scholars have viewed it as productive of anxiety and despair."[32]

This book will show that Flavel indeed understood the dangers of introspection and self-doubt and sought to alleviate such problems through directing his hearers toward Christ's work on their behalf and the Spirit's work in their hearts. His preaching exemplified Williams's description of the Puritans:

> They warned their hearers to examine their hearts for good as well as evil, and to be encouraged by the smallest graces; they directed troubled believers away from introspection and to obedience, for a sense of God's love would inevitably follow; and they encouraged those obsessed with self-examination to take up meditation on God's blessings.[33]

Flavel's concern was for the joy of his people, not only in eternity but also in their present life on earth. He believed that such delight in Christ could only be truly experienced if believers had assurance that they were in Christ. Flavel, then, like many of his Puritan peers, did not fit the decidedly dour connotation they have often been given. They were not "'prudish,' 'sexually repressed,' 'prohibitionist,' 'busybody snoops'—the types of things that led the twentieth century social critic H. L. Mencken to define puritanism as 'the fear that someone,

---

32. Jean Dorothy Williams, "The Puritan Quest for the Enjoyment of God: An Analysis of the Theological and Devotional Writings of Puritans in Seventeenth Century England" (PhD diss., University of Melbourne, 1997), 81.

33. Williams, "Puritan Quest," 81.

somewhere, may be happy.'"[34] This book will show that despite the many difficulties Flavel endured, he knew great joy in Christ, and ministered so that his people might as well.

Flavel's Life and Ministry: A Brief Sketch

John Flavel "was, by all measures, an English Puritan."[35] He was "a preacher, husband, father, nonconformist, sufferer, and victim of repeated persecution," who "had at one time more disciples than John Owen and Richard Baxter."[36] In addition, he "was a prolific preacher and writer—his collected works filling six volumes."[37] All this makes him an exemplar of the Puritan pastor.

He was born in Bromsgrove, Worcestershire, in 1630, into a family deeply rooted in the Puritan movement.[38] His father, Richard, was a Presbyterian minister, who, by all accounts, was a dedicated and esteemed pastor. "He was a person of such extraordinary piety, that those who conversed with him, said, they never heard one vain word drop from his mouth."[39] Flavel gives the following assessment of his father:

---

34. Francis J. Bremer, *Puritanism: A Very Short Introduction* (New York: Oxford University Press, 2009), 1.

35. Cosby, *John Flavel: Puritan Life*, 4.

36. Cosby, *John Flavel: Puritan Life*, 4. While Cosby does not cite the source of this assertion, it likely comes from an unknown contemporary of Flavel, recorded in Wood, *Athenae*, 323. Nathan Parker notes some question as to the validity of the quote being associated with this work, but not with its veracity as a whole; see Parker, "Proselytisation," 21n17.

37. Yuille, *Inner Sanctum*, 2.

38. Controversy surrounds the date of Flavel's birth. While many scholars point to the years 1627 or 1628 (so articulated by the anonymous biographer whose "The Life of the Late Rev. Mr. John Flavel, Minister of Dartmouth" begins vol. 1 of Flavel's *Works*), Cosby argues for the year 1630 due to the date of his baptism falling in that year. See Cosby, *John Flavel: Puritan Life*, 14. For those who agree with Cosby, see Chang, "John Flavel"; and James William Kelly, *Oxford Dictionary of National Biography*, eds. H. C. G. Matthew and Brian Harrison (Oxford: Oxford University Press, 2004), s.v. "Flavell, John (bap. 1630, d. 1691)." Those who argue the early date for Flavel's birth include the following: Yuille, *Inner Sanctum*; Embry, *Honest*; Joel R. Beeke and Randall J. Pederson, *Meet the Puritans* (Grand Rapids: Reformation Heritage Books, 2006).

39. "Life of the Late," 1:iii.

For my own part, I must profess before the world, that I have a high value for this mercy, and do, from the bottom of my heart, bless the Lord, who gave me a religious and tender father, who often poured out his soul to God for me: he was one that was inwardly acquainted with God; and being full of bowels to his children, often carried them before the Lord, prayed and pleaded with God for them, wept and made supplications for them. This stock of prayers and blessings left by him before the Lord, I cannot but esteem above the fairest inheritance on earth.[40]

While they were imprisoned in London for nonconformity, Flavel's parents contracted the plague. They died shortly after their release in 1665,[41] leaving behind three sons.[42]

Flavel followed in his father's footsteps by becoming a Puritan minister after attending University College, Oxford. Having come to a saving knowledge of Christ during college, Flavel accepted a call to ministry in 1650 to assist Mr. Walplate, the minister of Diptford, in the county of Devon.[43] Shortly after this appointment, he traveled to Salisbury to be ordained as a Presbyterian pastor.[44] While Flavel's time in Diptford was brief, it was not without significance. During these five years, he succeeded Mr. Walplate as pastor. In addition, he married, was widowed, and married again.[45]

---

40. Flavel, *Fountain*, 1:257. See also his statements concerning the significance of godly parents in 4:371–72, which likely also hint of his experience growing up in the Flavel home.

41. For a description of this event, see "The Life of the Late Rev. Mr. John Flavel," in *Works*, 1:iii–iv.

42. There is some confusion on this point. Flavel's biographer mentions only John and Phinehas, as does John Quick, but Richard's will includes a third son, Abiather, as well as three daughters: Anne, Elizabeth, and Deborah. See Edmund Calamy and A. G. Matthews, *Calamy Revised: Being a Revision of Edmund Calamy's Account of the Ministers and Others Ejected and Silenced, 1660–1662* (Oxford: Oxford University Press, 1988), 201; Chang, "John Flavel," 19; Cosby, *John Flavel: Puritan Life*, 27n10.

43. "Life of the Late," 1:iv.

44. Chang, "John Flavel," 22.

45. Flavel married Jane Randal, "a pious gentlewoman, of a good family, who died in travail of her child without being delivered." "Life of the Late," v. John mourned the loss of his wife and first child, writing in *A Token for Mourners*, "You cannot forget that in the years lately past, the Almighty visited my tabernacle with the rod, and in one year cut off from it the root, and the branch, the tender mother, and the only

In 1656, Flavel moved with his family to Dartmouth, where he would—except for a time of exile—minister for the rest of his life. He succeeded the recently deceased Reverend Anthony Hartwood, who had previously befriended Flavel, after witnessing his godly leadership during a provincial synod.[46] Flavel began his time in Dartmouth preaching alongside colleague Allen Geare, who was very ill and would eventually pass in December 1662.[47] As these two men worked together, "Flavell ministered in St Clement's, Townstal, the ancient parish church overlooking Dartmouth, and on alternate Wednesdays he lectured in St Saviour's, a daughter church in town."[48] During this time, Flavel's reputation as a godly minister and effective preacher increased.

Beginning in 1662, however, Flavel's ministry changed dramatically with the enactment of the Clarendon Code—a series of four legal statutes passed between 1661–1665.[49] The most significant of these statutes was the Act of Uniformity in August 1662.[50] It essentially put Puritan ministers to the supreme test: "Abandon your puritan principles or abandon your pulpit."[51] The subsequent Sunday "was remembered

---

son." John Flavel, *A Token for Mourners: Or the Advice of Christ to a Distressed Mother, Bewailing the Death of Her Dear and Only Son (1674)*, in *Works of John Flavel* (1820; repr., Edinburgh: Banner of Truth Trust, 2015), 5:604. Following the encouragement of friends, Flavel married his second wife, Elizabeth Morris. See Chang, "John Flavel," 23.

46. Chang, "John Flavel," 24.

47. Kelly, "Flavell, John." Cosby has Geare's death occurring four months after Flavel's arrival, but this seems to be a miscopy of Flavel's anonymous biography, which states that it was four months after Black Bartholomew Day. See Cosby, *John Flavel: Puritan Life*, 17; "Life of the Late," vi–vii.

48. Kelly, "Flavell, John."

49. Concerning this Code and its name, Coffey writes, "The Cavalier Parliament's laws against Dissent became known in the nineteenth century as the Clarendon Code. This is something of a misnomer, since Sir Edward Hyde, the Earl of Clarendon, was not the mastermind behind the legislation, and historians are divided over his attitude towards it." Coffey, *Persecution and Toleration in Protestant England, 1558–1689*, Studies in Modern History (Harlow, England: Longman, 2000), 167–68.

50. Technically, the beginning of the Clarendon Code was the passing of the Corporation Act in the preceding December, in 1661, which all but removed Puritans from public office. See Coffey, *Persecution*, 168.

51. Winship, Michael P., *Hot Protestants: A History of Puritanism in England and America* (New Haven, Conn.: Yale University Press, 2018), 205. The reasoning for such strong language is due to this Act's requirement that Puritan ministers were to be "episcopally ordained, to renounce the Solemn League and Covenant and to assent to

by puritans as 'Black Bartholomew's Day,' when the ancient feast of Saint Bartholomew was marked by the emptying out of the Church of England's puritan ministry."[52] Though stripped of his position, Flavel remained in Dartmouth, staying close to his congregation and serving a small Puritan school.[53] He continued to take every opportunity to teach and preach to his congregation.[54]

It was not until the passing of the Oxford Act (or Five-Mile Act) that Flavel was forced to move from Dartmouth to nearby Slapton. According to Winship, this act banned ministers "from coming within five miles of any town of any place where they had ministered unless they had taken an extremely harsh oath of loyalty."[55] Despite the government's attempts to curb the influence of Puritan ministers, Flavel continued to serve among his congregation. Members gathered to hear him preach whenever and wherever opportunity allowed. One of their favorite spots to convene was called Saltstone. Located in the Kingsbridge estuary, this strip of land was only accessible at low tide.[56] At times, Flavel disguised himself as a woman in order to meet with his people undetected. On one occasion, he plunged his horse into the sea to escape authorities.[57] As Joel Beeke and Randall Pederson write, "Once, soldiers rushed in and dispersed the congregation. Several of the fugitives were apprehended and fined, but the remainder brought Flavel to another wooded area where he continued his sermon."[58] Such was Flavel's fortitude. Amid persecution, he exemplified the resolve of an English Puritan minister, and honored his father's legacy.[59]

---

the new Prayer Book." Coffey, *Persecution*, 168. Such demands were simply too much for the majority of Puritans.

52. Winship, *Hot Protestants*, 206.

53. Kelly, "Flavell, John."

54. "Life of the Late," 1:vi.

55. Winship, *Hot Protestants*, 210.

56. Calamy and Matthews, *Calamy Revised*, 200.

57. Kelly, "Flavell, John."

58. Beeke and Pederson, *Meet the Puritans*, 247.

59. See Coffey, *Persecution*, 177. Coffey writes about such Puritan resolves, explaining, "Instead of fleeing, however, Dissenters generally chose to stay put and face up to persecution. The longing for theocracy had been displaced by a sense that tribulation was the lot of the godly" (177). While Dissenters included a larger swath than the Puritans, this statement can certainly be applied to the smaller Puritan group.

The constant need to flee and hide continued until Charles II issued a Declaration of Indulgence in 1672. With this new freedom, Flavel returned to Dartmouth and received ordination as a Congregational minister.[60] This time of peace was short-lived, however, as the Indulgence was struck down within the year.[61] Flavel (and his fellow Puritan ministers) experienced another fifteen years of persecution, with some of the worst moments occurring during this period. For Flavel, though his ministry continued amid the struggle, this period would prove to be his most productive as a writer, according to James Kelly:

> Over the next ten years he published *A Token for Mourners* (1674), *The Seaman's Companion* (1676), *Divine Conduct* (1678), *Sea Deliverances* (c. 1679), *The Touchstone of Sincerity* (1679), *The Method of Grace* (1681), *Navigation Spiritualized* (1682), *A Saint Indeed* (1684), and *Treatise on the Soul of Man* (1685).[62]

Flavel's family life seemed to echo these same highs and lows, as he lost his second wife early in this period, married his third wife, Agnes Downe, and later buried her in 1684, after she had given him two more sons.[63]

The worst persecution of this period occurred in the early 1680s. Coffey notes, "Between 1681 and 1686, Dissenters were to face persecution worse than anything they had previously encountered since the early 1660s, the other period when they had been seen as a genuine political threat."[64] During this time, Flavel was exiled to London. It

---

60. Chang, "John Flavel," 32. It is important not to make too much of this apparent transition, as C. E. Whiting explains: "After 1662 the distinction between the Presbyterians and the Independents necessarily ceased to be very sharp.... In the Indulgence licenses of 1672 it sometimes happens that the same minister is described as a Presbyterian in one place and a Congregationalist in another, or a Presbyterian is stated to have been licensed for a Congregational meeting-house." See C. E. Whiting, *Studies in English Puritanism from the Restoration to the Revolution, 1660–1688* (New York: Macmillan, 1931), 62–63.

61. Winship, *Hot Protestants*, 218.

62. Kelly, "Flavell, John." Parker's research disputes the dates of Flavel's *Navigation Spiritualized* and *A Saint Indeed*. He believes both were written much earlier. Parker, "Proselytisation," 296–315. Parker notes some other works written during these decades, which still demonstrate Flavel's increased output in this period of persecution.

63. Chang, "John Flavel," 31.

64. Coffey, *Persecution*, 173.

was also during this time that he married for a fourth and final time—
this time to Dorothy Jeffries.[65] Returning to Dartmouth in late 1684,
he resumed his ministry and remained there (despite multiple offers
to minister in London) until his death.

When James II ascended the throne in 1687, he issued a Declaration of Indulgence. It provided Flavel with the freedom to minister.
This continued for the rest of his life. Cosby explains,

> From that point on, Flavel was allowed to preach without state
> persecution and enjoyed a fruitful ministry until his death—
> preaching twice each Lord's Day, lecturing each Wednesday, and
> preaching on the Thursday before administering the Lord's Sup-
> per. His congregation built a large church upon his return to the
> pulpit in Dartmouth.[66]

While on his way to speak at an assembly of ministers on June 21,
1691, Flavel suffered a significant stroke, and died later that night.[67]
His anonymous biographer notes that among his last words were
these: "I know that it will be well with me."[68]

In this brief overview of his life and ministry, it is evident that Flavel
was indeed a Puritan's Puritan. He was a devoted pastor, prolific author,
and skilled preacher. Yet, as Embry notes, "Unlike other Puritans such
as Richard Sibbes, Thomas Goodwin, or John Owen, whose theolo-
gies are better known today, little is known about Flavel's ministry and
theology."[69] Such an oversight is unfortunate; for, as Sinclair Ferguson
states, "Flavel illustrated the Puritan vision of the godly minister and
the faithful preacher."[70] But Flavel also experienced much pain and persecution throughout his life. And yet, in the midst of it all, he had great
joy in Christ. This joy flowed from his certainty in Christ's work on

---

65. There seems to be some confusion as to when and where this marriage took
place. Chang has it occurring while Flavel was still in London, as does Flavel's
anonymous biographer. See Chang, "John Flavel," 33; "Life of the Late," ix. Kelly has it
happening just after Flavel's return to Dartmouth. See Kelly, "Flavell, John."

66. Cosby, *John Flavel: Puritan Life*, 20.

67. Kelly, "Flavell, John."

68. "Life of the Late," 1:xv.

69. Embry, *Keeper*, 3.

70. Kelly M. Kapic and Randall C. Gleason, eds., *The Devoted Life: An Invitation to
the Puritan Classics* (Downers Grove, Ill.: InterVarsity, 2004), 212.

his behalf and his standing in Christ, seen even in his last words noted above, "I know that it will be well with me."[71] It is no surprise that Flavel once wrote in his diary, "to make sure of eternal life is the great business which the sons of death have to do in this world."[72] This was an essential concern of Flavel's life and ministry, for he believed that this business held in its grasp the deepest joy of this life. It was this joy of assurance that formed the essence and expression of his spirituality.

71. "Life of the Late," 1:xv.
72. Chang, "John Flavel," 37.

Chapter 2

Flavel's Theology of Assurance

Flavel's Context: Understanding the Westminster Assembly on Assurance

The Westminster Confession of Faith is arguably the central exposition of English Puritan doctrine and one of the most influential theological works of the Reformed tradition.[1] It was written during some of the most tumultuous years of the English Reformation, in hopes of unifying England around a common yet robustly Reformed theology and ecclesiology. As Robert Letham states, "One of the main tasks facing the House of Commons in this national emergency was to establish an Assembly of Divines to provide a legal and theological basis for the Church, now that the regular order had been abolished."[2] He further explains that the "Assembly's mandate was largely doctrinal: the 'settling of the government and liturgy of the Church of England, and for

---

1. See J. V. Fesko, *The Theology of the Westminster Standards: Historical Context and Theological Insights* (Wheaton, Ill.: Crossway, 2014), 1–2; Robert Letham, *The Westminster Assembly: Reading Its Theology in Historical Context* (Phillipsburg, N.J.: P&R, 2009), 1; Chad Van Dixhoorn, introduction to *Confessing the Faith: A Reader's Guide to the Westminster Confession of Faith* (Edinburgh: Banner of Truth Trust, 2014), xvii–xxi; J. Ligon Duncan III, ed., introduction to *Westminster Confession into 21st Century*, 1:xii–xv.

2. Letham, *Westminster Assembly*, 30. The national emergency referred to in this quote was the result of a civil war that was taking place in England—a war of theology, between those who wanted to see the Reformation take greater hold in the country and region, and those who were more sympathetic to Catholicism. Led by the Long Parliament (1640–1660), those seeking the reign of Reformed theology, worship, and government in England gained power and eventually abolished the Episcopacy. This action led to the need and creation of the Westminster Assembly. For more details on these events see Letham, *Westminster Assembly*, 11–31; and Fesko, *Theology*, 33–55.

vindicating and clearing of the doctrine of said Church from all false calumnies and aspersions."[3]

The Westminster Assembly was both established and selected by the members of Parliament. It was convened on July 1, 1643.[4] Describing its makeup, Letham writes,

> When the members were finally chosen, the Assembly—composed almost exclusively of English subjects—consisted of 119 divines. Two came from each county in England, two from the Channel Islands, one from each county in Wales, two each from Oxford and Cambridge universities, and four from London. In addition to these, there were ten representatives from the House of Lords and twenty from the Commons. The majority were Presbyterian, but most not dogmatically so. There were a number of Episcopalians, a few Independents, and a few more Erastians.[5]

Much has been written about the composition of the Assembly, much of it praiseworthy, but some of it critical. While the Assembly lacked some of the notable theologians of its day, it was quite well-suited for its task. John Leith explains,

> The Assembly was composed of highly competent men who were fully able to utilize the accumulated theological work of more than a century. They were not creative minds so much as summarizers and interpreters of the tradition. They were for the most part preacher-teachers who wrote not theological masterpieces

---

3. Letham, *Westminster Assembly*, 30. While the focus was primarily doctrinal, the ecclesiastical focus would be added after a negotiation with their Scottish allies resulted in a "request that the brief be extended to include church government as a priority" (30).

4. Letham, *Westminster Assembly*, 31. For a helpful chronology of the events of the Assembly, see John H. Leith, *Assembly at Westminster: Reformed Theology in the Making* (Richmond, Va.: John Knox Press, 1973), 29–30.

5. Letham, *Westminster Assembly*, 32. For more information on the leaders and members of the assembly, see Chad Van Dixhoorn, *Oxford Dictionary of National Biography*, May 24, 2007, https://doi.org/10.1093/ref:odnb/92780, s.v. "Westminster Assembly"; Van Dixhoorn, *The Minutes and Papers of the Westminster Assembly 1643–1652*, vol. 1 (Oxford: Oxford University Press, 2012), 106–47.

but sermons and occasional theological treatises. On this level of theological work they are unsurpassed.[6]

Of course, little defense of these men's gifts is needed, since their labors yielded a product of unparalleled theological import. Though slightly overstated, their contemporary Richard Baxter's admiration is notable: "The Christian world since the days of the apostles had never a Synod of more excellent divines."[7]

The Assembly was adept on theological matters, and particularly familiar with the doctrine of assurance. Beeke remarks,

> The assembly's divines were doctrinally and pastorally well-versed on the subject of assurance. At least twenty-five members of the assembly wrote treatises pertinent to the doctrines of faith and assurance: John Arrowsmith, William Bridge, Anthony Burgess, Cornelius Burgess, Jeremiah Burroughs, Richard Byfield, Joseph Caryl, Daniel Cawdrey, Thomas Gataker, George Gillespie, Thomas Goodwin, William Gouge, William Greenhill, Robert Harris, John Ley, John Lightfoot, Philip Nye, Edward Reynolds, Samuel Rutherford, Henry Scudder, Obadiah Sedgwick, William Spurstowe, William Twisse, Richard Vines, and Jeremiah Whitaker.[8]

This list demonstrates both the significance of assurance to English Puritanism and the representative nature of the Assembly's discussion on assurance in the Westminster Confession. Beeke asserts that "by the 1640s English Puritan thought, notwithstanding various emphases, was nearly unanimous on several distinctives with respect to assurance."[9] It should not be surprising, therefore, that Flavel's understanding of assurance has much in common with the Assembly's exposition in the Westminster Confession.

---

6. Leith, *Assembly at Westminster*, 46.

7. As quoted in Alexander F. Mitchell, *The Westminster Assembly: Its History and Standards; Being the Baird Lectures for 1882* (Philadelphia: Presbyterian Board of Publication and Sabbath-School Work, 1897), 122.

8. Beeke, *Assurance of Faith*, 141–42.

9. Beeke, *Assurance of Faith*, 142.

Before proceeding to Flavel's theology of assurance, it is important to comprehend the statements on faith and assurance laid out in Westminster Confession of Faith 18. It makes four primary assertions.

The Availability of Assurance

The first statement opens by affirming that assurance is available to every believer: "Such as truly believe in the Lord Jesus, and love him in sincerity, endeavoring to walk in all good conscience before him, may in this life be certainly assured that they are in a state of grace, and may rejoice in the hope of the glory of God, which hope shall never make them ashamed."[10] Like Calvin, the Westminster Confession makes it clear that believers may be "certainly assured" of their salvation "in this life." For the Assembly, the Christian life is not to be marked by apprehension, dominated by constant doubt as to whether they are in a state of grace. Rather, as Chad Van Dixhoorn affirms, the Westminster divines argued that "Christians can really know they are Christians."[11] Such certainty, however, ought not to be embraced uncritically. It is for those who "truly believe in the Lord Jesus," who "love him in sincerity," and who endeavor "to walk in all good conscience before him."

These qualifiers are crucial. While assurance is possible, the danger of self-deception is real. "Hypocrites and other unregenerate men may vainly deceive themselves with false hopes and carnal presumptions of being in the favor of God and estate of salvation, which hope of theirs shall perish," the Westminster Confession of Faith states.[12] This caution points to the Assembly's deep concern over the prevalence of hypocrisy in the church. As Beeke explains,

> Even a cursory examination of Puritan literature will reveal that the expression, "false hopes and carnal presumptions," is weighted with significance.… The Puritans had taken to heart Christ's warning in the Sermon on the Mount that some who

---

10. WCF 18.1.

11. Van Dixhoorn, *Confessing the Faith*, 227.

12. WCF 18.1.

professed to serve Him would be told, "I never knew you: depart from me" (Matt. 7:23).[13]

Whereas Calvin ministered in a context in which most people doubted their eternal state, the Westminster divines ministered in a setting in which many presumed they were saved. Thus, the Westminster Confession of Faith affirms the reality of both assurance of salvation and self-deception.

Finally, the opening statement in the Westminster Confession asserts that it is possible to be a believer without knowing it. The Assembly expresses this with the addition of one word: *may*. The believer "may in this life be certainly assured" and "may rejoice in the hope of the glory of God." By adding the term *may*, the Confession argues that "believers may possess saving faith without knowing assuredly that they do possess it."[14] In doing so, as Beeke notes, the Westminster divines sought to communicate that "full assurance belonged more properly to the well-being (i.e., the healthy condition and robust prosperity) of faith, than to the being (i.e., the essence or state) of faith."[15] This distinction, as well as these three possibilities, are further developed in the final three statements on assurance found in Westminster Confession of Faith 18.

The Foundation of Assurance

The next statement in Westminster Confession 18.2 establishes the foundation for assurance. It declares that assurance is "not a bare conjectural and probable persuasion, grounded upon a fallible hope; but an infallible assurance of faith."[16] In opposition to the Roman Catholic dogma, as defined by the Council of Trent, the Assembly upholds the certainty of "infallible" assurance.

This infallibility is "founded upon the divine truth of the promises of salvation."[17] These promises constitute the "primary objective ground of assurance." It is objective because it is rooted in God's Word.

---

13. Beeke, *Assurance of Faith*, 148.
14. Beeke, *Assurance of Faith*, 150.
15. Beeke, *Assurance of Faith*, 150.
16. WCF 18.2.
17. WCF 18.2.

Beeke notes that it "affirms from the outset that the believer does not gain assurance by looking at himself or anything he has produced apart from God's promises, but primarily by looking to God's faithfulness in Christ as He is revealed in the promises of the gospel."[18] For the Westminster divines, assurance is firmly rooted in Christ's work, not the believer's work.[19]

While the divine promises in Scripture provide the primary ground of assurance, the Westminster Confession notes two other grounds. Christians can know they are in a state of grace through "the inward evidence of those graces unto which these promises are made."[20] This second ground means that one must examine his or her life for the fruit of God's work. R. M. Hawkes explains that the Puritans urged Christians to "examine their works, not as a replacement to faith, but as a work of faith, to see God's hand working within themselves."[21] What are these evidences of grace, and how does one discover them? Though not mentioned in the Westminster Confession, Beeke explains that many of the Puritans answered these questions by means of two syllogisms:

> The Puritans taught that two very closely related, yet distinct, syllogisms should be used to fortify assurance—the "practical syllogism" and the "mystical syllogism." The practical syllogism was based largely on the believer's sanctification and good works as evidenced in practical, daily life. It tended to accent the believer's life of new obedience which expressed and confirmed his experience of grace.... The mystical syllogism was based largely

---

18. Beeke, *Assurance of Faith*, 152. John Von Rohr explains, "It is not that this assurance is absolutely necessary for the life of the believer. The faith of assurance must never be confused with the faith of adherence.... There may well be faith and God's acceptance without an overpowering sense of it." John Von Rohr, *The Covenant of Grace in Puritan Thought*, Studies in Religion /American Academy of Religion 45 (Atlanta: Scholars Press, 1986), 156.

19. Thomas Brooks (1608–1680), for example, writes, "Let thy eye and heart, first, most, and last, be fixed upon Christ, then will assurance bed and board with thee." Thomas Brooks, *Heaven on Earth: A Treatise on Christian Assurance* (1654; repr., Edinburgh: Banner of Truth Trust, 2004), 307.

20. WCF 18.2.

21. Hawkes, "Logic," 251–52.

on the believer's internal exercises and progress in the steps of grace. It tended to focus on the inward man.[22]

The Puritans employed both of these syllogisms in their preaching and teaching to such an extent that they became intertwined with the "signs of grace."[23] They described the recognition of these signs in the heart as the reflex act of faith. This reflexive act is ultimately the work of the Holy Spirit. According to Thomas Goodwin (1600–1680), the Holy Spirit "first produceth all graces in us, and then teacheth our consciences to read his handwriting."[24]

The third ground of assurance is "the testimony of the Spirit of adoption witnessing with our spirits that we are the children of God: which Spirit is the earnest of our inheritance, whereby we are sealed to the day of redemption."[25] The Westminster Confession highlights the role of the Holy Spirit but does not explain precisely how He testifies that believers are the children of God. Beeke argues that this lack of precision was intentional: "One significant reason the assembly did not detail more specifically what the Spirit's testimony is in assurance was to allow for the freedom of the Spirit in His assuring witness."[26]

The Westminster Confession, then, allowed for different understandings as to the exact nature of the Holy Spirit's witness. For many Puritans, this witness was simply related to the second ground of assurance, meaning the Holy Spirit testifies that Christians are the children of God by producing and confirming the evidences of God's grace. For others, the witness of the Holy Spirit is made directly to the believer's spirit. John Von Rohr comments, "The Spirit also speaks directly to the believer, bringing an inner testimony of God's grace and love."[27] This direct testimony was viewed as an immediate witness that brought with it a unique and dramatic experience of assurance.[28]

------

22. Beeke, *Assurance of Faith*, 160.

23. For further discussion see Beeke, *Assurance of Faith*, 161.

24. Thomas Goodwin, *The Works of Thomas Goodwin, D. D.*, ed. John C. Miller (Edinburgh: James Nichol, 1861–1867), 6:27.

25. WCF 18.2.

26. Beeke, *Assurance of Faith*, 169.

27. Von Rohr, *Covenant of Grace*, 166. Studies in Religion / American Academy of Religion, no. 45 (Atlanta, Ga: Scholars Press, 1986)

28. Adam Embry argues that, for a season, Flavel held this view, and though there

Though distinctions existed, the Assembly was united that the Spirit and the Word are absolutely vital to assurance. Beeke states, "In every sense…these three groups are united in asserting that the Spirit's testimony is always tied to, and may never contradict, the Word of God."[29]

The Pursuit of Assurance

Chapter 18.3 of the Westminster Confession of Faith affirms that genuine faith in Christ is not always accompanied by assurance: "This infallible assurance doth not so belong to the essence of faith, but that a true believer may wait long, and conflict with many difficulties before he be partaker of it."[30] As previously stated, the Assembly understood assurance as belonging to faith's health, but not its essence. Assurance was not necessary for the Christian life and the Puritans recognized that many sincere believers struggle and long for it.

This is not an ideal situation, and therefore one must pursue a greater assurance. The Westminster Confession declares, "It is the duty of every one to give all diligence to make his calling and election sure; that thereby his heart may be enlarged in peace and joy in the Holy Ghost, in love and thankfulness to God, and in strength and cheerfulness in the duties of obedience, the proper fruits of this assurance."[31] This duty is accomplished by the work of the Holy Spirit through "the right use of ordinary means."[32]

The Assembly identified the fruit of assurance as consisting of "peace, joy, love, thankfulness, strength, and cheerfulness."[33] The

---

is some evidence to that end, I think it more accurate to say that for a short season he gave some allowance to the immediate witness view, without embracing it. For Embry's presentation, see Embry, *Keeper*. For an example of this view—which would eventually be tied up with "sealing of the Spirit" language—see Beeke's discussion on Goodwin in Beeke, *Assurance of Faith*, 171–73.

29. Beeke, *Assurance of Faith*, 172.

30. WCF 18.3.

31. WCF 18.3.

32. WCF 18.3. Van Dixhoorn expresses this sentiment as follows: "If you are a professing Christian now lacking assurance of your salvation, pay attention to the preaching of the Word and turn to the Lord in prayer. Remain in the church and make full use of the sacraments 'so that Christ may dwell in your heart through faith.'" Van Dixhoorn, *Confessing the Faith*, 230–31.

33. The worthwhileness of this pursuit of assurance, namely the joy that results

possibility of this fruit motivates believers to seek greater assurance. Though it is not necessary for salvation, it is instrumental for joy. As Thomas Brooks writes, "The being in a state of grace will yield a man heaven hereafter, but the seeing of himself in this state will yield him both a heaven here and a heaven hereafter."[34]

The Loss of Assurance

The final paragraph of Westminster Confession of Faith 18 deals with the reality that believers can falter and even, for a time, lose assurance. It begins by noting that "true believers may have their salvation divers ways shaken, diminished, and intermitted."[35] These "divers ways," the Assembly contended, could have their origin in the believer or God. Primarily, they insisted that assurance was weakened or forfeited "by negligence in preserving of it; by falling into some special sin, which woundeth the conscience, and grieveth the Spirit; by some sudden or vehement temptation."[36] Thus, the Westminster Confession concludes that one's assurance can be shaken by sin, neglect, and temptation. The implications of this conclusion are evident. Beeke explains,

> Such references as these in the WCF make plain the possibility of forfeiting assurance: The Christian cannot enjoy high levels of assurance when he persists in low levels of obedience. For the Puritan, this was a good thing. If assurance remained high while obedience was minimal, the believer would be prone to take for granted the great privileges of adopted sonship and soon grow spiritually lazy.[37]

Disobedience is the principal means by which assurance is forfeited, but it is not the only means. The Assembly points to the possibility that assurance can be shaken, diminished, and intermitted "by God's withdrawing the light of his countenance, and suffering even such as

---

from assurance, lies at the heart of Flavel's spirituality, which is the primary thesis of this book. It is important to note its appearance here in the Westminster Confession of Faith, though much more will be discussed in the following chapter.

34. Thomas Brooks, *The Works of Thomas Brooks*, ed. Alexander Balloch Grosart (1861–1867; repr., Edinburgh: Banner of Truth Trust, 1980), 2:14.

35. WCF 18.4.

36. WCF 18.4.

37. Beeke, *Assurance of Faith*, 183.

fear him to walk in darkness and to have no light."[38] Though less common, doubts and struggles with assurance might be the result, not of sin, but of God's providential withdrawing. Beeke explains, "We need to recognize that these divines firmly believed that such 'withdrawment' on God's part was often for holy reasons and purposes beyond the comprehension of the individual believer, who only had to trust that these reasons were intended by God for his welfare."[39]

Whatever the cause behind a believer's struggle with assurance, one should not despair: "They are never utterly destitute of that seed of God, and life of faith, that love of Christ and the brethren, that sincerity of heart and conscience of duty, of which, by the operation of the Spirit, this assurance may in due time be revived, and by which, in the meantime, they are supported from utter despair."[40] Assurance of faith, though hidden from view, is never completely absent; there is always hope that it will be revived. In the spirit of much of English Puritan preaching is Von Rohr's encouragement: "In the search for one's faith, one may be assured that it need not be perfect, but rather, the least spark of faith, even weak faith, can lay hold of God's promises and be the instrument for justification and salvation."[41]

Concluding Thoughts

In four concise statements, the Westminster Assembly manages to convey a convincing account of the doctrine of assurance. In so doing, they manage to avoid two errors that were prevalent in their day, as Beeke points out: "They eschewed two kinds of religion, one that separated subjective experience from the objective Word (both living and written) in an unbiblical form of mysticism, and one that presumed salvation on the fallacious ground of historical or temporary faith."[42] Navigating the dangerous waters of mysticism and formalism, the Westminster Confession of Faith presents the real possibility of assurance and its sturdy foundation, all the while encouraging believers to

---

38. WCF 18.4.

39. Beeke, *Assurance of Faith*, 185.

40. WCF 18.4.

41. Von Rohr, *Covenant of Grace*, 168.

42. Beeke, *Assurance of Faith*, 158.

pursue greater assurance, even and especially, in the midst of seasons of doubt and darkness. Though broad, it is a decidedly helpful summary of English Puritan thinking on this complex issue.

Flavel's View: A Pastoral Development of Westminster

Flavel ministered at the time of the Westminster Assembly. Undoubtedly, he followed its proceedings with great interest. Brian Cosby observes, "It should not be underemphasized that Flavel inherited the confessional theology and identity of the Westminster Standards, an identity he maintained until the end of his life."[43] This theological adherence is evident in Flavel's understanding of the doctrine of assurance. In fact, his writing and preaching on this doctrine constitute a pastoral development of Westminster Confession 18. Cosby asserts that Flavel took Westminster's theology of assurance and "clothed it with pastoral ministry."[44] Flavel's dependence on and development of chapter 18 is on full display in his exposition of the Westminster Shorter Catechism 36.[45] Here he provides a clear and concise analysis of the doctrine of assurance.[46]

The Possibility of Assurance

Flavel begins his explanation of assurance by clearly defending the possibility of attaining it in this life and by noting that "all Christians

---

43. Cosby, *John Flavel: Puritan Life*, 50.

44. Cosby, *Suffering and Sovereignty*, 109. Cosby is speaking specifically about the application of assurance to those suffering, but the phrase is an apt characterization for how Flavel articulates the doctrine as a whole.

45. John Flavel, *An Exposition of the Assembly's Shorter Catechism*, in *Works of John Flavel* (1820; repr., Edinburgh: Banner of Truth Trust, 2015), 6:200–201. WSC 36 reads, "What are the benefits which in this life do accompany or flow from justification, adoption, and sanctification? The benefits which in this life do accompany or flow from justification, adoption, and sanctification, are, assurance of God's love, peace of conscience, joy in the Holy Ghost, increase of grace, and perseverance therein to the end." Flavel explains each of these fruits in order—beginning with "assurance of God's love," which will be the focus of the following discussion.

46. For other accounts of Flavel's understanding of assurance, see Embry, *Keeper*, 1–12, 69–106; Cosby, *Suffering and Sovereignty*, 107–34; Cosby, *John Flavel: Puritan Life*, 114–16; Parker, "Proselytisation," 104–6; Allen, "Theologian as Pastor," 56–72; Ian Macleod, "True and Nominal Christians Distinguished," *Puritan Reformed Journal* 9, no. 1 (January 2017): 197–214.

are commanded to strive for it."[47] In similar fashion to Westminster Confession of Faith 18, Flavel emphasizes this possibility while still warning of the dangers of false assurance. Though aware of the prevalence of self-deception and hypocrisy, Flavel is adamant it should not lead Christians to believe that assurance is impossible. He writes, "That assurance is one of the great difficulties in religion, is a great truth; but that it is therefore unattainable in this world, is very false. Popish doctrine indeed makes it impossible; but that doctrine is practicably confuted in the comfortable experience of many souls: all are commanded to strive for it."[48] The experience of countless believers, and the clear commands of Scripture to pursue it, point to the possibility of assurance.[49]

Furthermore, the practical benefits of assurance in this life, and the eternal consequence of false profession in the next, require that believers pursue it. Flavel exhorts, "O then, give the Lord no rest, till your hearts be at rest by the assurance of his love, and the pardon of your sins; when you can boldly say the Lord *is your help*, you will quickly say what immediately follows, *I will not fear what man can do unto me*."[50] To be assured, then, is to say that the Lord is *my* help. It is not merely to know that Christ saves but to know that Christ saves a particular individual: "Assurance saith, I believe and am sure that Christ died for me, and that I shall be saved through him."[51] For Flavel, such assurance—while not guaranteed in this life—is attainable.

Objective and Subjective Assurance
Flavel notes two principal kinds of assurance: objective and subjective. Describing objective assurance, Flavel appeals to 2 Timothy 2:19:

---

47. Flavel, *Exposition*, 6:200.

48. John Flavel, *The Touchstone of Sincerity, or The Signs of Grace and the Symptoms of Hypocrisy*, in *Works of John Flavel* (1820; repr., Edinburgh: Banner of Truth Trust, 2015), 5:525.

49. The biblical command most often cited by Flavel in this context is found in 2 Peter 1:10.

50. John Flavel, *A Practical Treatise of Fear*, in *Works of John Flavel* (1820; repr., Edinburgh: Banner of Truth Trust, 2015), 3:304. Italics in the original.

51. John Flavel, *The Method of Grace in the Gospel Redemption*, in *Works of John Flavel* (1820; repr., Edinburgh: Banner of Truth Trust, 2015), 2:115.

"Nevertheless, the foundation of God standeth sure, having this seal, The Lord knoweth them that are his."[52] This "seal" is the sanctifying work of the Spirit in the soul of the believer.[53] Flavel writes, "When he [the Spirit] seals objectively, that is, when he sanctifies us really by the infusion of grace, he seals us by way of distinction from other men.... The sanctification of the Spirit makes a real difference in the state and temper of the person."[54] There is a sense, then, in which all true believers have assurance because they all have God the Spirit at work in them. Cosby also reads Flavel in this way, suggesting that "Flavel seems to equate saving faith with 'objective assurance,' which he sees as a seal that God has indeed saved His elect."[55]

Flavel gives far more attention to subjective assurance, or the personal assurance that Christ "loved me, and gave himself for me."[56] Flavel sometimes describes it as the "formal" seal. In short, it is the Holy Spirit's work "which clears and ratifies his [the believer's] interest in Christ and salvation."[57] Here, the Holy Spirit assures the Christian "by irradiating the soul with a grace-discovering light, shining upon his own work; and this in order of nature follows the former work; he first infuses the grace, and then opens the eye of the soul to see it."[58] This assurance is subjective, for though empowered by the Holy Spirit, it involves the believer's work as well. Adam Embry explains, "The Spirit subjectively seals believers when He illuminates His works of

---

52. Flavel, *Exposition*, 6:200.

53. John Flavel, *Twelve Sacramental Meditations Upon Select Places of Scripture, to Prepare Believers for the Ordinance of the Lord's Supper*, in *Works of John Flavel* (1820; repr., Edinburgh: Banner of Truth Trust, 2015), 6:402. See also Flavel, *Fountain*, 1:95; and Flavel, *Method*, 2:343.

54. Flavel, *Twelve Sacramental Meditations*, 6:404–5. Flavel's reason for seeing the objective sealing here as the same as the objective assurance mentioned in his *Exposition* is the use of 2 Tim. 2:19 in both of these descriptions.

55. Cosby, *Suffering and Sovereignty*, 114; see also Embry, *Keeper*, 75–76.

56. Flavel, *Exposition*, 6:200. In describing subjective assurance here, Flavel cites Gal. 2:20 as its primary scriptural foundation.

57. Flavel, *Twelve Sacramental Meditations*, 6:404.

58. John Flavel, *A Saint Indeed: or The Great Work of a Christian Explained and Applied*, in *Works of John Flavel* (1820; repr., Edinburgh: Banner of Truth Trust, 2015), 5:434.

grace in their soul, enabling them to see that they are indwelt by the Spirit, that is, united to Christ."[59]

The Difficulty of Assurance

Flavel is quick to acknowledge that subjective assurance will never be perfect in this life: "It admits of doubts and fears, which interrupts it, and it is not always at one height."[60] Much like the Westminster Confession 18.4, Flavel recognizes that the believer's personal assurance will often be "shaken, diminished, and intermitted."[61] It is for this reason that Flavel does not hold that assurance is necessary for salvation but that "a man may be saved, and in Christ, without it."[62] He understands that assurance belongs to the well-being of faith and not the being of faith.[63] It is possible to be a believer while still doubting that one truly believes in Christ. Flavel explains, "There is many a true believer to whom the joy and comfort of assurance is denied.... A true believer may 'walk in darkness, and see no light,' Isa. 50:10."[64] A lack of assurance, therefore, is not merely the result of failure or forgetfulness, for even the faithful Christian may experience seasons of darkness and difficulty.

Flavel agrees with the Westminster Confession that believers often lack assurance due to sinfulness and negligence. He asserts that "negligence in duty starves it" and "sinning against light stabs it."[65] The idle Christian should not expect to gain or retain assurance, for "God doth not usually indulge lazy and negligent souls with the comforts of assurance; he will not so much as seem to patronize sloth and carelessness; he will give it, but it shall be in his own way: his command hath united our care and comfort together."[66] Believers, then, must be watchful, seeking to be obedient to the Word of God. As Flavel exhorts, "The comfort of our souls doth much depend upon the keeping of our

---

59. Embry, *Keeper*, 78.
60. Flavel, *Exposition*, 6:200.
61. WCF 18.4.
62. Flavel, *Exposition*, 6:201.
63. Beeke, *Assurance of Faith*, 150.
64. Flavel, *Method*, 2:114.
65. Flavel, *Exposition*, 6:201.
66. Flavel, *Saint Indeed*, 5:435.

hearts; for he that is negligent in attending his own heart, is (ordinarily) a great stranger to assurance, and the sweet comforts flowing from it."[67] While assurance is the gift of God, worked in the believer by the Holy Spirit, believers are not passive in receiving it: "We have it not for our holiness, but we always have it in the way of holiness."[68]

The Testimony of the Holy Spirit

Personal assurance is built, writes Flavel, "upon the testimony of God's Spirit witnessing with ours."[69] Agreeing with the primary assertion of Westminster Confession 18.2, Flavel is clear that the Holy Spirit is the "author of assurance," "the keeper of the great seal of heaven; and it is his office to confirm and seal the believer's right and interest in Christ and heaven, Rom. 8:16."[70] Among the Puritans, there is little disagreement as to the primacy of the Holy Spirit's work in assuring believers, but there is some difference of opinion as to how He accomplishes this work. Does the Holy Spirit witness *with* or *to* the believer's spirit? According to the former, the Holy Spirit enables Christians to see the evidence of His sanctifying work in their lives. According to the latter, the Holy Spirit communicates directly to believers in an extraordinary manner. The first witness is mediated by means of the Word of God, while the second is immediate—the Holy Spirit directly witnesses to one's spirit.

Flavel affirms that the testimony of the Holy Spirit is a mediated witness by the ordinary means of Scripture. He explains,

> In sealing the believer he doth not make use of an audible voice, nor the ministry of angels, nor immediate and extraordinary revelations, but he makes use of his own graces implanted in our hearts, and his own promises written in the scriptures; and in this method he usually brings the doubting trembling heart of a believer to rest and comfort.[71]

---

67. Flavel, *Saint Indeed*, 5:433.
68. Flavel, *Method*, 2:401.
69. Flavel, *Exposition*, 6:200.
70. Flavel, *Twelve Sacramental Meditations*, 6:402.
71. Flavel, *Twelve Sacramental Meditations*, 6:403.

On occasion, Flavel appears to give some credence to the view of the Holy Spirit's testimony as an immediate witness to one's spirit. He writes, "There is a witness of the Spirit, distinct from that of water and blood, that is, a witness, or sealing, which comes not in an argumentative way, by reasoning from either justification or sanctification, but seems to come immediately from the Spirit."[72]

One might be tempted to interpret this remark as implying that Flavel held (if only for a season) that the testimony of the Holy Spirit is immediate.[73] Such a conclusion, though, does not reflect Flavel's larger teaching. It would seem unwise to place Flavel among those Puritans who held to an immediate witness view based on this statement alone. Rather, it would be more accurate to maintain that Flavel articulated and taught the witness of the Spirit as fundamentally coming through the Word of God and the ordinary means of grace, while allowing for the very rare experience of an immediate witness.[74] This best fits with the fact that Flavel never encourages believers to seek any sort of experience that would align with the immediate witness.

While the testimony of the Holy Spirit is the only ground listed in Flavel's exposition of assurance in this section, he speaks of the other two grounds (listed in WCF 18.2) throughout his works. It is likely that Flavel is here highlighting the primacy of the role of the Holy Spirit in assurance and includes these other two grounds under this heading for the purposes of brevity. Throughout his ministry, Flavel points to the Holy Spirit's use of the promises of God and the inward evidences of grace to assure His people. Especially in his preaching, he frequently points to the doctrines of election, the covenant of grace,

---

72. John Flavel, *Pneumatologia: A Treatise of the Soul of Man*, in *Works of John Flavel* (1820; repr., Edinburgh: Banner of Truth Trust, 2015), 3:59.

73. See Embry's discussion, *Keeper*, 83–88.

74. Such allowance, however, is rarely given by Flavel for his current day. Thus, he writes, "But these immediate ways are ceased; no man may expect by any new revelation or sign from heaven, by any voice or extraordinary inspiration, to have his salvation sealed, but must expect that mercy in God's ordinary way and method, searching the scriptures, examining our own hearts, and waiting on the Lord in prayer." Flavel, *Twelve Sacramental Meditations*, 6:405–6.

adoption, and union with Christ as truths to which believers should cling when seeking greater assurance.[75]

Flavel's collection of sermons on Christ, *The Fountain of Life*, reveals how he grounds assurance in the words and works of the triune God. For example, in his third sermon, he writes, "But when we look to the covenant of redemption there is nothing to stagger our faith, both the federates being infinitely able and faithful to perform their parts; so that there is no possibility of failure on their parts."[76] The power and faithfulness of the Father and the Son, in light of their covenant together to redeem humanity, ought to buttress weak assurance. Thus, Flavel concludes, "Happy were it, if puzzled and perplexed Christians would turn their eyes from the defects that are in their obedience, to the fulness and completeness of Christ's obedience; and see themselves complete in him, when most lame and defective in themselves."[77] In expounding a thoroughly biblical Christology, Flavel again points his readers to the uses and inferences of this theology in establishing assurance.[78]

The Signs of Assurance

Recognizing the primary role of the Holy Spirit in assuring believers, Flavel is adamant that He does make use of signs. He cites 1 John 3:14 and verse 24 as evidence, noting that the Holy Spirit ordinarily utilizes certain marks to strengthen the believer's assurance.[79] Flavel then speaks to two of these signs, answering how true assurance is to be discerned from presumption.

First, he proposes that "true assurance humbles the soul; Gal. 2:20."[80] A mark of the Holy Spirit's work in the believer, one which ought to increase his or her assurance, is the presence of genuine

---

75. For an explanation of Flavel's use of these doctrines for grounding assurance, see Cosby, *Suffering and Sovereignty*, 119–26.

76. Flavel, *Fountain*, 1:59.

77. Flavel, *Fountain*, 1:59.

78. See Flavel, *Fountain*, 1:117, 174, 255, 269–70, 291, 328, 352, 448–49, 499–501.

79. Flavel, *Exposition*, 6:201. Flavel quotes 1 John 3:14, 24: "We know that we have passed from death unto life, because we love the brethren…. Hereby we know that he abideth in us, by the Spirit which he hath given us."

80. Flavel, *Exposition*, 6:201.

humility. Such humility differs from the false humility prevalent among the presumptuous. Flavel writes, "The humility and self-denial of our hearts in duties, will try what they are for their integrity and sincerity towards God…. But if the heart be upright indeed, it will express its humility, as in all other things, so especially in its duties wherein it approaches the great and holy God."[81] Flavel guides his readers and does not leave them with some sort of vague notion of humility; instead, he describes this humility as expressing itself in a high view of God and a low view of themselves. True believers, then, have "awful and reverential apprehensions" of God and "low and vile thoughts" of themselves and their works.[82] Such humility is most evident in their "renouncing all their duties in point of dependence, and relying entirely upon Christ for righteousness and acceptance."[83] Those who have been saved in Christ and sealed by the Holy Spirit will grow in humility, both as a sign of their true identity in Christ and as a result of the Holy Spirit's work of assurance in their hearts.

The second mark is obedience or holiness. Flavel writes that true assurance "makes the soul afraid of sin; 2 Cor. 7:1."[84] Assurance and obedience are close companions, for, as Flavel warns, "Assurance is unattainable without obedience; we will never be comfortable Christians except we be strict and regular Christians."[85] There is both a negative and positive aspect to this obedience—the believer is to both mortify sin and pursue righteousness. Neither can be excluded by the true Christian seeking greater assurance. For "the death of your sin is as evidential as any thing in the world can be of your spiritual life for the present, and of your eternal life with God hereafter. Mortification is the fruit and evidence of your union, and that union is the firm

---

81. Flavel, *Touchstone*, 5:570; see also *Fountain*, 1:95; and *Method*, 2:365, 395.

82. Flavel, *Touchstone*, 5:570–71.

83. Flavel, *Touchstone*, 5:570–71. Flavel does not, however, minimize duty and obedience, as will be evidenced in the next point. Rather, as he concludes the above paragraph, "They have special regard to duties in point of obedience, but none at all in point of reliance" (571).

84. Flavel, *Exposition*, 6:201.

85. Flavel, *Method*, 2:401.

ground-work and certain pledge of your glorification."[86] The assured believer is conscious of the danger and destruction of sin. But Flavel also contends that obedience in the positive sense is essential to assurance. "Faith improves by obedience…. Diligence in obedience in the work of God is the direct way to the assurance of the love of God. This path leads you into a heaven upon earth."[87] Again, both of these function as signs and fruits of true assurance. These two signs, however, are not the only signs of true assurance—rather, they are exemplary of a much longer list.[88]

The Fruit of Assurance

As the present work demonstrates, Flavel understood joy to be the premier fruit of assurance.[89] Assurance brings one "joy unspeakable amidst outward troubles."[90] This joy, in turn, provides a foretaste of heaven in the present. Flavel states, "All the joys of heaven are not to come; but some communicated in this life."[91] The joy of assurance, for Flavel, is the grandest of all pleasures that can be had in this life. To know with certainty that one is a child of God is the chief blessing of the Christian life. As Flavel remarks,

> You that have received Jesus Christ truly, give yourselves no rest till you are fully satisfied that you have done so; acceptance brings you to heaven hereafter, but assurance will bring heaven into your souls now. O, what a life of delight and pleasure doth the assured believer live! What pleasure is it to him to look back and consider where he once was, and where he now is? To look

---

86. Flavel, *Method*, 2:370.

87. Flavel, *Method*, 2:408.

88. As this work demonstrates in subsequent chapters, in addition to humility and holiness, Flavel also often includes faithfulness in the means of grace, perseverance in suffering, love for the brethren, etc., as signs which ought to strengthen assurance.

89. Joy being the primary fruit of assurance for Flavel is evident in the fact that it is the only fruit he mentions in answer to the question, "What is the fruit of assurance?" Moreover, he mentions joy twice in his response, "joy unspeakable amidst outward troubles" and "not only so, but we also joy in God, through our Lord Jesus Christ, by whom we have now received the atonement." See Flavel, *Exposition*, 6:201.

90. Flavel, *Exposition*, 6:201.

91. Flavel, *Exposition*, 6:201.

forward, and consider where he now is, and where shortly he shall be![92]

It is this delight that makes the pursuit of assurance a worthy endeavor. The joy of assurance is so great that Flavel confidently concludes, "There is nothing in this world, which true Christians more earnestly desire, than to be well assured and satisfied of the love of Jesus Christ to their souls."[93]

This point is especially evident in Flavel's ministry to sufferers. Cosby rightly acknowledges that the comforts of assurance were central to Flavel's teaching to those in the midst of difficult trials.[94] Flavel understood the "time of greatest sufferings for Christ" to be the "usual season of assurance,"[95] and trials to be the "highway to assurance."[96] Such assurance is God's grace to struggling believers, which enables them to thrive in the midst of difficulty. Flavel explains,

> In a word it is a sweet support, in all the troubles and afflictions on this side of the grave. Let the assured soul be cast into what condition the Lord pleases; be it upon a bed of sickness; yet this gives his soul such support and comfort, that he shall not say, I am sick. Sin being forgiven, the soul is well, when the body is in pain, Isa. 33:24. Let him be cast into a prison, here is that which will turn a prison into a paradise, Acts 5:41. Let him be pinched with outward want; this will supply all: "As having nothing, and yet possessing all things," 2 Cor. 6:10. Thus you see how desirable it is for its own excellency.[97]

It is no wonder that assurance held such a central place for Flavel and his peers, for its benefits are experienced now and forever. Though often seen as a troubled exercise, the pursuit of greater assurance, for Flavel, is the pursuit of greater joy.[98]

---

92. Flavel, *Method*, 2:138.

93. Flavel, *Twelve Sacramental Meditations*, 6:451.

94. See Cosby, *Suffering and Sovereignty*, 111–33.

95. Flavel, *Exposition*, 6:201.

96. Flavel, *Touchstone*, 5:581.

97. Flavel, *Twelve Sacramental Meditations*, 6:453.

98. This is not to exclude other fruits of assurance but to show Flavel's emphasis on the fruit of joy. On those who saw the Puritan pursuit of assurance as anxiety-inducing, see Williams, "Puritan Quest," 81.

Conclusion

The principal aim of this chapter was to lay out John Flavel's understanding of the doctrine of assurance. He has pastorally developed and contextualized the Westminster Confession's articulation of the doctrine of assurance, without veering from it on any point. Additionally, even from this brief exploration of his teaching on assurance, its prevalence in his ministry is inescapable. That he and his congregation be rightly assured of their union with Christ is clearly one of the primary concerns of Flavel's life. Lastly, the final note of this chapter on the joy of assurance for Flavel is at the very center of this work and will be the chief concern of the next chapter.

Chapter 3

Flavel's Joy in Assurance

Compared to other prominent Puritans, little is written about the life and character of John Flavel, but among that which is, there is hardly any disagreement: he was an exceptional Christian pastor and person.[1] Marked by the fruit of the Spirit, all record Flavel as a "godly, gifted, and wise minister of the gospel."[2] What was likely well-known by those close to him, however, seems often neglected in writings about him today. For he was not only a competent and caring pastor but he was also a joyous Christian. Flavel, like many of his contemporaries, believed the Christian life to be one of great delight. Indeed, in light of the mercies of God in Christ, Flavel considered joy to be the Christian's duty: "And yet you will not come up to your duty in all this, except you be joyful in the Lord, and rejoice evermore, after the receipt of such mercies as these."[3]

Such joy was not found just in his exhortations but in his life. As his biographer reveals,

> These things being previously dispatched, he tried himself by the scripture marks of sincerity and regeneration; by this means he

---

1. The following words by John Galpine, a contemporary and friend of Flavel's, exemplifies this description of him: "As to his character, all that knew him or have seriously perused the books he has put forth must need suffrage with me, that he was a man of choice and excellent parts, both natural and acquired; of a sound and solid judgment, of warm and lively affections, of a quick and fruitful invention, and of a ready expression and elocution; all which he had mightily improved by many years' study and labors in the word and doctrine." Galpine, "Short Life," in *Flavel, the Quaker*, 14–15.

2. Cosby, *John Flavel: Puritan Life*, 21.

3. Flavel, *Method*, 2:33.

attained to a well-grounded assurance, the ravishing comforts of which were many times shed abroad in his soul; this made him a powerful and successful preacher, as one who spoke from his own heart to those of others. He preached what he felt, what he had handled, what he had seen and tasted of the word of life, and they felt it also.[4]

Flavel's preaching and ministry were characterized by a joy with which he was well acquainted. He had experienced great delight in Christ. This joy, which for Flavel rested deeply in the assurance that he was in Christ, constituted the very essence and expression of his spirituality. Such a focus was not rare among the Puritans.

The Puritans and Joy

To say that the Puritans espoused a vision for the Christian life that exuded joy would surprise, if not stun, many today. The term *puritanical* is often used to describe a person who is solemn, stern, and stiff. While this perception has seemingly always accompanied the term, its widespread modern-day popularity is likely due to its dominance among the scholarship of the early twentieth century. As Jean Williams explains, "The Puritan was seen as a somber, guilt-ridden figure, who imposed on himself unremitting activity and ascetic devotion, in order to satisfy himself that he had been elected to salvation by a distant and arbitrary Deity."[5] More recently, however, many scholars have begun to challenge this long-held assertion. Alec Ryrie, for example, notes,

> It was a truism of Protestant pastoral theology that true Christians can and ought to be happy. The best-selling Protestant devotional books of the period include titles like *The iewell of ioye, The perpetuall Reioyce of the godly, Hearts delight, A discourse about the state of true happinesse, A Helpe to true Happinesse* or *The way to true happiness.*[6]

---

4. "The Life of the Late Rev. Mr. John Flavel," in Flavel, *Works*, 1:xi–xii.

5. Williams, "Puritan Quest," 2. See also S. Bryn Roberts, *Puritanism and the Pursuit of Happiness: The Ministry and Theology of Ralph Venning* (Suffolk, England: Boydell Press, 2015), 1–4.

6. Alec Ryrie, *Being Protestant in Reformation Britain* (Oxford: Oxford University Press, 2015), 77. It is significant to note that what Ryrie calls "early modern

Such writings demonstrate a Puritan spirituality that understood joy as the hallmark of the Christian life. It would not be an overstatement to say that, at their core, English Puritans were those who sought greater joy in Christ. It was a reforming movement, and as J. I. Packer notes, their understanding of reformation centered on renewal: "The essence of this kind of 'reformation' was enrichment of understanding of God's truth, arousal of affections Godward, increase of ardour in one's devotions, and more love, joy, and firmness of Christian purpose in one's calling and personal life."[7]

A Joyous Spirituality

This purpose of increasing love and joy is evident not just in the titles of their devotional works, it is seen throughout the writings of the English Puritans. Richard Sibbes (1577–1635), who lived in the generation before Flavel, seems to take aim at a dour view of Puritan spirituality by emphatically highlighting the centrality of joy as the purpose for ministry. Sibbes asserts,

> The end of the ministry is not to tyrannise over people's souls, to sting and vex them, but to minister comfort, to be helpers of their joy; that is, to help their salvation and happiness, which is here termed joy, because joy is a principal part of happiness in this world and in the world to come. Now, the end of the ministry is to set the people's hearts into a gracious and blessed liberty, to bring them into the kingdom of grace here, and to fit them for the kingdom of glory, to help forward their joy. This is the end, both of the word and of the dispensation of the word, in the ordinances of salvation, in the sacraments, and all, that our joy may be full; as our blessed Saviour saith, "These things have I spoken, that your joy may be full," John 15:11. It is the end of all our communion with the Father, Son, and Holy Ghost, and with the ministry, and one with another; as it is, 1 John 1:4, "These things have I written that your joy may be full;" you have

---

Protestantism"—the Protestantism of Britain from ca. 1530–1640—overlaps with what this work refers to as English Puritanism.

7. Packer, *Quest*, 26–27.

communion with the Father, Son, and Holy Ghost, and with us, "that your joy may be full." All is for spiritual joy.[8]

Puritan pastors, like Sibbes, understood themselves to be helpers of people's joy. The end of their ministry of the Word was a greater joy in Christ for their hearers—for delight in God was a peak of Puritan spirituality, a center point of the Christian life. John Howe (1630–1705), in his *A Treatise of Delighting in God*, expresses,

> The Lord himself is your portion. It becomes both your state and spirit to apply yourselves to a holy delight in him; to let your souls loose, and set them at liberty to satiate themselves with those undefiled and satisfying pleasures, to which you have a right, and in which you will find the loss and want of their meaner enjoyments abundantly made up to you.... It is plain that it is the common duty of *all to delight in God*.[9]

Clearly, the Puritans were not killjoys but rather those who ardently pursued joy in every aspect of their lives. It should be noted, however, that their pursuit of joy differed greatly from the worldly strivings of many around them.[10]

A Different Kind of Joy

To understand the joy of the Puritans, then, it is crucial to comprehend what they meant by it. First, they strongly asserted the possibility and reality of experiencing a false joy. Such joy was "an irrational and frivolous emotion, unrelated to God and His salvation."[11] The great majority of Puritans had no interest in pursuing such fleeting joy. As Ryrie explains, "Were early modern Protestants happy? In the normal sense of the word, perhaps not, but they scorned that sense....

---

8. Richard Sibbes, *The Complete Works of Richard Sibbes*, ed. A. B. Grosart (London: James Nisbet, 1862), 3:506.

9. John Howe, *A Treatise of Delighting in God*, ed. C. Matthew McMahon and Therese B. McMahon (Coconut Creek, Fla.: Puritan Publications, 2012), 11, Google Books, https://books.google.com/books?id=-bFDBQAAQBAJ.

10. Thus, Alec Ryrie writes, "For while Protestants of all stripes wanted to insist that they could be joyful, they also wanted to make it clear that they did not mean worldly joy." Ryrie, *Being Protestant*, 78.

11. J. Gwyn-Thomas, "The Puritan Doctrine of Christian Joy," in *Puritan Papers: Vol. 2, 1960–1962*, ed. J. I. Packer (Phillipsburg, N.J.: P&R, 2001), 122.

They would not have traded [their joy] for the mess of what the world around them called happiness."[12]

For the Puritans, joy concerned a reality much deeper and much more enduring than worldly happiness. Their joy was profoundly rooted in their experience of and relationship with God. J. Gwyn-Thomas notes that, for the Puritans, "the road to true joy is to see that we have strong, reasonable, and spiritual grounds for rejoicing, and that such joy be always linked with its Source and Object."[13] Joy was the fruit of living in communion with God and such communion was experienced only in union with Christ. As Tom Schwanda observes, "Both delight and enjoyment were significant experiences of being in union and communion with Jesus."[14]

The Puritans had a distinct view of union with God (also expressed as union with Christ), especially in comparison with much of the mysticism that surrounded them. Williams describes this uniqueness:

> Union with God was an objective reality founded on the forensic exchange of conversion, rather than a growing enjoyment of God after conversion; but it was also a mysterious spiritual and personal oneness, an intimate and loving unity. The union between God and believers was less like a business agreement or legal contract, than like the loving union of marriage, at once enduring, covenantal, mysterious, personal, and affectionate.[15]

It should be evident from this that union and communion were intimately related in the minds of most Puritans. To be in Christ is to know and experience the benefits and blessings of Christ. J. Stephen Yuille rightly clarifies, "In other words, by virtue of the mystical union, believers participate in Christ's spiritual privileges; namely, they have communion with Him in His names, titles, righteousness, holiness,

---

12. Ryrie, *Being Protestant*, 95. See also Ryrie, *Being Protestant*, 78; Adam Potkay, "Spenser, Donne, and the Theology of Joy," *Studies in English Literature* 46, no. 1 (Winter 2006): 48; Gwyn-Thomas, "Puritan Doctrine," 120–22.

13. Gwyn-Thomas, "Puritan Doctrine," 122–23.

14. Tom Schwanda, *Soul Recreation: The Contemplative-Mystical Piety of Puritanism* (Eugene, Ore.: Pickwick, 2012), 58.

15. Williams, "Puritan Quest," 66.

death, resurrection, and glory."[16] Such participation was not some hypothetical ideal but an experienced reality. Williams again expounds, "Union was the enduring reality of oneness with God established at conversion, undisturbed by sin and admitting of no variation; communion was the variable and growing experience which developed from this union, culminating in moments of ecstatic joy."[17]

It was for this reason that so many Puritans believed joy to be the duty of the Christian. Sibbes, in light of these benefits and blessings in Christ, thus writes, "Joy is that frame and state of soul that all that have given their names to Christ either are in, or should labour to be in."[18] True Christian joy, for the Puritans, is the fruit of communion with God, which occurs only in union with Christ. Vital to the experience of joy is the knowledge that one is truly in Christ, for it is only in Christ that one can know the blessings of His inheritance. Thus, for Sibbes, "A Christian, which way soever he look, hath matter of joy. God the Father is his, Christ is his, the Holy Ghost is his Comforter, the angels are his, all are his, life or death, things present or things to come, all are his, 1 Cor. 3:22."[19]

The Joy of Assurance

The confidence that one is in Christ, then, is a crucial element for the Puritan understanding and experience of joy. Such confidence was the focus of their doctrine of assurance, which was central to Puritan theology and spirituality.[20] Joy and assurance, as the Puritans saw them, were intimately related. For one, joy is a vital sign of assurance, as it is the product of the work of the Spirit in the life of a believer. Adam Potkay maintains, "For the individual soul seeking signs of its salvation, joy, no less than 'good works,' is a proof or 'earnest' of its sanctification by the Holy Spirit."[21] Thus, there is a real sense in which the joy of the Christian brings about a greater assurance of union with Christ. The

---

16. Yuille, *Inner Sanctum*, 45.

17. Williams, "Puritan Quest," 72.

18. Sibbes, *Complete Works*, 3:506.

19. Sibbes, *Complete Works*, 3:507.

20. Chapter 2 of the present volume provides an outline of the Puritan view of this doctrine, focusing on the Westminster Confession of Faith and Flavel's *Works*.

21. Potkay, "Spenser," 43.

joy of salvation, for the Puritans, ought to increase one's assurance of that salvation.

Primarily, however, the Puritans spoke of the joy of assurance itself, for there was immense delight in knowing one was secure in Christ. Indeed, without the assurance of one's standing in Christ, one's joy could only be fleeting if present at all. Williams notes that for the Puritan believer "it was not enough to be forgiven for sin at conversion; in order to experience the security and delight which flowed from union with God, it was necessary to become certain that one was indeed saved from God's judgement."[22] That one could be certain of such final salvation in Christ was, as noted in the previous chapter, the gift of the Reformation to the people of God in their day. Assurance of salvation was the balm of Reformation soteriology against the Roman Catholic "doctrine of doubting," which denied any such assurance.[23]

This certainty of one's salvation brought about a joy that Puritans often described in the language of heaven coming to earth. Thomas Brooks, for example, in his treatise on assurance, writes,

> It will bring down heaven into your bosoms; it will give you a possession of heaven, on this side heaven. An assured soul lives in paradise, and walks in paradise, and works in paradise; and rests in paradise; he hath heaven within him, and heaven about him, and heaven over him; all his language is Heaven, heaven! Glory, glory![24]

Since the true believer's salvation is guaranteed in Christ, a guarantee which can be known and experienced through the work of the Spirit in one's life, eternal joy can also be experienced now on earth, though only in part. The Puritan doctrine of assurance, in essence, makes the Christian's heavenly eternity so real and sure that it enters into the present.[25] As Ryrie asserts, "This claim—that moments of joy now are

---

22. Williams, "Puritan Quest," 75–76.

23. See Mark Dever, "Calvin, Westminster and Assurance," in *The Westminster Confession into the 21st Century*, ed. J. Ligon Duncan III, vol. 1 (Fearn, Scotland: Christian Focus, 2003), 310.

24. Brooks, *Heaven*, 139.

25. See Gwyn-Thomas, "Puritan Doctrine," 138–40.

glimpses of heaven to come—was pastorally very powerful."[26] So powerful, that these joys of assurance were used as "an *a fortiori* argument: if 'the little sponkes of that joy' are so overwhelming, how much more joyful must Heaven itself be?"[27]

Such reasoning demonstrates how genuine these joyous experiences of assurance were for the Puritan. John Winthrop (1588–1649), like many Puritans around him, tasted this joy of assurance, and described it in soaring language. Ryrie records Winthrop's recollection of encountering this joy at age thirty when his soul closed with Christ and he immediately knew a "rest there with sweet content, so ravished with his love, as I desired nothing nor feared anything, but was filled with joy unspeakable."[28] The language of "ravished" and "joy unspeakable" in Winthrop's words must not be overlooked, for this was how the Puritans often expressed the ecstasy they felt in such extraordinary moments. Williams explains,

> By far the most common descriptive terms used to describe ecstasy, which virtually became code-words for intense delight, were the Biblical clauses "peace that passeth understanding" and "joy unspeakable and full of glory."... The Biblical language of "ravishment" was also frequently borrowed from the Song of Songs, for it implied the abrupt and overpowering nature of ecstasy.[29]

Such speech, then, was used by the Puritans in those times "when a sense of God's love overwhelmed the soul."[30] As Winthrop's experience demonstrates, these ecstatic moments of exceptional joy often arose from the certainty of one's salvation in Christ.

The Pursuit of Joy

Though such experiences were typically quite brief, especially in light of the scope of one's life, the effects were long-lasting. Ryrie points out that "these experiences were, as a matter of chronological fact, occasional

---

26. Ryrie, *Being Protestant*, 86.
27. Ryrie, *Being Protestant*, 86.
28. John Winthrop, quoted in Ryrie, *Being Protestant*, 83.
29. Williams, "Puritan Quest," 116–17.
30. Williams, "Puritan Quest," 114.

and passing. But the experience itself contained a sense of timeless constancy."[31] Of course, these occasions of joy, though intermittent, were cultivated by the Spirit as the believer communed with God. This communion centered on what the Puritans referred to as the ordinary means of grace—those means which arose out of the Word of God and which brought that same Word deeper into the believer's heart.[32] The Puritans held that communion with God was the fruit of union with Christ and that such communion occurred through the Word of God.

Here, then, the Puritans recognized that joy was both a gift from God as well as a goal to be pursued. Joy came chiefly from the work of the Holy Spirit, but not to the neglect of all responsibility on the part of the believer. Gwyn-Thomas is right to conclude that joy "is the fruit of the new birth; God has wrought in man the nature which is capable of rejoicing in spiritual things. Not only is God the object of joy but He too is the one who has made it possible for us to rejoice in Himself. This He has done by His regenerating activity and His gift of the Holy Spirit."[33] Christians, because of the indwelling of the Spirit, have both the ability and the power to rejoice in God in all circumstances. This power is not their own, certainly, but the power the Spirit graciously gives to all who are in Christ. Such tension can be seen clearly in the thinking of Howe:

> You must expect to be dealt with as a sort of creature capable of understanding your own concernments; not to be hewed or hammered as senseless stones that are ignorant of the artist's intent, but as living ones, to be polished and fitted to the spiritual building by a hand that reasonably expects your own compliance. Unto which design though you must know you are to be subservient, and must do something; yet you must withal consider you can be but subservient, and of yourselves alone can

---

31. Ryrie, *Being Protestant*, 83.

32. For a brief explanation of these means, WSC 88 explains, "What are the outward and ordinary means whereby Christ communicateth to us the benefits of redemption? The outward and ordinary means whereby Christ communicateth to us the benefits of redemption, are his ordinances, especially the word, sacraments, and prayer; all which are made effectual to the elect for salvation." Schaff and Schaff, eds., *Creeds of Christendom*, 3:695.

33. Gwyn-Thomas, "Puritan Doctrine," 126–27.

do just nothing. Therefore if ever you would know what a life of spiritual delight means, you must constantly strive against all your spiritual distempers that obstruct it, in the power of the Holy Ghost. And do not think that is enjoining you a course wholly out of your power; for though it be true that the power of the Holy Ghost is not naturally yours, or at your disposal; yet by gracious vouchsafement and ordination it is.[34]

The Puritans assert that joy comes from God alone but also maintain that, by His grace, such joy can and must be sought by the people of God.

The responsibility of the Christian to seek joy necessitated a clear and accessible path on which one could pursue this delight in God. This Puritan path of piety, as noted above, centered on the Word of God and the means of grace. Though not a guarantee for joy in God, these means, for the Puritans, were the way God ordained for His people to commune with Him. Williams contends that these "devotional disciplines were the main mechanism God used to commune with the soul, and spiritual joy could never be expected without them."[35] Of chief significance among these disciplines were that of reading Scripture, prayer, and focused meditation on the things of God.[36] These

---

34. John Howe, *The Works of John Howe: As Published during His Life* (London: William Tegg, 1848), 1:590.

35. Williams, "Puritan Quest," 217.

36. Williams provides a helpful summary of the "typical daily pattern" for the devotional life recommended by popular handbooks of the day: "When you awake, let your first thoughts be centred on God; as you dress, meditate on the vanity of clothes and on your spiritual nakedness and need to be covered with the garment of Christ's righteousness; spend some time in private Bible reading, meditation on the Bible or a set topic, and a prayer in which you confess your sin, thank God for his preservation during the night, and pray for blessing during the coming day; engage in family Bible reading, prayer, and Psalm singing; in your secular calling, be honest and diligent; during the day, pray or meditate spontaneously and briefly as you go about your business; at dinner and supper, pray before and after the meal; let your conversation centre on spiritual things; in the evening, hold family duties, and then engage in private duties; as you remove your clothes, meditate on the fact that the day is coming when you will be stripped of all you have; before you sleep, review the day's sins and mercies; keep a written record of them; pray and repent of the day's sins, thank God for the day's blessings, and ask for preservation during the night; as you go to bed, meditate on sleep as an image of death—your last thoughts should be centred

means were to be pursued, both routinely and spontaneously, as individuals and as families, throughout the day as the believer sought to commune with and enjoy God.

The Puritan pursuit of joy through the means of grace was principally focused on Scripture. For them, Scripture was where one met God. Thus, Packer contends, "In the Puritans' communion with God, as Jesus Christ was central, so Holy Scripture was supreme."[37] Scripture was the "foundation, rule, and guide of the whole church, the spiritual food and means of life to all its members."[38] The path to joy in God, then, necessarily included immersing oneself in Scripture. The Puritans called one another to frequent reading of God's Word, to diligent study of its truth, and to consistent hearing of its proclamation. This last point was not to be neglected, as Charles Hambrick-Stowe points out, "For Perkins and other late sixteenth-century Puritans, chief of among the means of grace was the Word of God preached by godly ministers of the gospel."[39] Also central to the Puritans' engagement with Scripture was their emphasis on the significance of meditation. As Thomas Hooker (1586–1647) explains, meditation was "a serious intention of the mind, whereby we come to search out the truth and settle it effectually upon the heart."[40] It has been noted that "the Puritans believed that such meditation should be used to stir up our affections to glorify God and to arouse our minds to dutiful, holy resolutions."[41]

Such meditation was not only to be upon Scripture but was to include all things that encourage one's mind and heart Godward. Concerning the pursuit and experience of joy in God, the Puritans specifically sought to meditate on the realities of heaven and the

---

on God; sleep frugally; if you wake during the night, pray or meditate." Williams, "Puritan Quest," 219–20.

37. Packer, *Quest*, 24.

38. Mariano Di Gangi, ed., *Great Themes in Puritan Preaching* (Guelph, Ont.: Joshua Press, 2007), 21.

39. Charles Hambrick-Stowe, quoted in John Coffey and Paul C. H. Lim, eds., *The Cambridge Companion to Puritanism*, Cambridge Companions to Religion (Cambridge: Cambridge University Press, 2008), 195.

40. Thomas Hooker, quoted in Joel R. Beeke and Mark Jones, *A Puritan Theology: Doctrine for Life* (Grand Rapids: Reformation Heritage Books, 2012), 533.

41. Beeke and Jones, *Puritan Theology*, 533.

eternal joy that awaited them. They desired to be truly heavenly-minded. As Dewey Wallace describes, "Heavenly mindedness was the spiritual person's foretaste of the joys of heaven through meditation."[42] Thus, John Downame (1571–1652) writes that meditation "increaseth our sweet communion with God.... It exalteth our minds and souls above…worldly things, and causeth us…whilest we carry about with us this body of flesh, to be heavenly minded, and partakers of the Divine nature."[43] Ryrie is certainly correct to conclude that "the implication was that a serious effort at meditation could generate joy."[44]

The final principal way the Puritans sought joy was through prayer.[45] Both their engagement with Scripture and their meditation led the Puritans to pray. Such prayer was "to involve one's whole person, and it must be done regularly so it becomes a habit. The best way to pray is to pray the Scriptures, using the very words of the Bible as the content of our prayers."[46] After hearing from God in His Word, the Puritans endeavored to respond to God through prayer. Deeply saturated in Scripture, and aided by the Holy Spirit, prayer was often understood to be the culmination of communion with God and the time of most immense joy in God. Williams explains, "Private prayer was greatly valued by the Puritans, as the place where communion with God was most intimate, and enjoyment of God reached new heights."[47] Note how Thomas Brooks describes these blessings of prayer and how closely he ties them to communion with God:

> There is no service wherein souls have such a near, familiar, and friendly intercourse with God, as in this of prayer; neither is there any service wherein God doth more delight to make known his grace and goodness, his mercy and bounty, his beauty and glory, to poor souls, than this of prayer. The best and the sweetest flowers of paradise, God gives to his people when they are upon their

---

42. Dewey D. Wallace Jr., ed., introduction to *The Spirituality of the Later English Puritans: An Anthology* (Macon, Ga.: Mercer University Press, 1987), xvii.

43. John Downame, quoted in Williams, "Puritan Quest," 239.

44. Ryrie, *Being Protestant*, 87.

45. The rest of this work focuses specifically on Flavel's pursuit of joy in assurance, which proves to be a helpful example of the joy-centered spirituality of the Puritans.

46. Beeke and Jones, *Puritan Theology*, 533.

47. Williams, "Puritan Quest," 227.

knees…. God loves to lade the wings of prayer with the choicest and chiefest blessings. Ah! how often, Christians! hath God
kissed you at the beginning of prayer, and spoke peace to you in
the midst of prayer, and filled you with joy and assurance, upon
the close of prayer![48]

Prayer, for the Puritans, was not simply a prescribed add-on to the
spiritual life but a necessary means of communing with God and of
experiencing the joy of salvation in God.

Summary

The Puritans, often misidentified as sullen killjoys, were actually quite
emphatic about the necessity of joy for the Christian. They understood true joy to be at odds with the cultural norms of their day but
no less real and significant. Joy was at the heart of their spirituality,
for it flowed from communion with God in Christ. Essential to the
experience of joy, then, was the confidence the Spirit gives sincere
believers that they are indeed in Christ. This assurance undergirded
their delight and led them to pursue joy in God in all aspects of their
lives. Understanding joy to be the gift of the Spirit, they also held that
it was to be pursued through the ordinary means of grace. Thus, joy
was both the duty and the blessing of the Christian.

John Flavel and Joy

Flavel exemplifies the joy-centered spirituality of the Puritan movement, as his life and ministry exuded a profound delight in God. This
central emphasis on joy, while arising predominantly from his study
of Scripture, likely also found roots in his own experience. In his
A Treatise of the Soul of Man Flavel recounts an encounter with God
of particular significance.[49] Having determined to make the most of a

---

48. Thomas Brooks, *The Complete Works of Thomas Brooks*, ed. A. B. Grosart
(London: James Nisbet, 1866), 2:368–69.

49. See Flavel, *Pneumatologia*, 3:57–58. Flavel writes this story in the third
person and introduces it by saying, "I have, with good assurance, this account of a
minister," though it seems most likely that he is recalling an event from his own life.
The anonymous *Life of Rev. John Flavell, of Dartmouth* also takes this view: "In this
work he relates, in the third person, the following singular experience, which his
biographer states to refer to himself." *Life of Rev. John Flavell, of Dartmouth*, Christian

solitary journey, he spent his day traveling and meditating on the state of his soul and the hope of heaven. While meditating, "his thoughts began to swell, and rise higher and higher, like the waters in Ezekiel's vision, till at last they became an overflowing flood."[50] What followed was an experience of the joy of assurance that would mark his life:

> Such was the intention of his mind, such the ravishing tastes of heavenly joys, and such the full assurance of his interest therein, that he utterly lost a sight and sense of this world, and all the concerns thereof; and, for some hours, knew no more where he was, than if he had been in a deep sleep upon his bed.... He many years after called that day one of the days of heaven, and professed he understood more of the light of heaven by it, than by all the books he ever read, or discourses he ever had entertained about it. This was indeed an extraordinary fore-taste of heaven for degree, but it came in the ordinary way and method of faith and meditation.[51]

Such an encounter, however, was but a sample of a life lived in the joy of God. Flavel, through much persecution, faithfully ministered to his people with a heart that continually rejoiced in the goodness of God to him in Christ. As one of his biographers expressed,

> What he believed, his heart appears to have felt, and it influenced his conduct. His religion was not theological speculation, nor was it mere feeling; but that divine all-pervading principle which sanctifies the heart, elevates the affections, brings into near and delightful communion with God, by its progressive influence, fits a man for the society of angels, and the presence of God.[52]

In fact, so central was delight to his ministry that his last days were spent writing on the topic. As Increase Mather notes, "He also began some meditations on the joys of heaven; but before he had an opportunity to express what had been in his heart, the Lord Jesus said unto

---

Biography (London, 1834), 49. The degree of specificity of the account, especially the descriptions of the individual's inner thoughts, makes such a judgment nearly certain.

50. Flavel, *Pneumatologia*, 3:57.

51. Flavel, *Pneumatologia*, 3:57–58.

52. *Life of Rev. John Flavell*, 71.

him, 'Enter thou into the joy of thy Lord.'"[53] It is clear that Flavel experienced and exhibited great joy throughout his life in Christ. It was the essence and the expression of his spirituality.

Understanding Flavel's Joy

To discern Flavel's conception of joy it seems best to begin at his clearest explication of it, which is found in *An Exposition of the Assembly's Catechism*. Written toward the end of his life, Flavel lays out the basics of his understanding of Christian joy. He initiates his discussion by highlighting three different sorts of joy found in the world: sensitive, sinful, and spiritual.[54] The broadest of these categories, sensitive joy, is that which arises from one's receiving of God's common grace through the good things he has dispersed in the world (Acts 14:17). Such joy, while finding its source in the goodness of God, may be experienced at any time by all humanity.

There is, however, a joy that does not arise from God's goodness. Sinful joy, for Flavel, is a joy that is grounded upon the delusion of carnal security and presumptuous hope. Concerning this false joy of the unregenerate, he writes,

> They rejoice in corn, wine, and oil, in their estates and children, in the pleasant fruition of the creature; yea, and they rejoice also in Christ and the promises, in heaven and in glory: with all which they have just such a kind of communion as a man hath in a dream with a full feast and curious music; and just so their joy will vanish when they awake.[55]

This delight of the unregenerate includes both a real, though fleeting, carnal joy in the things of the world and a deceptively foolish joy in things spiritual. Regarding the former, Flavel sometimes refers to it as "creature joy," as he takes pains to clearly delineate what it does and does not offer. For instance, he explains,

> It is true, they [unbelievers] abound in creature-comforts; they live in pleasure upon earth; joy displays its colours in their faces;

---

53. Increase Mather, "An Epistle to the Reader," in Flavel, *Exposition*, 6:140.

54. Flavel, *Exposition*, 6:203.

55. Flavel, *Method*, 2:290.

> but for all this, there is not the least drop of true consolation in their hearts; they have some comfort in creature, but none in Christ: that little they gather in from the creature now, is all their portion of joy.[56]

There is pleasure in sin and in the worldly life, but such pleasure is always divided and temporary. In the end, it cannot stand. Flavel continues,

> And while they do enjoy it, it is mixed with many gripes of conscience, Job 14:13. Whatever consolation any unbeliever speaks of besides this, is but by rote; for when the day of his distress cometh, and the terrors of conscience shall awake him out of his pleasant dreams, all his sensual joys will vanish from him, and the doors of true consolation will be shut against him.[57]

Sin ultimately offers a half joy—that which never fully satisfies, even in the moment, and that which proves utterly destructive in the end.

Perhaps more dangerous, though, is the illusory spiritual joy of those who think they know Christ. Flavel is quick to point out that there is a joy in spiritual things that seems genuine but proves otherwise. Such joy is dreamlike—tangible in the moment but mere fantasy in reality. He proposes that such delusional joy springs from "church-privileges, natural ignorance, false evidences of the love of God, slight workings of the gospel, self-love, comparing themselves with the more profane, and Satan's policy managing all these in order to their eternal ruin."[58] Such are the "many springs to feed and maintain this life of delusion in the unregenerate."[59] Flavel recognizes the perils of false joy and is careful to condemn it at every point. Unimpressed with the carnal comforts of his culture, however, he does not contend against joy altogether.

For Flavel, the final category of spiritual joy is the only true joy to be found in this life. It is "this only that deserves the name of true solid consolation."[60] While Flavel speaks of spiritual joy in many ways

---

56. Flavel, *Method*, 2:249.
57. Flavel, *Method*, 2:249–50.
58. Flavel, *Method*, 2:290.
59. Flavel, *Method*, 2:290.
60. Flavel, *Method*, 2:245.

throughout his writings, he defines it simply as that which "is nothing else but the cheerfulness of our heart in God, and the sense of our interest in him, and in his promises."[61] Such delight brings real consolation, a close companion to joy for Flavel, which is "the cheerfulness of a man's spirit, whereby he is upheld, and fortified against all evils felt, or feared.... [It is] the refreshment, peace, and joy, gracious souls have in Christ, by the exercise of faith, hope, and other graces."[62] The uniqueness of this spiritual joy when compared with sinful joy is clear, then, as it is whole, unwavering, and transforming. It is "joy unspeakable and full of glory."[63] Where worldly joy always leaves one wanting, spiritual joy leaves one overflowing; so much so, writes Flavel, that "when a good man had but a little more than ordinary joy of the Lord poured into his soul, he was heard to cry, Hold, Lord, hold! thy poor creature is but a clay vessel, and can hold no more!"[64]

Delight in God is also unwavering and can buoy the soul in the most difficult of seasons. While it might not always include a natural or sensual joy, "there is no season wherein spiritual joy and comfort in God is unseasonable."[65] Flavel is insistent that neither man nor circumstance should triumph over the joy of God that resides in the believer's heart. A little perspective is all that is needed—for one step back from the worst of situations should quickly reveal that *the saints have infinitely more cause to rejoice, than to be cast down. There is more in one of their mercies to comfort them than in all of their troubles to deject them.*[66] Furthermore, not only do believers have more comfort

---

61. John Flavel, *Divine Conduct or the Mystery of Providence: A Treatise upon Psalm 57.2*, in *Works of John Flavel* (1820; repr., Edinburgh: Banner of Truth Trust, 2015), 4:429.

62. Flavel, *Method*, 2:244–45.

63. Flavel, *Exposition*, 6:203.

64. Flavel, *Pneumatologia*, 3:45.

65. Flavel, *Divine Conduct*, 4:428.

66. Flavel, *Divine Conduct*, 4:429. I have slightly altered this quotation of Flavel, putting it in the indicative where he originally asks a rhetorical question; however, the sense is the same. Here is the original in its larger context: "Why should we lay by our joy in God, upon the account of sad providences without, when at the very worst and lowest ebb, the saints have infinitely more cause to rejoice, than to be cast down? there is more in one of their mercies to comfort them than in all their troubles to deject them."

in Christ than woe in the world but their God can also change their difficulties to delight. As Flavel proclaims, "Your troubles in the world have been turned into joy, but your comforts in Christ can never be turned into trouble."[67] Spiritual joy is steadfast and resolute: "It is not in the power of men to deprive the saints of it."[68]

While true joy in God is both profound and persevering, it is also purposeful. As Flavel explains, "It makes the soul free and cheerful in the ways of obedience."[69] Delighting in God has a sanctifying effect on the soul of the believer. The more joy believers experience in God, the more they want of God. Joy and obedience are constant companions, for joy is found in obedience and obedience arises out of joy. Flavel sees this truth, for instance, in the sowing and reaping language of Scripture. He writes, "Every gracious action is the seed of joy; and every sinful action the seed of anguish and sorrow to the soul that soweth it."[70] Such rewards and consequences, however, are not always immediate or even apparent but they are definite. Flavel reminds his readers that "though the fruit or consequence of holy actions, for the present may seem bitter, and the fruit of sinful actions, sweet and pleasant; yet there is nothing more certain than that their future fruits shall be according to their present nature and quality."[71] Obedience to God will undoubtedly lead to greater joy in God. Such obedience, however, is only possible for those who have tasted true delight in God. Flavel states, "Now the wheels of the soul being oiled with the joy and comfort of the Spirit, run nimbly in the ways of obedience. The joy of the Lord is your strength."[72] The joy of the Spirit transforms the soul and leads us to greater holiness and even greater joy.

---

67. Flavel, *Method*, 2:251.

68. Flavel, *Exposition*, 6:203.

69. Flavel, *Exposition*, 6:203.

70. John Flavel, *Husbandry Spiritualized; Or, The Heavenly Use of Earthly Things*, in *Works of John Flavel* (1820; repr., Edinburgh: Banner of Truth Trust, 2015), 5:122. See also *Pneumatologia*, 3:161.

71. Flavel, *Husbandry Spiritualized*, 5:123.

72. Flavel, *Twelve Sacramental Meditations*, 6:408. It is significant to note that the "joy and comfort of the Spirit" that Flavel speaks of here is that which is brought forth through the sealing (or assuring) work of the Spirit. Again, Flavel ties joy and assurance together.

Like many of his Puritan contemporaries, therefore, Flavel understood joy to be the duty of all sincere Christians.[73] In answer to the question, "What should be the main care of a Christian in this world?" he replies, "To maintain his joy in God to the last."[74] The joy of the Christian is both his delight and his duty. For Flavel, it could not be otherwise, for joy is the only reasonable response to the mercies of God in Christ. Thus, he asks, "How rational is the joy of Christians, above the joy of all others in the world?"[75] Joy, for the Christian, is eminently sensible. Again, Flavel asks, "What is the Christian's work, but 'with joy to draw water out of the wells of salvation?'"[76] Thus, one should not be surprised that the command to rejoice is found throughout Scripture. Flavel explains that "joy in the way of the Lord is made the duty of the saints" (Pss. 97:12; 132:9, 16; Luke 7:22; Phil. 4:4).[77] Such duty, of course, is not burdensome for the true believer, for this duty is their delight. It is the longing of every new creature in Christ. Thus, Flavel asserts,

> When our work is our delight, we never faint nor tire at it. This inclination to God is to the soul as wings to a bird, or sails to a ship. This carries the soul easily through every duty.... For the hypocrite takes not delight in the spiritual and inward part of duty, but is secretly weary of it.... But now the upright heart goes to God as his joy.[78]

Joy, then, for Flavel is both the experience and the expectation of the Christian. While markedly different from its worldly counterfeits, it is profoundly palpable and powerful.

Flavel's Joy in the Triune God

Flavel captures the heart of the Puritan understanding of joy, which is

---

73. For example, see Sibbes, *Complete Works*, 3:506–7.

74. Flavel, *Exposition*, 6:204.

75. Flavel, *Method*, 2:276.

76. Flavel, *Husbandry Spiritualized*, 5:37.

77. Flavel, *Husbandry Spiritualized*, 5:38.

78. John Flavel, *Preparations for Suffering, in the Worst Times*, in *Works of John Flavel* (1820; repr., Edinburgh: Banner of Truth Trust, 2015), 6:35.

uniquely centered in God. True joy is to be found in God alone. The Puritans, in line with their Reformation forebears, asserted a strong doctrine of the Trinity.[79] This emphasis on the triune God is especially evident in Flavel's exposition of joy. He does not simply exhort his readers to a generic joy in God but rather a joy in God the Father, God the Son, and God the Spirit. While never separating or denying their unity, Flavel does highlight each especially, demonstrating a robust Trinitarian concept of joy.

Though less prominent in his discussions of joy, Flavel still clearly features God the Father as the source and center of all true delight. In his exposition of the glory of the preincarnate Son from Proverbs 8:30, he describes the Father as the "fountain, ocean and centre of all delights and joys."[80] He then expresses the richness of the Son's experience with the Father:

> To be wrapt up in the soul and bosom of all delights, as Christ was, must needs be a transcending apprehension; to have the fountain of love and delight letting out itself so immediately, and fully, and everlastingly, upon this only begotten darling of his soul, so as it never did communicate itself to any; judge what a state of transcendent felicity this must be.[81]

Flavel describes here the vibrant fellowship and communion within the Godhead, as he asserts the great joy that the Son has in the Father. Such delight in the Father, then, is what the Son shares with His people. Flavel explains,

---

79. For more on the Puritan understanding and emphasis on the Trinity, see Beeke and Jones, *Puritan Theology*, 85–100. The most substantial seventeenth-century Puritan work on the Trinity was Francis Cheynell's *The Divine Triunity of the Father, Son, and Holy Spirit* (London, 1650); also see John Owen, *Of Communion with God the Father, Son, and Holy Ghost, Each Person Distinctly, in Love, Grace, and Consolation; or, The Saint's Fellowship with the Father, Son, and Holy Ghost Unfolded*, in *Works of John Owen*, ed. William H. Gould (1850–53; repr., Edinburgh: Banner of Truth Trust, 1980). For more on Flavel's understanding of the Trinity, see Cosby, *John Flavel: Puritan Life*, 73–75; Brian H. Cosby, "The Christology of John Flavel," *Puritan Reformed Journal* 4, no. 1 (2012): 116–34.

80. John Flavel, *Fountain: A Display of Christ in His Essential and Mediatorial Glory*, in *Works of John Flavel* (1820; repr., Edinburgh: Banner of Truth Trust, 2015), 1:46.

81 Flavel, *Fountain*, 1:46.

> It shews us the peculiar happiness and privilege of believers above all people in the world: these only are they which shall be brought to God by Jesus Christ in a reconciled state.... Believers only are brought to God in the Mediator's hand, as a reconciled Father, to be made blessed for ever in the enjoyment of him.[82]

It is this felicity in the Father that is the great desire of humanity and the satisfaction of souls. Humanity's only true delight is in God, for He alone is its source, and all other so-called joys are mere fantasy outside of Him. Flavel is clear "that the chief happiness of man consisteth in the enjoyment of God: that the creature hath as necessary dependence upon God for happiness, as the stream hath upon the fountain, or the image in the glass upon the face of him that looks into it."[83]

With God the Father as the source of all joy, Flavel is quick to highlight the significant role of the Son as the one in whom believers have joy.[84] For while there is no joy that does not originate with the Father, there is also no experience of joy outside of the person and ministry of Jesus Christ. As Flavel writes, "[The knowledge of Jesus Christ] is fundamental to all comforts: all the comforts of believers are streams from this fountain. Jesus Christ is the very object of a believer's joy."[85] Here the doctrine of the Trinity is on full display, as Flavel describes both the Father and the Son as the fountain of joy, and yet still upholds their unique roles in the believer's experience of it. God the Father is the source while Christ is the object, but both are indispensable. Thus, Flavel proclaims, "Take away the knowledge of Christ, and a Christian is the most sad and melancholy creature in the world: again, let Christ but manifest himself, and dart the beams of his

---

82. Flavel, *Method*, 2:281.

83. Flavel, *Method*, 280. Elsewhere, Flavel states, "What is it for God to be all in all? First, That all the saints shall be filled and satisfied from God alone. Secondly, That there shall be no need of other things out of which they were wont to fetch comfort. Thirdly, That all other things, as heaven, angels, saints, shall be loved and enjoyed in God." *Exposition*, 6:215.

84. This section includes only a brief discussion of this role, as the next chapter focuses entirely on Flavel's concern for his congregation to look to Jesus for their joy.

85. Flavel, *Fountain*, 1:35.

light into their souls, it will make them kiss the stakes, sing in flames, and shout in the pangs of death, as men divide the spoil."[86]

The essential nature of Christ for believers' joy is due partly to the fact that it is He who has secured their joy through His life, death, and resurrection. All delight that the believer experiences arises only from His gracious work on one's behalf. As Flavel reminds his readers, "All spiritual good things are purchased by the blood of Christ for them."[87] And "this most precious grace is the dear purchase of our Lord Jesus Christ; yea, all that peace, joy, and spiritual comfort, which are the sweet fruit of faith, are with it purchased for us by his blood."[88] All the joyous benefits of His people's salvation have been procured by Him, and such benefits bring about an incalculable delight. Thus, Flavel proclaims, "He would not only obtain joy for them, but a full joy."[89] Of course, such joy is not to be found purely in that which Christ has secured but in His very person. Flavel is careful to never divorce Christ from His benefits and ensures that one grasps that joy is found not in His things but in His person. He asserts that "the gospel is glad tidings of great joy; but that which makes it so is Jesus Christ, whom it imparts and reveals to us."[90] The gospel is the good news of salvation, but that salvation is none other than the reconciliation of Christ's people to Himself. It is He that is their great reward and joy.

While the importance of the Father and the Son cannot be overlooked, it is the Spirit who holds prominence in Flavel's teaching on joy.[91] Flavel repeatedly uses the phrase "joy in the Holy Ghost" in his works, and such use demonstrates this principal role of the Spirit.[92] Flavel asks, "Why is spiritual joy called joy in the Holy Ghost?" He

---

86. Flavel, *Fountain*, 1:35.

87. Flavel, *Fountain*, 1:192.

88. Flavel, *Fountain*, 1:192.

89. Flavel, *Fountain*, 1:249.

90. Flavel, *Method*, 2:244. Flavel cites Luke 2:10–11 as support for such a statement.

91. This section includes only a brief discussion of the Spirit's role, as chapter 5 focuses entirely on Flavel's concern for his congregation to discern the Spirit for their joy.

92. For Flavel's most extensive treatment of this phrase, see John Flavel, *England's Duty under the Present Gospel Liberty*, in *Works of John Flavel* (1820; repr., Edinburgh: Banner of Truth Trust, 2015), 4:218–19.

responds simply, "Because the Holy Ghost is the author of it."[93] Joy is the fruit of the Spirit's ministry in the life of believers; thus, it is He who writes it into their souls. Again, Flavel's Trinitarianism is evident as he describes the Spirit, much like the Father and the Son, as the fountain of joy. "This life infused by the regenerating Spirit, is a most pleasant life. All delights, all pleasures, all joys, which are not fantastic and delusive, have their spring and origin here, Rom. 8:6."[94] All true spiritual joy arises out of the gracious work of the Spirit in applying the benefits of salvation obtained by Christ.

Flavel is insistent that it is not just the products of the Spirit that bring joy but His person. The presence of the Spirit in the life of the believer is itself great delight. As Flavel asks rhetorically, "Is it matter of all joy to have the Comforter himself, who is the Spirit of all consolation, taking up residence in thy heart, cheering, comforting, and refreshing it with such cordials as are unknown things in all the unbelieving world?"[95] The resounding *yes* to this question exhibits the grandeur of both the Spirit and the Spirit's joy.

While the Spirit's very presence brings some joy into the life of the believer now, His presence is also a guarantee of an exceedingly greater joy for all eternity. As will be discussed in the following section, Flavel is always quick to stress the indispensable nature of assurance for the experience of any spiritual joy in this life. The Spirit's assuring or sealing work, then, is of utmost import in His bringing joy to the believer. As Flavel explains, "This joy of the Holy Ghost is a spiritual cheerfulness streaming through the soul of a believer upon the Spirit's testimony, which clears his interest in Christ, and glory. No sooner doth the Spirit shed forth the love of God into the believer's heart, but it streams and overflows with joy."[96] All three persons of the triune God are featured in the joy of the believer; the joy of the Father brought to the Christian through the work of Christ and made known

---

93. Flavel, *Exposition*, 6:203. He also states, "Whence it become excellently expressive of the nature and use of the Spirit of grace, who is the cause and author of all joy in believers, John xvii. 13." *Method*, 2:143.

94. Flavel, *Method*, 2:90.

95. Flavel, *England's Duty*, 4:226.

96. Flavel, *England's Duty*, 4:218.

by the testimony of the Spirit. Spiritual joy, for Flavel, was deeply Trinitarian and consisted of delighting in the Father, Son, and Holy Spirit.

Flavel's Joy of Assurance

At the center of Flavel's understanding of joy lies the doctrine of assurance. If true spiritual joy is to be found only in God, then its experience necessarily clings to the certainty of one's standing before God. As Flavel asserts, "Evidence is requisite to joy and comfort; yea, so necessary, that even interest and propriety afford no sensible sweetness without it.… If I am registered in the book of life, and know it not, what comfort can my name there afford me?"[97] The experience of spiritual joy in this life is tied as directly to one's experience of assurance as to one's salvation. All the delight to be had in the benefits of salvation rest on the knowledge that believers have indeed been saved. It is for this reason that Flavel can so confidently declare, "All the solid delight and comfort of life results from the settlement and security of a man's great concern in the proper season thereof."[98] All delight and comfort in this life hang on the security of man's great concern—the salvation of his soul. In fact, for Flavel, this joy is the very fruit of assurance. "What is the fruit of assurance? Joy unspeakable amidst outward troubles."[99] The joy of assurance is that which even the most sizable trials and tribulations of this world cannot extinguish.

Such an understanding, however, does not mean that Flavel held assurance, and therefore joy, to be guaranteed for the true Christian. As noted earlier in this work, Flavel believed it was not only possible but even likely that sincere believers would experience seasons of doubts concerning their interest in Christ. He explains, "There is many a true believer to whom the joy and comfort of assurance is denied; they may say of their union with Christ, as Paul said of his vision; whether in the body or out of the body, I cannot tell; so they, whether in Christ

---

97. Flavel, *Method*, 2:23.

98. Flavel, *Pneumatologia*, 3:233. The "season" that Flavel speaks of here refers to the "seasons and opportunities for the application of Christ and his benefits, to their own souls" (227). Thus, the settlement and security of one's great concern is the gaining of assurance of their salvation in the proper season of its application to their souls.

99. Flavel, *Exposition*, 6:201.

or out of Christ, they cannot tell."[100] It is possible to be a Christian and not experience the certainty of that reality. And while this state does not affect the eternal joy of the believer, it profoundly alters one's current experience of it. There is little so lamentable for Flavel than doubting Christians who do not know the joy of their salvation. As Flavel expresses, "What though this state of friendship can never be dissolved, yet it is a dreadful thing to have it clouded: You may lose the sense of peace, and with it all the joy of your hearts, and the comforts of your lives in this world."[101] It is a dreadful affair indeed, to be in a state of clouded friendship with Christ and have your joy diminished.

It is this tragic plight that prompted Flavel to push his hearers to greater assurance and consequently, greater joy. While he understands this joy of assurance to be the gracious gift of the Spirit, Flavel still maintains that believers have a role to play in pursuing it.[102] He writes, "The comfort of our souls doth much depend upon the keeping of our hearts; for he that is negligent in attending his own heart, is (ordinarily) a great stranger to assurance, and the sweet comforts flowing from it."[103] The sincere Christian, then, in order to know true joy in God, must persist with all diligence in keeping his or her heart. For, as Flavel exhorts,

> God doth not usually indulge lazy and negligent souls with the comforts of assurance; he will not so much seem to patronize sloth and carelessness; he will give it, but it shall be in his own way: his command hath united our care and comfort together; they are mistaken that think the beautiful child of assurance may

---

100. Flavel, *Method*, 2:114. See chapter 2 of the present volume for more on Flavel's view of assurance.

101. Flavel, *Method*, 2:66.

102. See Flavel, *Saint Indeed*, 5:434. Here Flavel explains that the Spirit assures by witnessing to one's adoption in two ways: objectively and effectively. Objectively, "by working those graces in our souls which are the conditions of the promise, and so the Spirit and his graces in us, are all one: the Spirit of God dwelling in us, is a mark of our adoption." Effectively, "by irradiating the soul with grace-discovering light, shining upon his work…he first infuses the grace, and then opens the eye of the soul to see it." For more on this role of the Spirit in assurance, see chapter 2 of the present volume.

103. Flavel, *Saint Indeed*, 5:433.

be born without pangs; ah, how many solitary hours have the people of God spend in heart-examination![104]

The pursuit of assurance takes substantial effort, for self-examination of the heart can be an exceedingly painful task. Flavel is quick to point out, though, that it is a proven way. He writes, "It is the course that Christians have taken in all ages, and that which God hath abundantly blessed to the joy and encouragement of their souls."[105] It is not an easy exercise, but it is the only way to true and lasting comfort and joy. For Flavel, then, it is decidedly worth it. There exists no more significant duty for the believer: "Since, then, the joy of our life, the comfort of our souls, rises and falls with our diligence in this work, keep your hearts with all diligence."[106]

Finally, Flavel wants to be sure his hearers comprehend the immense power of this joy of assurance. Such joy cannot be contained, nor can it be overcome. Its power transforms all persons and all problems. Thus, Flavel exclaims, "What heart hath largeness and strength enough to receive and contain the joy and comfort which flow from a cleared interest in Christ!"[107] So exceptional is this joy, that "if there were no other heaven, [it would be] an abundant recompence."[108] Unsurprisingly, then, Flavel believes this joy to have the ability to enable Christians to withstand any situation that might come their way. It is a delight that encourages and enlivens the soul. Without it, there is only hardship; but with it, only hope. Flavel contends,

> Let God but give a person a little of this joy into his heart, and he shall presently feel himself strengthened by it, either to do or to suffer the will of God. Now he can pray with enlargement, hear with comfort, meditate with delight: and if God call him

---

104. Flavel, *Saint Indeed*, 5:435.

105. John Flavel, *A Brief Account of the Rise and Growth of Antinomianism, with Reflections upon the Errors of the Sect*, in *Works of John Flavel* (1820; repr., Edinburgh: Banner of Truth Trust, 2015), 3:590.

106. Flavel, *Saint Indeed*, 5:435.

107. Flavel, *Method*, 2:386.

108. Flavel, *England's Duty*, 4:219.

to suffer, this joy shall strengthen him to bear it. This was it that made the martyrs go singing to the stake.[109]

It is no wonder that Flavel sees this joy of assurance as the center and culmination of all joy in God.

Conclusion

Throughout his life and ministry, John Flavel had joy in his sights. It was not merely a theme of his preaching but a reality in his experience. He knew joy in God—a joy that arose out of his confidence that he was indeed in Christ. And it is at this point that one begins to see how the joy of assurance informs his spirituality. In a word, the heart of his spirituality is the pursuit of a joy which is known best by way of assurance. Thus, for Flavel, the pursuit of assurance is the pursuit of deepest joy, meaning they follow identical paths. Moreover, the motivation for assurance is joy. And this is what makes the joy of assurance the essence and expression of Flavel's spirituality.

---

109. Flavel, *England's Duty*, 4:219.

Chapter 4

Joy in Looking to Christ

At the foundation of John Flavel's theology and spirituality is his doctrine of Christ.[1] As far as he is concerned, there is nothing more significant: "There is no doctrine more excellent in itself, or more necessary to be preached and studied, than the doctrine of Jesus Christ, and him crucified."[2] The prominence of this doctrine is evident throughout Scripture. "The knowledge of Jesus Christ," says Flavel, "is the very marrow and kernel of all the Scriptures; the scope and centre of all divine revelations: both testaments meet in Christ."[3] Such knowledge is not primarily theoretical, but practical—that is to say, it is "fundamental to all graces, duties, comforts, and happiness."[4]

It should not be surprising, then, that much of Flavel's writing and preaching focuses on Christ's person and work. This is an important observation, given that some scholars criticize the Puritans for neglecting Christology. Marshall Knappen, for example, argues that there is a "surprising lack of Christological thought in this avowedly Christian movement" and that "the person of Christ figures very little in their literature."[5] But is this really the case? Even a cursory

---

1. For more on Flavel's Christology see Cosby, *John Flavel: Puritan Life*; Cosby, "Christology of John Flavel," 116–34; Yuille, *Inner Sanctum*; Chang, "John Flavel"; McCallum, "Christology of John Flavel"; and Peter Beck, "'The Fountain of Life': The Excellency of Christ in the Preaching of John Flavel," *Puritan Reformed Journal* 5, no. 1 (2013): 43–57.

2. Flavel, *Fountain*, 1:34.

3. Flavel, *Fountain*, 1:34.

4. Flavel, *Fountain*, 1:34.

5. M. M. Knappen, *Tudor Puritanism* (Chicago: University of Chicago Press, 1939), 376.

glance at Puritan literature seems to indicate the opposite. As Joel Beeke and Mark Jones observe, "Puritan theologians produced outstanding studies in the area of Christology…and it is a great mystery as to why so little secondary literature has been written on Puritan Christology."[6] For example, Thomas Goodwin, John Owen (1616–1683), John Arrowsmith (1602–1659), Isaac Ambrose (1604–1664), William Gouge (1575–1653), and James Durham (1622–1658) all wrote significant works on Christology.[7]

For his part, Flavel produced *The Fountain of Life Opened Up; or, A Display of Christ in His Essential and Mediatorial Glory*, which Brian Cosby describes as "the most extensive study of the person and work of Christ published in English Puritanism during the seventeenth century."[8] What makes it so unique is that it is not merely a scholastic study but a preeminently practical one. Peter Beck explains, "Expounding on the person and work of Christ, Flavel sought to move the beauty and importance of these doctrines beyond the justifying of the soul to the sanctifying of the man."[9] In other words, Flavel's principal aim is transformational; he wants his readers to grow in the grace and knowledge of Christ (2 Peter 3:18).

Flavel's Doctrine of Christ

Flavel is not an innovator—which is not a criticism but an

---

6. Beeke and Jones, *Puritan Theology*, 335. For an assessment of Knappen's critique, see Mark Jones, *Why Heaven Kissed Earth: The Christology of the Puritan Reformed Orthodox Theologian, Thomas Goodwin (1600–1680)* (Gottingen: Vandenhoeck & Ruprecht, 2010), 28–29.

7. See Thomas Goodwin, *The Heart of Christ in Heaven towards Sinners on Earth*, in *Works of Thomas Goodwin D. D.*, vol. 5 (London, 1681–1704); and Goodwin, *Of Christ the Mediator*, in *Works of Thomas Goodwin D. D.*, vol. 5 (London, 1681–1704). See also John Owen, *Christologia, or, A Declaration of the Glorious Mystery of the Person of Christ*, in *Works of John Owen*, vol. 12 (London: Johnstone and Hunter, 1850–1855). See also John Arrowsmith, *Theanthropos; or, God-Man: Being an Exposition upon the First Eighteen Verses of the First Chapter of the Gospel according to St John* (London, 1660); Isaac Ambrose, *Looking unto Jesus; A View of the Everlasting Gospel* (London, 1658); William Gouge, *A Learned and Very Useful Commentary upon the Whole Epistle to the Hebrews* (London, 1655); James Durham, *Christ Crucified; or, The Marrow of the Gospel in 72 Sermons on Isaiah 53* (Edinburgh, 1683).

8. Cosby, *John Flavel: Puritan Life*, 76.

9. Beck, "Fountain of Life," 43.

acknowledgment that he does not deviate from his confessional tradition. This confessional commitment is clearly evident in his Christology. Jones explains, "The evidence suggests that the Reformed orthodox, particularly in the seventeenth century, had a view of Christ's person—if all of the particulars are included—unique to their own theological traditions, but nevertheless firmly rooted in Chalcedonian orthodoxy."[10] This is certainly the case with Flavel, who holds to an orthodox Christology as articulated in the creeds of the early church. These creeds are always present, implicitly and explicitly, in his writings. For example, in his sermon, "Of Christ's Wonderful Person," Flavel mentions both the Council of Nicaea and the Council of Chalcedon. Concerning the divine nature of Christ, he writes, "The least tread awry may ingulph us in the bogs of error. Arius would have been content, if the council of Nice would but have gratified him in a letter."[11] Concerning the two natures of Christ, Flavel remarks, "The divine and human, are not confounded; but a line of distinction runs betwixt them still in this wonderful person. It was the heresy of the Eutychians, condemned by the council of Chalcedon, to affirm, that there was no distinction betwixt the two natures in Christ."[12] Clearly, Flavel sees himself as the heir of a theological tradition found in the creeds that emerged from the early church councils.

In addition to Nicaea and Chalcedon, Flavel was committed to Westminster. "Flavel's theology," says Cosby, "was consistent with many of his Puritan contemporaries during the later-Stuart period. He was an heir of the Westminster Assembly (1642–1652) and wrote one of the earliest expositions of the Westminster Shorter Catechism."[13] The work of the Westminster Assembly loomed large in Flavel's doctrine of Christ. This is evident in his *Exposition of the Assembly's Shorter Catechism*.[14] It is also apparent in his acceptance of the *communica-*

---

10. Jones, *Why Heaven Kissed Earth*, 3.

11. Flavel, *Fountain*, 1:74. Flavel is referring, of course, to the difference between the two Latin terms *homoiousios* and *homoousios*. This was a major point of contention at the Council of Nicaea.

12. Flavel, *Fountain*, 1:78. Flavel also mentions the Nicene Creed in *Fountain*, 1:514; *Pneumatologia*, 2:477–78; *Divine Conduct*, 3:440; *England's Duty*, 4:35.

13. Cosby, "Christology of John Flavel," 118.

14. Flavel, *Exposition*, 6:178–81.

tio idiomatum,[15] as affirmed in the Westminster Confession: "Christ, in the work of mediation, acteth according to both natures; by each nature doing that which is proper to itself; yet, by reason of the unity of the person, that which is proper to one nature is sometimes, in Scripture, attributed to the person denominated by the other nature."[16] Flavel agrees wholeheartedly: "The two natures being thus united in the person of the Mediator, by virtue whereof the properties of each nature are attributed, and do truly agree in the whole person; so that it is proper to say, the Lord of glory was crucified, and that the blood of God redeemed the Church."[17]

In sum, it is important to note that, when it comes to his doctrine of Christ, Flavel is both orthodox (Chalcedon) and Reformed (Westminster).[18] He viewed any departure from this confessional tradition as heterodoxy and ultimately detrimental to the believer's spiritual well-being.

The Person of Christ

When considering the doctrine of Christ, Flavel distinguishes between His person and work. He summarizes his doctrine of Christ's person

---

15. Beeke and Jones, *Puritan Theology*, 339.

16. WCF 8.7.

17. Flavel, *Fountain*, 1:79.

18. While this introduction focuses primarily on those people and movements that have positively influenced Flavel's doctrine of Christ, it should be noted that his Christological writings are often polemical. He was deeply engaged in refuting the errors of his day, including Socinianism. This movement began in the late sixteenth century in opposition to major tenets of Reformation theology, including Christology. Proponents denied the full deity of Christ and interpreted Christ's work on the cross as an example, rather than a substitutionary atonement. Flavel explicitly mentions the Socinians in the following: *Fountain*, 1:60, 79, 481; *Method*, 2:252, 415; *The Occasions, Causes, Nature, Rise, Growth, and Remedies of Mental Errors*, in *Works of John Flavel* (1820; repr., Edinburgh: Banner of Truth Trust, 2015), 3:433, 445, 455, 464, 475, 563–64; *Navigation Spiritualized: A New Compass for Seaman*, in *Works of John Flavel* (1820; repr., Edinburgh: Banner of Truth Trust, 2015), 5:286; *Vindiciae Legis et Foederis, or A Reply to Mr. Philip Cary's Solemn Call in which He Contends Against the Right of Believers' Infants to Baptism*, in *Works of John Flavel* (1820; repr., Edinburgh: Banner of Truth Trust, 2015), 6:320–21; *Twelve Sacramental Meditations*, 6:434; and *The Reasonableness of Personal Reformation and the Necessity of Conversion*, in *Works of John Flavel* (1820; repr., Edinburgh: Banner of Truth Trust, 2015), 6:473. For more on Flavel's rejection of Socinianism, see McCallum, "Christology of John Flavel."

as follows: "Ye know he is (1) true and very God; (2) true and very man; (3) that these two natures make up but one person, being united inseparably; and (4) that they are not confounded or swallowed up in one another, but remain still distinct in the person of Christ."[19] Three essential truths emerge from Flavel's summary.

Christ is God. In the second of his forty-two sermons on the excellency of Christ, Flavel uses Proverbs 8:30 to "set forth Christ in his essential and primeval glory."[20] He explains in detail the Son's relationship with the Father, noting, "The condition and state of Jesus Christ before his incarnation, was a state of the highest and most unspeakable delight and pleasure, in the enjoyment of his Father."[21] The cause of this joy is the profound unity of the Father and the Son—they are one. Flavel writes, "Now Jesus Christ was not only near and dear to God, but one with him; 'I and my Father are one,' John 10:30, one in nature, will, love and delight."[22] This unity is unlike anything on earth: "This was no natural oneness; no child is so one with his father, no husband so one with the wife of his bosom, no friend so one with his friend, no soul so one with its body, as Jesus Christ and his Father were one."[23] This unique relationship exists because the Son is "true and very God," equal with the Father in every respect. Flavel declares, "'To be equal with God, and to be in the form of God,' (i.e.) to have all the glory and ensigns of the majesty of God; and the riches which he speaks of, was no less than all that God the Father hath…and what he now hath in his exalted state, is the same he had before his humiliation."[24]

Christ is man. For Flavel, the oneness of the Father and the Son in "nature, will, love, and delight" makes the incarnation even more extraordinary. He exhorts, "Adore, and be for ever astonished at the love of Jesus Christ to poor sinners; that ever he should consent to

---

19. Flavel, *Fountain*, 1:81.

20. Flavel, *Fountain*, 1:42. Prov. 8:30 says, "Then I was by him, as one brought up with him: and I was daily his delight, rejoicing always before him."

21. Flavel, *Fountain*, 1:44.

22. Flavel, *Fountain*, 1:46.

23. Flavel, *Fountain*, 1:46.

24. Flavel, *Fountain*, 1:44.

leave such a bosom, and the ineffable delights that were there, for such poor worms as we are. O the heights, depths, lengths, and breadths of unmeasurable love!"[25] For Flavel, the incarnation means "that Jesus Christ did really assume the true and perfect nature of man, into a personal union with his divine nature, and still remains true God, and true man, in one person for ever."[26] This is the *hypostatic* union—the union of the divine nature and human nature in the person of Christ. Flavel is careful to explain that it is not the same as the essential union of the three persons in the Godhead, nor is it the same as the mystical union between believers and Christ.[27] Rather, by the incarnation, the Son (fully God) assumed to Himself a human nature, so that He now has two natures in His one person. Flavel writes,

> But this assumption of which I speak, is that whereby the second Person in the Godhead did take the human nature into a personal union with himself, by virtue whereof the manhood subsists in the second person, yet without confusion, both making but one person, *theanthropos*, or Immanuel, God with us.[28]

This was not a partial assumption—rather, "Christ took a complete and perfect human soul and body, with all and every faculty and member pertaining to it."[29] Therefore, Christ is "true and very man" in body and soul.

Christ is one person with two distinct, yet inseparable, natures. Following Chalcedon, Flavel insists that the incarnation does not entail the mixture of the divine nature and human nature, nor does it infer the creation of some sort of merged nature. Rather, "the human nature is so united with the divine, as that each nature still retains its own essential properties distinct. And this distinction is not, nor can be,

---

25. Flavel, *Fountain*, 1:49.

26. Flavel, *Fountain*, 1:74.

27. Flavel, *Fountain*, 1:75. For more on his understanding of the mystical and hypostatic unions, see Yuille, *Inner Sanctum*, 13–14. On the relationship between these unions, Yuille notes Flavel's assertion that "Christ must become one with us hypostatically in order for us to become one with Him mystically."

28. Flavel, *Fountain*, 1:76.

29. Flavel, *Fountain*, 1:76–77.

lost by that union."[30] Flavel is quick to point out that such a distinction does not imply that the two natures can be separated from one other. Although they are distinct, they are "united inseparably" in the person of Christ. Flavel makes clear, "The union of the two natures in Christ, as an inseparable union; so that from the first moment thereof, there never was, nor to eternity shall be, any separation of them."[31]

The Work of Christ

According to Flavel, the person of Christ leads directly to the work of Christ. In fact, it is impossible to separate the two: "Christ, who is the same yesterday, today, and for ever; so that he is the true and only Mediator betwixt God and men: no other is revealed in Scripture; no other is sufficient for it; no other needed beside him."[32] As the "only Mediator betwixt God and men," Christ came to redeem His people from their captivity to, and misery in, sin.[33] Flavel affirms that even the name *Jesus Christ* speaks to this reality: "The name Jesus, notes his work about which he came; and Christ, the offices to which he was anointed; and in execution of which he is our Jesus."[34] These offices include His work as prophet, priest, and king.[35]

------

30. Flavel, *Fountain*, 1:77.

31. Flavel, *Fountain*, 1:78. Flavel is in agreement with WCF 8.2: "The Son of God, the second person in the Trinity, being very and eternal God, of one substance, and equal with the Father, did, when the fullness of time was come, take upon him man's nature, with all the essential properties and common infirmities thereof, yet without sin: being conceived by the power of the Holy Ghost in the womb of the Virgin Mary, of her substance. So that two whole, perfect, and distinct natures, the Godhead and the manhood, were inseparably joined together in one person, without conversion, composition, or confusion. Which person is very God and very man, yet one Christ, the only mediator between God and man." WCF 8.2.

32. Flavel, *Fountain*, 1:113–14.

33. Flavel, *Exposition*, 177–78.

34. Flavel, *Fountain*, 1:108.

35. Christ's threefold office is known as the *munus triplex Christi*. J. V. Fesko explains, "Though popularly attributed to Calvin, the threefold office had been spoken of in the earliest days of the church, appears in Patristic authors such as Eusebius of Caesarea (ca. 263–339) and medieval authors such as Thomas Aquinas (1226–1274), and was anticipated by Johannes à Lasco (1499–1560) before Calvin." Fesko, *Theology*, 185. Calvin popularized this designation through his *Institutes*: "Therefore, in order that faith may find a firm basis for salvation in Christ, and thus rest in him, this principle must be laid down: the office enjoined upon Christ by the Father consists of

Christ as prophet. In the *The Fountain of Life*, Flavel commits two sermons to the prophetic office of Christ, focusing first on His work of revelation and second on His work of illumination. He summarizes, "His prophetical office consists of two parts; one external, consisting in a true and full revelation of the will of God to men.... The other in illuminating the mind, and opening the heart to receive and embrace that doctrine."[36] Thus, Christ is the chief prophet of the church, the one who fully and finally reveals God and His ways to us. "It belongs to a prophet to expound the law, declare the will of God, and foretell things to come: all these meet, and that, in a singular and eminent manner, in Christ our prophet."[37] Christ's preeminence as a prophet arises from the perfection of His person. As Flavel notes, "It implies the divinity of Christ, and proves him to be true God; forasmuch as no other can reveal to the world, in all ages, the secrets that lay hid in the heart of God, and that with such convincing evidence and authority."[38] Christ, truly God and truly man, is uniquely equipped to disclose the truth of God to the people of God.

The prophetic work of Christ does not end with His declaration of the things of God. He must illumine His people, so that we know and love what He has revealed. "The opening of the mind and heart," says Flavel, "effectually to receive the truths of God, is the peculiar prerogative and office of Jesus Christ."[39] We stand in need of such illumination because our mind is darkened through sin, and we cannot

---

three parts. For he was given to be prophet, king, and priest." John Calvin, *Institutes of the Christian Religion*, ed. John T. McNeill, trans. Ford Lewis Battles (Louisville: Westminster John Knox Press, 2006), 1:494. While Calvin may have popularized this classification, it became standard in the next century. Alister McGrath states, "This understanding of the threefold office was formalized during the seventeenth century, and is given full justification in the writings of Protestant theologians of this period." Alister McGrath, *Christian Theology: An Introduction*, 5th ed. (Chichester, England: Wiley-Blackwell, 2011), 321. This idea is found in WSC 23: "Christ, as our Redeemer, executeth the offices of a Prophet, of a Priest, and of a King, both in his estate of humiliation and exaltation."

36. Flavel, *Fountain*, 1:118–19.

37. Flavel, *Fountain*, 1:119.

38. Flavel, *Fountain*, 1:122. He explains in a footnote, "If the doctrine of Christ, and his discourses be examined, it will be as clear as sunshine, that his words are not the words of a man, or some prophet, but of the Father himself, that is, of the true God."

39. Flavel, *Fountain*, 1:133.

open our own hearts. Our sinfulness prevents us from knowing God, for "one of the great miseries under which lapsed nature labours, is spiritual blindness."[40] Mercifully, Christ brings the "eye-salve" which alone can "cure it."[41] He opens the heart through the proclamation of the gospel by the use of the ordinary means of grace, and through the work of His Spirit upon the heart. These two—the Word and the Spirit—cannot be separated. As Flavel explains,

> But the ordinances in themselves cannot do it, as I noted before; and therefore Christ hath sent forth the Spirit, who is his *Pro-rex*, his vicegerent, to carry on this work upon the hearts of his elect. And when the Spirit comes down upon the souls in the administration of the ordinances, he effectually opens the heart to receive the Lord Jesus, by the hearing of faith.[42]

The unity of Christ's work of revelation and illumination is evident here, for what He reveals His people declare, and what His people declare His Spirit applies. Douglas McCallum rightly observes "the pneumatological emphasis in Flavel's Christology, an emphasis that was, in the history of dogmatic development, a largely Reformed insight."[43]

Christ as priest. Flavel devotes five sermons to Christ's priestly work—more than what he devotes to the other two offices combined.[44] At the center of these sermons is his presentation of the two primary acts of Christ's priestly work: oblation and intercession.

> [These are] answerable to the double office of the High-priest, offering the blood of the sacrifices without the holy place, which typed out Christ's oblation; and then once a year bring the blood before the Lord into the most holy place, presenting it before

---

40. Flavel, *Fountain*, 1:333.

41. Flavel, *Fountain*, 1:333.

42. Flavel, *Fountain*, 1:137.

43. McCallum, "Christology of John Flavel," 50.

44. This emphasis is consistent with other Puritan theologians. Jones notes, "With regard to Christ's state of humiliation, Goodwin focuses the bulk of his attention on Christ as priest. This is, of course, perfectly understandable given the context of the seventeenth century where the Socinians, in particular, vigorously attacked the Reformed orthodox understanding of Christ's priestly office." Jones, *Why Heaven Kissed Earth*, 216–17.

God, and with it sprinkling the mercy-seat, wherein the intercession of Christ was in a lively manner typified to us.[45]

The first component of Christ's priestly work is oblation—the
offering of His own self for the sins of His people. Flavel describes
Christ's oblation as vicarious, penal, particular, and propitiatory.[46]
As a vicarious sacrifice, Christ offered Himself as a substitute for His
people. "And when Christ came to offer his sacrifice," says Flavel, "he
stood not only in the capacity of a priest, but also in that of a surety:
and so his soul stood in the stead of ours, and his body in the stead
of our bodies."[47] Such an offering was necessary due to the immense
consequences of sin. In order to save His people, Christ had to suffer
the full penalty due to them for their sin, so that God might "be just,
and the justifier" (Rom. 3:26). God "required from him, as our surety,
the penalty due to us for our sin. And so Christ had to do immediately with God, yea, with a God infinitely wronged, and incensed
by sin against us. To this incensed Majesty, Christ our High-priest
approached, as to a devouring fire, with the sacrifice."[48] Flavel's har-
rowing description of the ramifications of our sin accents the power
and pathos of Christ's priestly work.

According to Flavel, Christ offered this oblation on behalf of the
elect: "The persons for whom, and in whose stead he offered himself
to God, was the whole number of God's elect, which were given him
of the Father, neither more nor less: so speak the Scriptures."[49] The

---

45. Flavel, *Fountain*, 1:154.

46. For more on the Puritans' view of the atonement, see Beeke and Jones, *Puritan
Theology*, 359–70; Fesko, *Theology*, 185–205; and Jones, *Why Heaven Kissed Earth*,
212–53. For more on Flavel's view of the atonement, see Cosby, *John Flavel: Puritan
Life*, 76–78; Cosby, "Christology of John Flavel," 127–130; Yuille, *Inner Sanctum*, 17–19;
Chang, "John Flavel," 77–81; and McCallum, "Christology of John Flavel," 44–85.

47. Flavel, *Fountain*, 1:156.

48. Flavel, *Fountain*, 1:159.

49. Flavel, *Fountain*, 1:159. Evidently, Flavel holds a form of what is often referred
to as definite (or limited) atonement. Cosby states, "He is very clear, too, that Christ's
death was an atoning sacrifice only for the 'sins of the elect.'" Cosby, *John Flavel: Puritan
Life*, 77. The four primary views of his day were as follows: (1) universal satisfaction
for all; (2) sufficiency for all (and applied in some sense to all), but efficacious for the
elect; (3) sufficiency for all, but efficacious for the elect; and (4) efficacious for the
elect. Fesko, *Theology*, 191. Flavel fits in the third category. He states, "It is confessed,

result of Christ's oblation was satisfaction—the propitiation of God and the restoration of His people to Him. "The design and end of this oblation was to atone, pacify, and reconcile God, by giving him a full and adequate compensation or satisfaction for the sins of these his elect."[50] Christ offered Himself, body and soul, for the elect, to satisfy the justice of God, in order that His people might be reconciled to Him. This is "the making up of that breach caused by sin, between us and God, and restoring us again to his favour and friendship."[51] Such was Christ's priestly work of oblation.

In addition to offering Himself for us to God, Christ intercedes for us before God. Flavel writes, "Jesus our High-priest lives for ever, in the capacity of a potent Intercessor, in heaven, for believers."[52] This means that Christ's priestly work did not end when He ascended to heaven—rather, He continues, as our mediator, to represent, inter-cede, and advocate for us before God. In the first place, Christ's work of intercession means that He presents "himself before the Lord in our names, and upon our account."[53] This presentation ensures God's mercy and love toward us.[54] In addition, he actively presents His blood and suffering on our behalf. Flavel proclaims, "Those wounds he received for our sins on earth, are, as it were, still fresh bleeding in heaven: a moving and prevailing argument it is with the Father, to give our mercies he pleads for."[55] Finally, standing before the Father, with

---

there is sufficiency of virtue in this sacrifice to redeem the whole world, and on that account some divines affirm he is called the 'Saviour of the world,' John 4:42." Flavel, *Fountain*, 1:159. Such an understanding places Flavel within the confessional standards of the Westminster Assembly: "The Lord Jesus, by his perfect obedience and sacrifice of himself, which he through the eternal Spirit once offered up unto God, hath fully satisfied the justice of his Father, and purchased not only reconciliation, but an ever-lasting inheritance in the kingdom of heaven, for all those whom the Father hath given unto him." WCF 8.5. For more on the various views, see Fesko, *Theology*, 187–203.

50. Flavel, *Fountain*, 1:160.

51. Flavel, *Fountain*, 1:160.

52. Flavel, *Fountain*, 1:167.

53. Flavel, *Fountain*, 1:168.

54. Flavel states, "As when God looks upon the rainbow, which is the sign of the covenant, he remembers the earth in mercy: so when he looks on Christ, his heart must needs be toward us, upon his account; and therefore in Rev. 4:3 Christ is compared to a rainbow encompassing the throne." Flavel, *Fountain*, 1:168.

55. Flavel, *Fountain*, 1:169.

His wounds on full display (so to speak), Christ presents our prayers to God. Like the high priest in Israel, He enters God's presence "with the names of the children of Israel on his breast, with the blood of the sacrifice, and his hands full of incense."[56]

Christ as king. Christ rules over His people extensively, as He claims authority in their hearts and in their world. "Christ hath a twofold kingdom," writes Flavel, "the one spiritual and internal, by which he subdues and rules the hearts of his people; the other providential and external, whereby he guides, rules, and orders all things in the world, in a blessed subordination to their eternal salvation."[57] Christ is king over all—His people and His world—and His rule is to the delight and blessedness of His people. First, Christ rules in the hearts of His people. Having purchased them by means of His priestly work, He conquers their hearts, removing all their defenses and bringing about their willful obedience to His rule. For Flavel, this authority includes six principal actions: (1) He "imposes" a new law upon them, (2) He "rebukes and chastises" them for disobeying His law, (3) He keeps them "from iniquity," (4) He "protects them in his ways," (5) He "rewards" their obedience, and (6) He "pacifies all inward troubles."[58] Christ, the king, executes all this "powerfully, sweetly, and suitably" for the joy of His people.[59]

Christ's kingly rule does not end in the hearts of His people but extends to all that is around them. Flavel remarks, "All the affairs of the kingdom of providence are ordered and determined by Jesus Christ, for the special advantage, and everlasting good of his redeemed people."[60] He exercises authority over all creation, and He employs His authority for the good of His people (Rom. 8:8). He does so by "supporting, permitting, restraining, limiting, protecting, punishing, and rewarding those over whom he reigns providentially."[61] This provi-

------

56. Flavel, *Fountain*, 1:169–70.
57. Flavel, *Fountain*, 1:199.
58. Flavel, *Fountain*, 1:203–6.
59. Flavel, *Fountain*, 1:206.
60. Flavel, *Fountain*, 1:212.
61. Flavel follows this statement with an explanation of each of Christ's acts. See Flavel, *Fountain*, 1:213–16.

dential rule ought to move His people to trust Him and obey His law. Flavel asks, "Hath God left the government of the whole world in the hands of Christ, and trusted him over all? Then do you also leave all your particular concerns in the hands of Christ too, and know that the infinite wisdom and love, which rules the world, manages every thing that relates to you."[62]

Having considered Christ's offices separately, it is important to remember that none of them stands alone. What Christ accomplishes in His kingly work is dependent upon His work as prophet and priest, and the execution of His prophetic and priestly offices offers nothing if His kingly work is left undone. Christ's work as mediator necessarily encompasses all three. Flavel summarizes,

> Had he not, as our Prophet, opened the way of life and salvation to the children of men, they could never have known it; and if they had clearly known it, except, as their Priest, he had offered up himself, to impetrate and obtain redemption for them, they could not have been redeemed virtually by his blood; and if they had been so redeemed, yet had he not lived in the capacity of a King, to apply this purchase of his blood to them; for what he revealed as a Prophet, he purchased as a Priest; and what he so revealed and purchased as a Prophet and Priest, he applies as a King.[63]

Flavel's Delight in Christ

Christ, fully God and fully man, is our prophet, priest, and king. For Flavel, this makes Him the centerpiece of our salvation and, unsurprisingly, the centerpiece of our joy. In short, there is no true joy outside of the person and work of Christ. Flavel declares,

> Jesus Christ is the very object matter of a believer's joy, Phil. 3:3, "Our rejoicing is in Christ Jesus." Take away the knowledge of Christ, and a Christian is the most sad and melancholy creature in the world: again, let Christ but manifest himself, and dart the beams of his light into their souls, it will make them kiss the

---

62. Flavel, *Fountain*, 1:219.
63. Flavel, *Fountain*, 1:198–99.

stakes, sing in flames, and shout in the pangs of death, as men that divide the spoil.[64]

For this reason, Flavel continually calls his hearers to look to Christ for their joy, reminding them of the inexhaustible riches that are found in Christ alone. So great is this joy in Christ that we will never tire of rejoicing in Him. Flavel built his life and ministry on this reality:

> We used to say, one thing tires, and it is true that it doth so, except that one thing be virtually and eminently all things, as Christ is; and then one thing can never tire; for such is the variety of sweetness in Christ, who is the *deliciae humani generis*, the delights of the children of men, that every time he is opened to believers from pulpit or press, it is as if heaven had furnished them with a new Christ; and yet he is the same Christ still.[65]

This delight in Christ is the application of Flavel's doctrine of Christ. Joy in Christ is not optional for the Christian; it is the very essence of what it means to know Christ.

The Joy of Christ

Christ is the object of joy because of His person and work. This means the joy of Christ flows from who He is and what He has done. The loveliness of His person is delightful enough, but when coupled with the greatness of His work, the grandeur of His joy is incomparable. While it is impossible to separate Christ's person from His work, it is helpful to see how Flavel speaks of the believer's joy in relation to both.

Joy in Christ's person. Christ brings great delight to the Christian, for the splendor of His person is unequaled in all creation. Flavel declares,

> O what a fair One! what an only One! what an excellent, lovely, ravishing One, is Christ! Put the beauty of ten thousand paradises, like the garden of Eden, into one; put all trees, all flowers, all smells, all colours, all tastes, all joys, all sweetness, all loveliness in one; O what a fair and excellent thing would that be? And yet it should be less to that fair and dearest well-beloved

---

64. Flavel, *Fountain*, 1:35.
65. Flavel, *Fountain*, 1:23.

Christ, than one drop of rain to the whole seas, rivers, lakes, and fountains of ten thousand earths. Christ is heaven's wonder, and earth's wonder.[66]

Since Christ is "true and very God," He is more glorious than anything in the universe. As the cause is greater than the effect, so the Creator is greater than His creation. To enjoy Christ is to delight in the one in whom there is no imperfection or limitation.

We enjoy Christ, says Flavel, because He is altogether lovely.[67] His loveliness is qualitatively and quantitatively greater than all other loveliness. First, all other loveliness is "derivative and secondary," but Christ's loveliness is "original and primary."[68] All that is beautiful and desirable is so because it originates in Christ; in other words, it is lovely because Christ is lovely. Any creaturely excellence is but a shared excellence, derived from its Creator. Christ alone is the fountain of all that is excellent. His loveliness, therefore, is of a different sort. He is desirable in and of Himself, while everything else is desirable on account of Him.

Second, all other loveliness is "fading and perishing," but Christ's loveliness is "fresh to all eternity."[69] Since He is the eternal God, His loveliness is eternal. All other delights will ultimately cease to satisfy, but Christ's joy knows no end. We can never drink His excellencies to the last drop. The pleasures of His person will never dull or dim.

---

66. Flavel, *Fountain*, 1:68.

67. Flavel's use of the terms *lovely* and *loveliness* is rooted in a tradition going back to Bernard of Clairvaux (1090–1153). Bernard greatly influenced the piety of the Puritans, especially through his exposition of the Song of Songs. As Arie de Reuver observes, "These four themes [God's love, meditation on Christ, bridal mysticism, and union with God]…involve components of his spirituality." Arie de Reuver, *Sweet Communion: Trajectories of Spirituality from the Middle Ages through the Further Reformation* (Grand Rapids: Reformation Heritage Books, 2007), 36. The intimate marital language expressed in the Song of Songs is interpreted allegorically by Bernard as descriptive of the believer's profound experience of the love of God in Christ. Flavel, and many Puritans, make use of this tradition to describe the joy of union with Christ. For more on the mystical elements in Puritan spirituality, see Williams, "Puritan Quest."

68. Flavel, *Method*, 2:216.

69. Flavel, *Method*, 2:217.

Christ alone can fully satisfy the soul, for He is "every way adequate" to its "vast desires."[70] Flavel remarks,

> The loveliness of every creature is of a cloying and glutting nature; our estimation of it abates and sinks by our nearer approach to it, or longer enjoyment of it: creatures, like pictures, are fairest at a due distance, but it is not so with Christ; the nearer the soul approacheth him, and the longer it lives in the enjoyment of him, still the more sweet and desirable is he.[71]

Christ grows in loveliness the closer we come to Him and increases in desirability the more we know Him. From first to last, from top to bottom, and from end to end, Christ is altogether lovely.

Such loveliness produces a joy that is unrivaled among earthly joys: "Draw the comparison how you will betwixt Christ and all other enjoyments, you will find none in heaven nor on earth to equal him.… He is more than all peace, all comfort, all joy, as the tree is more than the fruit."[72] So great is the delight of Christ that even heaven would be barren without Him. Heaven without Christ is no heaven at all. Flavel writes, "If Christ should say to the saints, take heaven among you, but as for me I will withdraw myself from you; the saints would weep, even in heaven itself, and say, Lord, heaven will be no more heaven to us, except thou be there, who are by far the better half of heaven."[73] The joy of Christ is so splendid that even heaven itself, in all its perfections, would bring nothing but sorrow without His presence. Such is the joy of Christ's person.

Joy in Christ's work. It is the work of Christ that enables us to experience the glorious joy of the person of Christ. Due to our sinfulness, we are unable to enjoy Christ, and we are captivated by lesser (and ultimately empty) earthly delights. We need the redeeming work of Christ to rescue us from our idolatry and empower us to rejoice in Him. For this reason, we find great joy in Christ, our prophet, priest, and king.

---

70. Flavel, *Method*, 2:218.
71. Flavel, *Method*, 2:217.
72. Flavel, *Method*, 2:206.
73. Flavel, *Method*, 2:207.

There is much delight in the prophetic work of Christ, as He reveals the truth of God and enables us to understand it. As Flavel explains, "We are, by nature, blind and ignorant, at best but groping in the dim light of nature after God. Jesus Christ is a light to lighten the Gentiles. When this great prophet came into the world, then did the day-spring from on high visit us."[74] Christ is the "original and fountain of all that light which guides us to salvation."[75] All the joy of salvation comes about by Christ's guiding light. He dispels the clouds of confusion, ignorance, and doubt by His prophetic work, as He teaches, illumines, and guides His people into all truth through His Word and Spirit. Flavel declares, "If light be pleasant to our eyes, how pleasant is that light of life springing from the Sun of righteousness!"[76] The knowledge of truth is a remarkable delight, and Christ, as the source of all that is true, brings such delightful truth into the minds and hearts of His people.

In Flavel's estimation, it is Christ's priestly work that most often draws His people into the fullness of joy and comfort. As noted above, Flavel believes that Christ (our priest) has offered Himself as a sacrifice for His people, paying the penalty for our sin, thereby reconciling us to God. While inseparable from His work as prophet and king, it is Christ's priestly work that actually purchased our salvation. This makes Christ's work on the cross a particular delight to the Christian. Flavel proclaims, "O what a joyful sound is this! What ravishing voices of peace, pardon, grace, and acceptance, come to our ears from the blood of the cross?… Reader, the word assures thee, whatever thou hast been, or art, that sins of as deep a dye as thine, have been washed away in this blood."[77] As we encounter the shame of sin, the distress of doubt, and the torment of temptation, we need only to look to the cross to be reminded of Christ's priestly work on our behalf.

This wondrous work is finished: "Jesus Christ hath perfected and completely finished the great work of redemption, committed to him

---

74. Flavel, *Method*, 2:218.

75. Flavel, *Exposition*, 6:182.

76. Flavel, *Method*, 2:219.

77. Flavel, *Fountain*, 1:328.

by God the Father."[78] Christ's words upon the cross—"It is finished"—bring unspeakable delight to believers. As Flavel explains, "It is but one word in the original; but in that one word is contained the sum of all joy; the very spirits of all divine consolation."[79] It is a great joy to know, no matter our flaws and failings, that we are complete in Christ, for God has reckoned Christ's perfect righteousness to us. This means we rejoice that "though we have no righteousness of our own; yet of God, Christ is made unto us righteousness; and that righteousness of his is infinitely better than our own: instead of our own, we have his. O blessed be God for Christ's perfect righteousness!"[80]

In addition to redeeming His people by means of His priestly work, Christ has purchased all good things for them as an inheritance. First, He has given them all temporal goods for their joy. "Not that they have the possession, but the comfort and benefit of all things.... The saints *utuntur mundo, et fruuntur Deo,* 'use the world, and enjoy God' in the use of it. Others are deceived, defiled, and destroyed by the world; but these are refreshed and furthered by it."[81] Since we have been redeemed by the blood of Christ, we are now able to enjoy God in our enjoyment of the world. What was previously a temptation to idolatry is now a blessing to savor.

Christ has also purchased all spiritually good things for His people. Through His oblation, His people receive all the benefits of salvation—justification, sanctification, adoption, and so forth. Flavel writes, "This most precious grace is the dear purchase of our Lord Jesus Christ; yea, all that peace, joy, and spiritual comfort, which are the sweet fruits of faith, are with it purchased for us by this blood."[82] Lastly, Christ has secured all eternal good things for believers. We know present joy, but a far greater joy awaits us in heaven. "Heaven, and all the glory thereof," says Flavel, "is purchased for you that are believers, with this price.... Therefore to complete our happiness, and

---

78. Flavel, *Fountain*, 1:431.
79. Flavel, *Fountain*, 1:430.
80. Flavel, *Fountain*, 1:437.
81. Flavel, *Fountain*, 1:191–92.
82. Flavel, *Fountain*, 1:192.

fill up the uttermost capacity of our souls, all the good of eternity is put into the account and inventory of the saints' estate and inheritance."[83]

What Christ accomplished for His people through His prophetic and priestly offices, He applies to them as their king. Christ reigns in our hearts as He claims for us all of the blessings of the kingdom of God. These privileges include "freedom from the curse of the law," "freedom from the dominion of sin," "protection in all trouble and dangers," "bearing of burdens and infirmities," "sweet peace and tranquility of soul," and "everlasting salvation."[84] These are but a few of the many delights that the people of God receive from Christ their king. In fact, Flavel is adamant that all life, liberty, comfort, and joy come from the caring hand of Christ. He explains,

> It is Christ that doth all for you that is done. He looks down from heaven upon all that fear him; he sees when you are in danger by temptation, and casts in a providence, you know not how, to hinder it. He sees when you are sad, and orders reviving providences, to refresh you. He sees when corruptions prevail, and orders humbling providences to purge them. Whatever mercies you have received, all along the way you have gone hitherto, are the orderings of Christ for you.[85]

Christ, as the portion of His people, must be their prized joy. It is in Him alone that we know true and lasting joy. Flavel comments,

> Out of the several offices of Christ, as out of so many fountains, all the promises of the new covenant flow, as so many soul-refreshing streams of peace and joy: all the promises of illumination, counsel and direction flow out of the prophetical office; all the promises of reconciliation, peace, pardon, and acceptation flow out of the priestly office, with the sweet streams of joy, and spiritual comforts depending thereupon; all the promises of converting, increasing, defending, directing, and supplying grace, flow out of the kingly office of Christ; indeed,

---

83. Flavel, *Fountain*, 1:193.
84. Flavel explains each of these benefits in Flavel, *Fountain*, 1:206–8.
85. Flavel, *Fountain*, 1:219.

all promises may be reduced to the three offices: so that Jesus Christ must needs be altogether lovely in his offices.[86]

The excellency of Christ's work demonstrates the loveliness of His person. We should, therefore, fix our eyes on Christ, so that we might know the infinite riches of joy that He alone offers. This "looking" is the means by which the Holy Spirit increases our delight in Christ.

The Joy of Assurance

Because Christ possesses all joy, we only experience joy in union with Him. It is for this reason that Flavel insists that we must be sure of our interest in Christ.[87] If we have no assurance of salvation, we can know only little joy in Christ. Flavel asks, "How little comfort can any man take in his present enjoyments and accommodations in the world, whilst it remains a question with him, whether he be delivered from the wrath to come?"[88] A lack of assurance puts all future joy in jeopardy, while stifling present joy, for the believer finds no consolation outside of Christ:

> Nothing can comfort the soul without Christ! he is the soul that animates all comforts; they would be dead things without him. Temporal enjoyments, riches, honours, health, relations yield not a drop of true comfort without Christ. Spiritual enjoyments, ministers, ordinances, promises, are fountains sealed and springs shut; till Christ open them, a man may go comfortless in the midst of them all.[89]

Without the sure knowledge that we are in Christ, even the good things of life prove barren and unable to provide any lasting joy. Heaven itself, argues Flavel, is no joy without an interest in Christ: "The Spirit of the Lord gives the believing soul not only a sight to discern the transcendent excellency of these spiritual objects, but a sight

---

86. Flavel, *Method*, 2:219.

87. For examples see Flavel, *Fountain*, 1:27, 61–62, 197, 482, 499, 534; *Method*, 2:245, 385; *Pneumatologia*, 3:233–34; *England's Duty*, 4:218–19; *Touchstone*, 5:525–27; and *Twelve Sacramental Meditations*, 6:455.

88. Flavel, *Fountain*, 1:472.

89. Flavel, *Method*, 2:247.

of his interest in them. This is my Christ, and this the glory prepared for me. Without interest, heaven itself cannot be turned unto joy."[90]

It is of utmost importance, therefore, that we are confident of our standing in Christ. Flavel exhorts, "Give not sleep therefore to thine eyes, reader, till thou hast got good evidence, that thou art of that number who Jesus hath delivered from the wrath to come. Till thou canst say, he is a Jesus to thee."[91] There is little joy in knowing that Christ is Savior, for true delight resides in the knowledge that Christ is "my" Savior. This delight is incomparable, as Flavel asserts, "There is nothing in all the world would give him such joy, as to be well assured of an interest in [Christ]."[92] The knowledge that Christ is mine and I am Christ's guarantees the fullest joy in Christ.

For Flavel, this realization should overwhelm our hearts: "What heart hath largeness and strength enough to receive and contain the joy and comfort which flow from a cleared interest in Jesus Christ! Certainly, Christian, the tranquility and comfort of your whole life depend upon it; and what is life without the comfort of life?"[93] All the comfort of life rests on assurance. To know that "Christ is ours, with the unspeakable joys that are inseparably connected therewith, is that 'white stone, and new name, which none know but he that receives it;' for no words can possibly signify to another what that soul tastes and feels in such an hour as that is."[94]

So wonderful is the joy of a settled interest in Christ that Flavel speaks of it as possessing two heavens. "You have two heavens, one in hand, the other in hope."[95] Assurance in Christ brings such present delight that it is to experience heaven on earth. As such, it is a great advantage in the midst of trials, especially in the day of death. Because Christ is ours, the most difficult hardship is no cause for despair. Flavel proclaims, "It is this blessed hope that must support you under all the troubles of life, and in the agonies of death. The securing of a blessed

90. Flavel, *England's Duty*, 4:218.
91. Flavel, *Fountain*, 1:473.
92. Flavel, *Method*, 2:125.
93. Flavel, *Method*, 2:386.
94. Flavel, *Touchstone*, 5:511.
95. Flavel, *Touchstone*, 5:528.

resurrection to yourselves, is therefore the most deep concernment you have in this world."[96] Because Christ is the representative of His people, His resurrection ensures our resurrection. To be in Christ means that one day we will rise to new life as Christ did. Such hope removes fear and makes even death, in one sense, a means of joy:

> Though some Christians shun death…yet others there be, who seeing their title clear, their work done, and relishing the joys of heaven, in the prelibations of faith, are willing to be unclothed, and to be with Christ. Their love of Christ hath extinguished in them the love of life; and they can say with Paul, *I am ready*.[97]

In sum, for Flavel, the joy of assurance in Christ is the greatest delight: "The weakest Christian is exalted above all other men; but the assured Christian hath a preference before all other Christians."[98] This delight resides in the knowledge that Christ is ours. He is our prophet, priest, and king. All the joy that belongs to His person and work is ours, to be experienced through union with Him. And the many doubts and difficulties of this life are no match for His conquering mercies. Thus, "the assured Christian is at rest, from those tormenting fears and jealousies…that are as cruel as the grave, and as insufferable as coals of fire in a man's bosom. He can take Christ into the arms of faith, and say, 'My beloved is mine, and I am his. Return to thy rest, O my soul, for the Lord hath dealt bountifully with thee!'"[99] Nothing in all of creation can dispel the joy of those who are in Christ. Flavel states, "For let the sealed and assured believer consider, and compare; and he must needs find a joy and pleasure, beyond the joy of the whole earth…. Put Christ into the sensible possession of a believer, and joy is no more under his command for that time: he cannot forbear to rejoice."[100]

Looking to Christ for the Joy of Assurance
Given the relationship between joy and assurance, it is little wonder that Flavel devotes much of his ministry to helping believers grow in

---

96. Flavel, *Fountain*, 1:499.
97. Flavel, *Pneumatologia*, 2:597. Italics in the original.
98. Flavel, *Twelve Sacramental Meditations*, 6:452.
99. Flavel, *Twelve Sacramental Meditations*, 6:452.
100. Flavel, *Twelve Sacramental Meditations*, 6:452.

assurance thereby increasing their joy. His principal word of counsel is to look to Christ, who is both the source of assurance and joy. By looking to Christ, assurance is cultivated and joy is strengthened. It is this conviction that ultimately led Flavel to write *The Fountain of Life*:

> There be many things dispersed through this treatise, of Christ, to animate such joy, and excite such longings.... O when you shall consider what he hath done, suffered, and purchased for you, where he is now, and how much he longs for your coming, your very hearts should groan out those words, Phil. 1:23, "I desired to be dissolved, and to be with Christ."[101]

Flavel's forty-two sermons are intended to exalt the matchless glories of Christ, so that we might fix our eyes on Him. "What cause have all the saints to love their Lord Jesus with an abounding love? Christian, open the eyes of thy faith, and fix them upon Christ, in the posture he lay in the garden, drenched in his own blood: and see whether he be not lovely in these his dyed garments."[102] Again, Flavel declares,

> The eye of faith is a precious eye, and the visions of Christ by faith, are ravishing visions: and he that beholds Christ, the Lamb of God, by a steady fixed eye of faith, cannot but admire, and be deeply affected with such a sight of him. The views of Christ by faith, are ravishing and transporting views.[103]

Flavel's use of the term "ravishing" is significant. As J. D. Williams explains, "The Biblical language of 'ravishment' was also frequently borrowed from the Song of Songs, for it implied the abrupt and overpowering nature of ecstasy."[104] This eyeing of Christ produces unspeakable delight. "Certainly, the admiration, love, delight, and joy of our hearts, are all at the command of faith: for let us but consider what ravishing excellencies are in Christ, for the eye of the believer to behold and admire."[105]

---

101. Flavel, *Fountain*, 1:27.

102. Flavel, *Fountain*, 1:283.

103. Flavel, *Twelve Sacramental Meditations*, 6:412. Flavel's sermon is based on John 1:29.

104. Williams, "Puritan Quest," 116–17.

105. Flavel, *Twelve Sacramental Meditations*, 6:412.

Looking to Christ entails effort on our part. It is to study, admire, and imitate Him. Flavel explains, "A saving, though immethodical knowledge of Christ, will bring us to heaven, but a regular and methodical, as well as saving knowledge of him, will bring heaven into us."[106] This looking involves a consistent study of Christ, so that we develop a "saving knowledge" of Him. This is essential for our enjoyment of Christ, for it helps us grow in assurance. As Flavel notes, it is a "sweet and comfortable knowledge; to be studying Jesus Christ, what is it but to be digging among all the veins and springs of comfort? and the deeper you dig, the more do these springs flow upon you. How are hearts ravished with the discoveries of Christ in the gospel?"[107]

When we look to Christ and see the perfection of His work on our behalf, our doubts and fears give way to delight and comfort. In order to gain such assurance, we must first look away from our own failures and then look to His faithfulness. Flavel explains, "Happy were it, if puzzled and perplexed Christians would turn their eyes from the defects that are in their obedience, to the fulness and completeness of Christ's obedience; and see themselves complete in him, when most lame and defective in themselves."[108] To see the obedience of Christ, and know that it is our obedience, assures and delights us. It is not enough to glance at Christ; we must meditate on, and rejoice in, the knowledge of our Savior. Flavel exhorts, "The love of God in Jesus Christ still rises higher and higher in every discovery of it. Admire, adore, and be ravished with the thoughts of his love!"[109] To look at Christ with the eyes of faith is to love Him more and more. This continual looking to Him leads to continual rejoicing in Him.

Flavel is adamant that this adoration of Christ ultimately leads to imitation of Christ. In short, to look at Him is to live like Him. "But above all," says Flavel, "thine eyeing the great pattern of patience, Jesus Christ; whose Lamb-like carriage, under a trial…is here recommended to thee. O how should this transform thee into a lamb, for

____

106. Flavel, *Fountain*, 1:21.
107. Flavel, *Fountain*, 1:36.
108. Flavel, *Fountain*, 1:59.
109. Flavel, *Fountain*, 1:430.

meekness also!"[110] When we look to Christ, we worship Him, not only with our words but with our lives. To imitate Christ, therefore, is the work of those whose eyes are fixed on Christ. Flavel explains, "But for thee, reader, be thou a follower of Christ, imitate thy pattern; yea, let me persuade thee, as ever though hopest to clear up thine interest in him, imitate him in such particulars as these that follow."[111]

Conclusion

Flavel's spirituality finds its essence and expression in the pursuit of joy. This chapter has demonstrated that such joy is found in Christ alone. Since He is "true and very God" and "true and very man," He is able to serve as our prophet, priest, and king. It is this threefold work that enables and empowers His people to experience joy in Him. To know joy, then, is to know Christ. This truth is front and center in Flavel's ministry, as he encourages believers to look to Christ for assurance and joy. As we do so, reveling and rejoicing in His person and work, we begin to reflect and imitate Him. Such fruit, in turn, leads us to greater assurance and joy.

---

110. Flavel, *Fountain*, 1:368.

111. Flavel, *Fountain*, 1:439. These particulars include: (1) beginning to work for God early in life, (2) working with zeal and purpose, (3) working diligently for the time is short, (4) working diligently while guarding against vanity, (5) working with resolve amidst discouragement, and (6) working until the day of death (439–40).

Chapter 5

Joy in Discerning the Spirit

If Christ stands at the center of John Flavel's theology and spirituality, then the Spirit is its heart.[1] It is the Spirit who drives the life of the Christian, points to Christ, convicts of sin, empowers obedience, and comforts the soul. Such an emphasis on the Spirit was one of the hallmarks of the Reformers. As Geoffrey Nuttall writes, "A return of interest in the doctrine of the Holy Spirit, and a fresh conviction of its centrality for Christian faith and experience, are characteristics of the Reformation."[2] This renewed interest was especially prominent in John Calvin and his successors. Richard Lovelace notes that Calvin's doctrinal work on the Spirit has earned him the ascription "the theologian of the Holy Spirit," and that the English Puritans who followed him gave "us the most profound and extensive biblical-theological studies of the ministry of the Holy Spirit which exist in any language."[3] While Flavel did not produce a major work on pneumatology, his writings continually feature the Spirit and His necessary work in the believer's life.

For Flavel, the Spirit is the "fountain of all spiritual life," for there is no life in Christ without the Spirit of Christ.[4] The life of the Christian,

---

1. For other treatments of Flavel's pneumatology, see Embry, *Keeper*; Embry, "John Flavel's Theology of the Holy Spirit," *The Southern Baptist Journal of Theology* 14, no. 4 (Winter 2010): 84–99; and Cosby, *John Flavel: Puritan Life*, 78–80.

2. Geoffrey F. Nuttall, *The Holy Spirit in Puritan Faith and Experience* (Chicago: University of Chicago Press, 1992), 4.

3. Richard F. Lovelace, *Dynamics of Spiritual Life: An Evangelical Theology of Renewal* (Downers Grove, Ill.: InterVarsity, 1979), 120. J. I. Packer agrees, "The work of the Holy Spirit is the field in which the Puritans' most valuable contributions to the church's theological heritage were made." Packer, *Quest*, 179.

4. Flavel, *Method*, 2:86.

purchased by the work of Christ, begins with the work of the Spirit. He is the "author of faith."[5] This Spirit who gives life, says Flavel, "actuates the soul whom he regenerates, and by sanctifying it, causes it to live a divine life."[6] The Christian is born by the Spirit, sanctified by the Spirit, and sealed by the Spirit. He who is the author of faith, is also the author of grace and joy.[7] For Flavel, there is no spirituality without the Spirit—no spiritual life without its author. It is essential, then, that all Christians seek to discern the work of the Spirit in their lives. Their very life and joy depend on it.

Flavel's Pneumatology

Flavel's preaching and writing on the doctrine of the Holy Spirit is consistent with his seventeenth-century English Puritan context. As Adam Embry summarizes, "John Flavel's theology of the Spirit was not innovative but representative of Reformed Orthodoxy expressed among the English Puritans."[8] The best summary of this stream of English Puritan theology is found in the Westminster Confession of Faith, which was a particular favorite of Flavel's.[9] Similar to Flavel's own works, the Westminster Confession does not include a specific section laying out its theology of the Spirit. Rather, the "development of the doctrine of the Holy Spirit reflects the nature of scripture's teaching on the subject by integrating the person and work of the Spirit to the whole of God's eternal purposes as they have been expressed in creation and throughout redemption," according to O. Palmer Robertson.[10] Though he never provided a systematic presentation of the

____

5. John Flavel, *Vindiciarum Vindex: A Refutation of Mr. Philip Cary's Rejoinder to My Defence of the Right of Believers' Infants to Baptism*, in *Works of John Flavel* (1820; repr., Edinburgh: Banner of Truth Trust, 2015), 3:534. The Spirit is also the author of repentance. See *Exposition*, 6:266.

6. Flavel, *Method*, 2:89.

7. Flavel, *Exposition*, 6:203, 283.

8. Embry, "John Flavel's Theology," 95.

9. His appreciation for the work of the Westminster Assembly is most evident in his *Exposition*. He produced it toward the end of his life as a means to catechize his congregation. See Embry, "John Flavel's Theology," 95.

10. O. Palmer Robertson, "The Holy Spirit in the Westminster Confession of Faith," in *The Westminster Confession into the 21st Century*, ed. J. Ligon Duncan III, vol. 1 (Fearn, Scotland: Christian Focus, 2003), 98.

doctrine, Flavel's understanding of both the person and the work of the Spirit is clear and central in his writings.

The Person of the Spirit

Concerning the nature of the Spirit, Flavel is unmistakable in his belief that He is fully God. He asserts, "On account of his nature; for he is God co-equal with the Father and Son in nature and dignity.... So that you see he is God. The Rock of Israel. God omnipotent, for he created all things. God omnipresent, filling all things. God omniscient, who knows your hearts."[11] Thus, Flavel concludes, do not grieve the Spirit, "for in so doing you grieve God."[12] The full deity of the Spirit is also seen in that He is called the Holy Spirit. He is not simply the Spirit but the Spirit who is holy. Discussing the sealing work of the Spirit, Flavel reminds his readers of its author: "Consider the author of this work, the Spirit of God, who is an holy Spirit, as the text calls him, and the Spirit of truth, as Christ calls him."[13] The Spirit possesses all divine attributes, for He is God.

The full deity of the Holy Spirit is also seen in Flavel's repeated statements highlighting the Trinitarian nature of God. For instance, the Spirit, along with the Father and Son, are alone to be worshiped in heaven and on earth. Flavel writes, "In this they agree, that the worship above and below are both addressed and directed to one and the same object, Father, Son, and Spirit; all centers and terminates in God."[14] This triune nature of God lies always at the foundation of Flavel's thinking, and it is especially evident in his insistence on the full divinity of the Spirit. Of course, Flavel's Trinitarianism did not develop in a vacuum but is again indicative of his affirmation of the orthodoxy of the early church councils. In fact, Flavel describes God's providential protection of this orthodoxy as follows: "When, or wheresoever, venomous errors, and deadly heresies do arise, he hath his servants at hand with antidotes against them.... And as he had his

---

11. Flavel, *Fountain*, 1:512. Flavel quotes 2 Sam. 23:23; Gen. 1:2; Ps. 139:7; and Rom. 9:1 to support his assertion.

12. Flavel, *Fountain*, 1:512.

13. Flavel, *Twelve Sacramental Meditations*, 6:403.

14. Flavel, *Pneumatologia*, 3:49.

Athanasius to defend the Deity of Christ, so he wanted not his Basil to defend the doctrine of the Holy Spirit against Macedonius."[15] To deny the full deity of the Spirit, for Flavel, was to commit heresy and deny the faith altogether.

Flavel's upholding of the full deity of the Spirit, however, did not come at the cost of denying the Spirit's distinct personhood. The Spirit is not a divine power or force, as the Socinians of Flavel's day argued, but a divine person.[16] Flavel's understanding of the distinct personhood of the Spirit is evident in three main ways. First, Flavel consistently delineates the work of the Spirit as congruent, yet distinct from the work of the Father and the Son. Thus, when speaking of the reconciliation of God's people to God, he notes that this is a work of the triune God, in which "the scriptures point out the proper office of each Person. The Father receives us into favour; the Son mediates, and gives the ransom which procures it; the Spirit applies and seals this to the persons and hearts of believers."[17] The Spirit, then, like the Father and the Son, is a person of the triune God who works through His particular office for the salvation of His people.

Second, the personhood of the Spirit can be seen in the fact that He wills. The Spirit does as He pleases, He is not a mere power at the direction of another. For Flavel, He is Lord: "It is the Spirit that gives the word all that virtue it hath: he is the Lord of all saving influences: he hath dominion over the word, over our souls, over the times and seasons of conversion."[18] As Lord, the Spirit dispenses His blessings "arbitrarily," as He deems fit.[19] This reality does not mean that He operates outside of the Father and the Son but rather highlights His distinct personhood alongside the Father and the Son. Flavel is careful

---

15. Flavel, *Occasions*, 3:434.

16. It was Socinianism that contributed in part to the Puritans' emphasis on the doctrine of the Holy Spirit. Beeke and Jones explain, "The Puritan emphasis on the Spirit built on this ontological foundation of His deity and was a response to the rising threat of Sociniansim." Beeke and Jones, *Puritan Theology*, 420–21. These Socinians held that the Spirit "was merely the power of God" (421). For more on Socinianism in Flavel's day, see *Puritan Theology*, 420n9.

17. Flavel, *Fountain*, 1:160.

18. Flavel, *Method*, 2:58.

19. Flavel, *Method*, 2:58.

to uphold the unity of the Trinity: "The Father, Son, and Spirit work out their design in a perfect harmony and consent: as there was no jar in their council, so there can be none in the execution of it."[20] Thus, the Spirit is not an impersonal force at the employment of the Father and the Son but a distinct person working in harmony with the Father and the Son.

Finally, Flavel demonstrates the personhood of the Spirit through his persistent call for believers not to grieve Him. For example, he exhorts,

> I plead now on his behalf, who hath so many times helped you to plead for yourselves with God. He that hath so often refreshed, quickened, and comforted you, he will be quenched, grieved, and displeased by an impure, loose, and careless conversation; and what will you do then? Who shall comfort you when the Comforter is departed from you? When he that should relieve your souls is far off? O grieve not the holy Spirit of God by which you are sealed, to the day of redemption.[21]

Such stirring admonitions as these could never be made concerning a mere power or force. They necessitate that the Spirit be a person, for only a person can be grieved and displeased, and only a person can refresh, quicken, and comfort another.

Flavel, then, is orthodox in his understanding of the person of the Spirit. Throughout his writings, he repeatedly describes the glory of the Spirit, regularly defending both His full deity and full personhood. In all of his descriptions, he upholds the creed that emerged from the Council of Constantinople: "I believe in the Holy Ghost, the Lord and Giver of Life; who proceedeth from the Father and the Son; who with the Father and Son together is worshiped and glorified; who spake by the Prophets."[22] It is this Spirit, the "Lord and Giver of Life," who Flavel believed to be at the very heart of true Christian spirituality.

---

20. Flavel, *Method*, 2:21.
21. Flavel, *Fountain*, 1:542.
22. Schaff and Schaff, *Creeds of Christendom*, 2:59.

The Work of the Spirit

To understand Flavel's view of the Spirit's work, we must first grasp how he understands its relationship to Christ's work. For Flavel, the Spirit's work is to apply Christ's work to the believer. He asks, "Whose work or office is it to apply Christ to us? It is the office and work of God's Spirit."[23] Thus, the Spirit is a type of "vicegerent" to Christ, one who stands in and represents Christ to His people.[24] As such, the Spirit comes in the name and authority of Christ. Flavel explains, "The Spirit hath another office assigned him, even to apply, as Christ's vicegerent, the redemption designed by the Father, and purchased by the Son for us."[25] It is for this reason that the Spirit is often referred to as "the Spirit of Christ."[26] Again, Flavel's Trinitarianism is evident here, as it is clear that to experience the Spirit is to experience Christ. Much like Christ's claims that to see Him is to see the Father (John 14:9), so to know the Spirit is to know Christ. It is, therefore, the Spirit's very work "to take of Christ's and shew it to us…to take of his death, resurrection, ascension, yea, of his very present intercession in heaven, and shew it to us."[27] Flavel is adamant that the Spirit's work can only be rightly comprehended in light of Christ's work.

Flavel's exposition of the Spirit's work, then, follows closely with his explanation of the work of Christ. In fact, it is easiest to trace Flavel's understanding of the Spirit's work by looking at how he highlights it in relation to Christ's work in His threefold office. As Embry confirms, "Flavel's pneumatology developed in step with how Christ was revealed in Scripture as prophet, priest, and king."[28] Thus, Flavel shows how the Spirit's primary works of illumination, sanctification, direction, and consolation apply to Christ's work as prophet, priest, and king.

---

23. Flavel, *Exposition*, 190.

24. Flavel often identifies the Spirit as Christ's vicegerent. See Flavel, *Fountain*, 1:54, 137, 206; *Method*, 174; and *England's Duty*, 4:32.

25. Flavel, *Fountain*, 1:54.

26. For example, see Rom. 8:9 and Gal. 4:6.

27. Flavel, *Fountain*, 1:512.

28. Embry, "John Flavel's Theology," 87.

The Spirit's work of illumination. As prophet, Christ reveals truth to His people and illumines that truth so that they receive it. This prophetic act of illumination by Christ is carried out through the Spirit. Flavel explains, "There are two doors of the soul barred against Christ; the understanding by ignorance; and the heart by hardness: both these are opened by Christ. The former is opened by the preaching of the gospel, the other by the internal operation of the Spirit."[29] It is the Spirit who illumines the hearts of God's people so that they both understand the truth of Christ and delight in it. This illumination happens at the hearing of the Word of God but requires the special grace of the Spirit. Because the spiritual blindness of humanity is too great to be overcome by their mere reason, they must be illumined. "So the Spirit comes down at certain times in the word, and opens the heart," says Flavel, "and then it becomes the power of God to salvation."[30] If the preaching of the Word of God is to be effective, the Spirit of God must work in and through it.

The Spirit's work of illumination, then, is the opening up of the unbelieving heart so that it sees and worships the glory of Christ. Such work happens only in conjunction with the proclamation of the Word. As Flavel describes, "The Spirit of God, working in fellowship with the word, effectually turns the heart from sin."[31] This work of illumination, therefore, is a work of the Word and the Spirit. But it is the Spirit who gives the Word its power. Thus, Flavel asks,

> Whence the word of God hath all this power? And it is most certain, that it is not a power inherent in itself, nor derived from the instrument by which it is managed, but from the Spirit of the Lord, who communicates to it all that power and efficacy which it has upon our souls.[32]

The preaching of the Word without the Spirit lacks the power to revive the unbeliever's dead heart. Its effectiveness is found only in the wise, strong hands of the Spirit. This Word of God, however, "when it is

---

29. Flavel, *Fountain*, 1:132.
30. Flavel, *Fountain*, 1:135.
31. Flavel, *Method*, 2:297.
32. Flavel, *Method*, 2:298.

set home by the Spirit, is mighty to convince, humble, and break the hearts of sinners."[33] The Word, especially the preached Word, is the chosen instrument of the Spirit's work of illumination in the hearts of God's people.

This fellowship of Word and Spirit is central for Flavel and his Puritan contemporaries.[34] The reason for such an emphasis was due partly to the rise of Quakerism after the English Civil War (1642–1651).[35] The Quaker movement stressed an "illumination that came from the light within" and, therefore, they stressed the need to listen for a "divine inner voice."[36] As Beeke and Jones note, "The Quakers did not deny that God could and did speak to people mediately through the written text of Scripture, but they were convinced that they also knew and enjoyed the Spirit's immediate inspiration and guidance."[37] The heart of the controversy came down to whether the Scripture was to be tried by the Spirit, or the Spirit by the Scripture. Thus, George Fox (1624–1691), founder of the Quakers, describes another minister "as calling the Scriptures 'the touchstone and Judg' and himself as saying, 'ye holy ghost [that] gave them forth was the Judg and Touchstone.'"[38] Could the Spirit speak outside of the Scripture? Flavel's answer was clear:

> All teachings of God are agreeable with the written word: The Spirit of God, and the word of God do never jar…. When God speaketh unto the heart of man, whether in way of conviction, consolation, or instruction in duty, he always makes use of the express words of scripture, or speaks to the heart in language every way consentaneous and agreeable to scripture: So that the

---

33. Flavel, *Method*, 2:299.

34. For more on this see J. Stephen Yuille, introduction to *Great Spoil: Thomas Manton's Spirituality of the Word* (Grand Rapids: Reformation Heritage Books, 2019), xii–xvi.

35. For a helpful introduction to the Quaker movement, see Pink Dandelion, *An Introduction to Quakerism* (Cambridge: Cambridge University Press, 2007). To better understand the conflict between Quakerism and Flavel's Puritan contemporaries, see Beeke and Jones, *Puritan Theology*, 429–41. Flavel only mentions the Quakers explicitly three times: *Navigation Spiritualized*, 5:286; *Saint Indeed*, 5:499; and *Vindiciae Legis et Foederis*, 6:320–21.

36. Beeke and Jones, *Puritan Theology*, 433.

37. Beeke and Jones, *Puritan Theology*, 433.

38. As quoted in Nuttall, *Holy Spirit*, 27.

> written word becomes the standard to weigh and try all divine teachings.... Whatever is disagreeing or jarring with the scripture must not pass for an inspiration of God, but a deluding sophism, and insinuation of Satan.[39]

The Word of God cannot be separated from the Spirit of God. His work of illumination is therefore restricted to the written Word of God. The Spirit illumines the minds and hearts of believers to know and love the truth of Scripture. Thus, any and all supposed spiritual truth, must be tried by the explicit word of the Spirit, the written word of Scripture.

The Spirit's work of sanctification. Christ, as priest, gave his life for His people to redeem and reconcile them to God.[40] His work includes the purification of His people from both the guilt and pollution of sin. Flavel understood the latter as being cured by sanctification, which was purchased by Christ but performed by the Spirit. He explains, "And though it is proper to say the Spirit sanctifies, yet, it is certain, it was the blood of Christ that procured for us the Spirit of sanctification.... The pouring forth of Christ's blood for us, obtained the pouring forth of the spirit of holiness upon us."[41] Through His death Christ secured our holiness, and in so doing, gave us the Spirit to make us holy in actuality.

Pivotal to Flavel's understanding of the role of the Spirit in sanctification is his understanding of union with Christ.[42] It is through this union that the Spirit sanctifies the people of God. The believer is declared holy in Christ and becomes holy in Christ. But this union with Christ occurs only through the work of the Spirit: "The Spirit of Christ is the very bond of union betwixt him and our souls."[43] According

---

39. Flavel, *Method*, 2:325–26.

40. Flavel describes the four ends of Christ's death for this people as follows: (1) "That blood was shed and applied to deliver from danger," (2) "The blood was shed to make an atonement betwixt God and the people," (3) "That blood was shed to purify persons from their ceremonial pollutions," and (4) "That blood was shed to ratify and confirm the testament or covenant of God with the people." Flavel, *Fountain*, 1:468–69.

41. Flavel, *Fountain*, 1:479.

42. For more on Flavel's understanding of union with Christ, see Yuille, *Inner Sanctum*.

43. Flavel, *Method*, 2:329.

to Flavel, the Spirit Himself is the bond that unites the Christian to Christ. By means of this bond the Spirit both brings Christ to us and brings us to Christ, as Flavel describes:

> So that the Spirit's work in uniting or ingrafting a soul in Christ, is like the cutting off the graff from its native stock (which he doth by his illuminations and convictions) and closing it with the living, which it is thus prepared, and so enabling it (by the infusion of faith) to suck and draw the vital sap, and thus it becomes one with him.[44]

We are united to Christ by the Spirit and by faith, which is itself a gift of the Spirit. Our union with Christ, therefore, is all brought about by the work of the Spirit. "So that these two, namely, the Spirit on Christ's part, and faith, his work on our part, are the two ligaments by which we are knit to Christ," Flavel argues.[45]

Being thus united to Christ, believers are sanctified by the Spirit. For Flavel, this sanctification "notes an holy dedication of heart and life to God: Our becoming the temples of the living God, separate from all profane sinful practices, to the Lord's only use and service."[46] Thus, in sanctifying us, the Spirit indwells us, mortifies our sin, and vivifies our spirits; He makes us holy. This holiness comes to us by the work of the Spirit because of the work of Christ. Flavel closely associates these two workings: "As [Christ] died for sin, so the Spirit applying his death to us in the work of mortification, causes us to die to sin, by the virtue of his death: And as he was quickened by the Spirit, and raised unto life, so the Spirit applying unto us the life of Christ, causeth us to live, by spiritual vivification."[47] The Spirit makes us holy by applying the work of Christ to us and in us. As the apostle Paul wrote, it is Christ who is our "wisdom, and righteousness, and sanctification, and redemption" (1 Cor. 1:30). It is the work of the Spirit to unite us to Christ, whereby He becomes to us wisdom, righteousness, sanctification, and redemption.

---

44. Flavel, *Method*, 2:38.
45. Flavel, *Method*, 2:37–38.
46. Flavel, *Method*, 2:19.
47. Flavel, *Method*, 2:18–19.

The Spirit's work of direction. The kingship of Christ points to the reality of His rule both in the hearts of His people and in the world they inhabit. His work as king brings forth "all the promises of converting, increasing, defending, directing, and supplying grace," according to Flavel.[48] This kingly work, as with His prophetic and priestly works, is applied by the Spirit. Christ rules His people through His Spirit. As Flavel states, "And thus his eternal kingdom is administered by his Spirit, who is his *prorex*, or vicegerent in our hearts."[49] After Christ ascended to the right hand of the Father as king, He sent His Spirit to be His very presence among His people, to rule, guide, and direct them.[50]

The Spirit applies Christ's kingly work by indwelling the people of God and ruling in their hearts. Flavel explains, "Look as the holy Spirit of God dwells and rules in sanctified souls, walks in them as in hallowed temples, guiding and comforting the souls of the saints."[51] The soul of the Christian is the dwelling place of the Spirit, the sphere in which Christ is king and His authoritative power is on display. It is the Spirit who subdues the heart of sinners by the word of the gospel and directs them to Christ. Since Christ's work as king never fails, so this potent work of the Spirit cannot be thwarted: "Neither is there any defect in the applying cause, the Spirit of God, who hath already begun to work upon thy heart, and is able to break it and bow it, and bring it home fully to Christ, and to complete the work of faith upon thee with power."[52] The Spirit, as He illumines and sanctifies the elect, brings home the work of Christ fully and powerfully, guiding and directing each heart.

Such direction, as with all of God's works among His people, is for our good. The Spirit's directing work is gracious and compassionate, and points to His role as comforter. Flavel reminds,

---

48. Flavel, *Method*, 2:219.

49. Flavel, *Fountain*, 1:206.

50. Thus, Flavel writes, "But in the next place, see that you abuse not the Spirit, whom God sent from heaven at his ascension, to supply his bodily absence among us, and is the great pledge of his care for, and tender love to his people." Flavel, *Fountain*, 1:511.

51. Flavel, *England's Duty*, 4:49.

52. Flavel, *England's Duty*, 4:156.

> It was he that so often hath helped your infirmities, when you knew not what to say; comforted your hearts when they were overwhelmed within you, and you knew not what to do; preserved you many thousand times from sin and ruin, when you have been upon the slippery brink of it in temptations.[53]

It is the Spirit who continually directs believers away from the malaise of sin and toward the mercy of Christ, all the while caring for them in their hurts and hardships and comforting them with the joy of communion with Christ.

The Spirit applies the work of Christ to the people of Christ. He illumines their hearts and minds, so that they see and love Christ. He sanctifies their souls as He unites them to Christ and empowers them to mortify sin and live unto Christ. Finally, He directs their hearts as He indwells them and brings them under Christ's rule, protecting and comforting them at every turn. The Spirit, then, opens the eyes of God's people so that they see the glory of Christ, purifies them through uniting them to Christ, and guides them by placing them under the authority of Christ.

Flavel's Joy of the Spirit

The person and work of the Spirit is central to Flavel's understanding of Christian joy. In fact, so central is the Spirit to joy that Flavel refers to Him as "the author, fountain, and spring of all graces and comforts."[54] For Flavel, the believer's every joy comes from the gracious hands of the Spirit. Thus, he describes the Spirit as the oil of gladness, the one who has been poured out on God's people:

> Oil was used at the instalment of sovereign princes, which was the day of the gladness of their hearts; and, among the common people, it was liberally used at all their festivals, but never upon their days of mourning. Whence it becomes excellently expressive of the nature and use of the Spirit of grace, who is the cause and author of all joy in believers, John 17:13.[55]

---

53. Flavel, *Fountain*, 1:512.
54. Flavel, *Fountain*, 1:192. See also *Exposition*, 203.
55. Flavel, *Method*, 2:143.

As the Spirit applies the work of Christ to us, He is the one who primarily communicates God's grace, love, peace, and joy to us. The joy of the triune God flows through the Spirit of God to the people of God. This joy is especially experienced by believers through His indwelling presence, His sanctifying work, and His sealing work.

The Joy of the Spirit's Presence

As it is the Spirit's work to communicate grace and joy, so He Himself is a grace and joy to the Christian. To have the Spirit is a matter of great delight for the believer. As Flavel asks rhetorically, "Is it matter of all joy to have the Comforter himself, who is the Spirit of all consolation, taking up residence in thy heart, cheering, comforting, and refreshing it with such cordials as are unknown things in all the unbelieving world?"[56] The answer, of course, is a resounding *yes*. There is no greater joy in all the world than knowing the comfort and kindness of the Spirit. These inward comforts are "the hidden manna which no man knows but he that eateth of it."[57] To enjoy the Spirit's presence is to know joy inexpressible.

The reason such joy is unknown in our world is because it is not of our world. The joy of the Spirit is an otherworldly joy: "Those comforts communicated by the Spirit to believers, are of the same kind with the joys of heaven, though in a far inferior degree."[58] Those in whom the Spirit dwells feel and taste the joys and comforts of the Spirit. Such delights are the foretastes of the eternal joy of heaven. To have the Spirit, then, is to have the first fruits of heaven. It is due to this reality that Flavel so often speaks of the joy of the Spirit as a "joy unspeakable, and full of glory" (1 Peter 1:8).[59]

Though this joy is not *of* this world, it is *for* this world. It is joy in the Spirit that empowers believers to mortify sin and live for Christ. Flavel explains, "If your hearts were once sanctified and brought under the government of the Spirit, you would quickly find a far more excellent pleasure in the crucifying of your lusts, than now you seek

---

56. Flavel, *England's Duty*, 4:226.
57. Flavel, *England's Duty*, 4:99.
58. Flavel, *England's Duty*, 4:221.
59. Flavel, *England's Duty*, 4:221.

in the gratification and fulfilling of them."[60] The presence of the Spirit, governing our hearts and lives, makes the life of holiness a far greater delight than the life of worldliness. The Spirit's presence and work reorients the heart so that it increasingly takes pleasure in that which God has designed for our joy. To live for Christ becomes our greatest delight. Such joy is a more stable and genuine joy. It is not like the carnal joy of the world that vanishes like a dream when we awaken from sleep.[61]

This joy of the Spirit is also a strengthening joy. To have His presence is to have that joy which not only withstands all hardships but enables us to persevere under all trials. There is nothing that can crush the zeal of those who have the Spirit. Flavel recounts the experience of the apostles: "You read of the apostles (Acts 16:25), how they sang in the prison: The Spirit of God made them a banquet of heavenly joys, and they could not but sing at it: Though their feet were in the stocks, their spirits were never more at liberty."[62] The presence of the Spirit is a joy that gives us, even in the harsh realities of this sin-cursed world, a foretaste of the world to come. Such a foretaste empowers us to turn from sin and rejoice in Christ in every circumstance.

The Joy of the Spirit's Sanctifying Work

Flavel is adamant that the sanctified life is the joyous life. It is the life of true change, available only to those in whom the Spirit dwells, as He transforms them by applying the work of Christ to their souls. This "application of Christ to us… [includes] all those works of the Spirit which are known to us in Scripture by the names of regeneration, vocation, sanctification, and conversion."[63] As the Spirit regenerates, calls, converts, and sanctifies His people, they experience the great

---

60. Flavel, *Pneumatologia*, 3:197.

61. Flavel speaks of the joy of the unregenerate in this way: "They rejoice in corn, wine, and oil, in their estates and children, in the pleasant fruitions of the creature; yea, and they rejoice also in Christ and the promises, in heaven and in glory: with all which they have just such a kind of communion as a man hath in a dream with a full feast and curious music; and just so their joy will vanish when they awake." Flavel, *Method*, 2:290.

62. Flavel, *Pneumatologia*, 3:142.

63. Flavel, *Method*, 2:19.

joy of knowing salvation in Christ. This alone is the good life. As Flavel asserts, "This life infused by the regenerating Spirit, is a most pleasant life. All delights, all pleasures, all joys, which are not fantastic and delusive, have their spring and origin here."[64] The life of true joy springs forth only from the work of the Spirit in the believer.

It is through this work of the Spirit that life and peace are found. Quoting Romans 8:6, Flavel explains, "'To be spiritually minded is life and peace,' i.e. a most serene, placid life; such a soul becomes, so far as it is influenced and sanctified by the Spirit, the very region of life and peace."[65] The sanctified soul becomes the arena for joy. The sanctifying work of the Spirit enables the believer to experience genuine joy and as the believer grows in holiness, so they grow in delight. For Flavel, this is the only true pleasure in life: "Regeneration is the term from which all true pleasure commences; you never live a cheerful day, till you begin to live to God: therefore it is said (Luke 15:24), when the prodigal son was returned to his father, and reconciled, then they began to be merry."[66] The life of joy is life with God, which is purchased by Christ and applied by the Spirit. The Spirit first brings delight to the believer through His work of regeneration; He then increases that delight through His sanctifying work; and, finally, one day He brings that delight to its culmination in His work of glorification.

Again, Flavel declares that this delight is inexplicable to those who do not have the Spirit. He writes, "None can make another, by any words, to understand what that pleasure is which the renewed soul feels diffused through all its faculties and affections, in its communion with the Lord, and in the sealings and witnessings of his Spirit."[67] So substantial is the joy of the spiritual life that all other supposed joys are negated in its wake. Flavel considers "all the delights in the sensual life, all the pleasure that ever your lusts gave you, are but as putrid, stinking waters of a corrupt pond, where toads lie croaking

---

64. Flavel, *Method*, 2:90.

65. Flavel, *Method*, 2:90. He later quotes Rom. 8:5–6 in full: "For they that are after the flesh do mind the things of the flesh; but they that are after the Spirit the things of the Spirit. For to be carnally minded is death; but to be spiritually minded is life and peace." Flavel, *Method*, 339.

66. Flavel, *Method*, 2:90.

67. Flavel, *Method*, 2:90.

and spawning, compared to the crystal streams of the most pure and pleasant fountain."[68] There is no comparing the pure, ever-flowing joys of the Spirit with the stale, stagnant pleasures of the world.

Lastly, it is this sanctifying work of the Spirit that makes the believer more enjoyable. As the Spirit gives us eyes to see the delightfulness of Christ, and the power to live for the delight of Christ, we actually become more delightful ourselves as we become more like Christ. Thus, Flavel exhorts, "Strive to be Christ-like, as ever you would be lovely in the eyes of God and man."[69] Such striving, of course, is effective only in the power of the Spirit, for only the Spirit can make the Christian holy, which He has promised to do. It is this increasing holiness that brings increasing joy. Flavel expounds,

> Certainly, my brethren, it is the Spirit of Christ within you, and the beauty of Christ upon you, which only can make you lovely persons; the more you resemble him in holiness, the more will you discover of true excellency and loveliness; and the more frequent and spiritual your converse and communion with Christ is, the more of the beauty and loveliness of Christ will be stamped upon your spirits, changing you into the same image, from glory to glory.[70]

The more the Spirit shapes us into the image of Christ, the greater joy we will know in this life. The Spirit's presence and work, therefore, is truly the spring and fountain of all delight.

The Joy of the Spirit's Sealing Work

Since joy is rooted in the Spirit, we must ensure we have the Spirit. In other words, to know the rich joys of the Christian life, we must be certain that we are in Christ. Without assurance, we have little reason to suppose that we will know the delight that comes from it. Fortunately, the Spirit, as Flavel continually asserts, is the "earnest" or "seal" of salvation in Christ.[71] It is by the Spirit that we know we are truly in Christ (1 John 3:24). For this reason, Flavel writes, "The giving of the

---

68. Flavel, *Method*, 2:91.

69. Flavel, *Method*, 2:224.

70. Flavel, *Method*, 2:224.

71. Flavel uses these terms interchangeably. For example, he states, "The light

Spirit to us, or his residing in us, as a sanctifying Spirit, is everywhere in scripture made the pledge and earnest of eternal salvation, and consequently must abundantly confirm and prove the soul's interest in Christ."[72] To have the Spirit of Christ is to be certain that we are in Christ. It is this sealing work of the Spirit, then, that is foundational to assurance and, by consequence, joy.[73]

The Spirit's sealing work. Flavel describes the sealing of the Spirit in two ways: an objective sense and a subjective (or effectual) sense. He states, "Now the Spirit seals two ways, Objectively and Effectually; the first is by working those graces in us, which are the conditions of the promises: the latter by shining upon his own work, and helping the soul to discern it."[74] The Spirit first seals believers objectively by sanctifying them and transforming them into the image of Christ. This sealing is true of all Christians, as every Christian is sealed by the Spirit in this sense. Flavel is resolute that "all gracious souls are sealed objectively, i.e. they have those works of grace wrought on their souls, which do… ascertain and evidence their title to glory."[75] The Spirit, however, also seals subjectively, meaning that He aids believers in seeing His gracious work in their own hearts and lives. He "first infuses the grace, and then opens the eye of the soul to see it."[76]

It is in this subjective sealing of the Spirit that the joy of assurance is found. There is great joy in the Spirit's presence and sanctifying work; however, an inability to see that work obviously stifles joy. The experience of the Spirit's subjective sealing, therefore, is not the same for all believers. As Flavel explains,

---

of the Spirit, superadded to both the former, which is sometimes called its *earnest,* sometimes its *seal.*" Flavel, *Preparations for Suffering,* 6:38.

72. Flavel, *Method,* 2:333.

73. For more on Flavel's understanding of the Spirit's sealing work in assuring believers, see Embry, *Keeper,* 69–94; Cosby, *Suffering and Sovereignty,* 107–34; Cosby, *John Flavel: Puritan Life,* 114–16; Parker, "Proselytisation," 104–6; Allen, "Theologian as Pastor," 56–72; Ian Macleod, "True and Nominal," 197–214.

74. Flavel, *Fountain,* 1:95.

75. Flavel, *Fountain,* 1:449.

76. Flavel, *Saint Indeed,* 5:434.

> The Spirit doth but plant the habits, excite and draw forth the acts, and also shine upon his own work, that the soul may see it; and that sometimes with such a degree of light as only begets peace, and quiets the heart, though it doth not fully conquer all the doubts of it. And at other times the heart is irradiated with so clear a beam of light, that it is able to draw forth a triumphant conclusion, and say, Now I know the things that are freely given me of God: I believe, and am sure.[77]

It is clear that while most believers experience some aspect of this subjective sealing of the Spirit, they do not experience it to the same degree. Such a reality, along with the potential of false assurance, leads Flavel to consider how the Spirit seals.

Among the Puritans in Flavel's day, there were two main views of the Spirit's sealing (or witnessing) work: immediate and mediate.[78] The Spirit's immediate witness, explains Flavel, is "distinct from that of water and blood (1 John 5:8), that is a witness, or sealing, which comes not in an argumentative way, by reasoning from either justification or sanctification, but seems to come immediately from the Spirit."[79] Some scholars have argued that Flavel, at least for a time, believed this immediate witness was one means to gain assurance.[80] Such a conclusion, however, seems to be overstated. While Flavel occasionally allows for such an immediate witness, he never encourages his readers to seek (or even expect) such an experience.

Flavel, instead, asserts that this witness of the Spirit is "extraordinary and immediate, vouchsafed only to some persons, at some special times and seasons."[81] He notes that while this may have been the experience of some New Testament believers, "these immediate

---

77. Flavel, *Preparations for Suffering*, 6:38.

78. To better grasp this debate among the Puritans, see Beeke, *Assurance of Faith*, 170–73, 253–59; and Packer, *Quest*, 179–89. See also chapter 2 of the present volume.

79. Flavel, *Pneumatologia*, 3:59.

80. For example, Embry writes, "Thus Flavel's doctrine of the sealing of the Spirit moves from dismissing an immediate sealing of the Spirit in 1667 to accepting it by 1685. In the 1685 publication of *The Soul of Man*, Flavel lists both mediate and immediate witness of the Spirit as viable options for obtaining assurance of salvation." Embry, *Keeper of the Great Seal*, 85.

81. Flavel, *Twelve Sacramental Meditations*, 6:405.

ways are ceased; no man may now expect by any revelation or sign from heaven, by any voice or extraordinary inspiration, to have his salvation sealed." Rather, such mercy should be expected to come "in God's ordinary way and method, searching the scriptures, examining our own hearts, and waiting on the Lord in prayer."[82] Thus, Flavel gives little credence to the immediate witness; instead, he repeatedly exhorts his people to seek the mediate witness of the Spirit, which he understands to be the superior way. He sums up his view as follows: "I will not deny but there may be an immediate testimony of the Spirit; but sure I am his mediate testimony by his graces in us, is his usual way of sealing believers."[83] An immediate witness of the Spirit, though possible in Flavel's mind, was not ordinary nor best for gaining assurance.

Flavel is resolved to show that it is the mediate testimony of the Spirit that we ought to seek and expect. This witness is "mediate, in, and by the previous use and exercise of faith, heart-examination, &c. The Spirit of God concurring with, and blessing such duties as these, helps the soul by them to a sight of its interest in Christ, and the glory to come."[84] Here, the Spirit witnesses with our spirit as we exercise faith through examining our hearts by prayerful meditation on Scripture and the things of God.

It is this ordinary means, writes Flavel, that "hath been the constant practice of the saints in all ages, to clear their title to the righteousness of Christ wrought without them, by the work of his Spirit wrought within them."[85] Instead of imparting some direct and immediate revelation to the soul, the Spirit seals believers by guiding them to see the evidences of His regenerating and sanctifying work in their lives. These evidences are highlighted as He helps them to understand the Scriptures and their own hearts, all the while empowering them to live for Christ. Flavel explains, "The Spirit of God is ready to seal you, it is his office and his delight so to do. O therefore, give diligence to this work, attend the study of the scriptures and of your own hearts

---

82. Flavel, *Twelve Sacramental Meditations*, 6:405–6.
83. Flavel, *Vindiciae Legis et Foederis*, 6:354.
84. Flavel, *Pneumatologia*, 3:57.
85. Flavel, *Occasions*, 3:459.

more, and grieve not the holy Spirit of God, and you may arrive to the very desire of your hearts."[86] The principal means by which the Spirit assures us that we are truly in Christ is, for Flavel, to see His work in our hearts and lives, and know that it is His work. The first act of the Spirit in sanctifying us is His objective sealing, while this second act of enabling us to clearly identify His work is His subjective sealing. It is through these two acts that the Spirit assures believers and brings about our greatest joy and consolation.

The joy of being sealed. It is the joy of the sealing work of the Spirit that Flavel describes as *the* joy of the Spirit. So significant is the delight that comes from the Spirit's assuring work that Flavel considers it to be the locus of all joy in the Spirit. For him, "this joy of the Holy Ghost is a spiritual cheerfulness streaming through the soul of a believer upon the Spirit's testimony, which clears his interest in Christ, and glory."[87] It is "the very quintessence and spirit of all consolation," "joy unspeakable and full of glory," and "no more under that soul's command."[88]

It is unsurprising, then, that Flavel equates this joy with experiencing a foretaste of heaven. Such joy proves "that all the joys of heaven are not to come; but some communicated in this life."[89] Even among spiritual delights, the joy of the Spirit's sealing work is clearly unique. Flavel states, "The conclusion or truth sealed is ravishing and transporting… [it is] to enjoy heaven upon earth, a joy beyond all joys of this world."[90] To be sealed by the Spirit and to have our interest in Christ cleared is to have our eternity with Christ guaranteed. It is to have our future heaven brought into the present and to have our eternal joy begin now. So, Flavel notes, it is this sealing work of the Spirit that has "a direct and clear aspect upon the life to come, and the happiness of our souls in the full enjoyment of God to eternity; for it

---

86. Flavel, *Method*, 2:138.

87. Flavel, *England's Duty*, 4:218.

88. Flavel, *England's Duty*, 4:218.

89. Flavel, *Exposition*, 201. See also *Method*, 335; *Pneumatologia*, 2:575; and *England's Duty*, 4:221.

90. Flavel, *Twelve Sacramental Meditations*, 4:407.

is to that life we are now sealed; and of the full sum of that glory, that these are the pledges and earnests."[91]

Finally, such joy is indestructible. The sealing work of the Spirit so establishes the souls of believers that while doubts, struggles, and temptations will come, none will ultimately dissolve their hope. Flavel asserts,

> Now temptations may come, great persecutions and sore afflictions may come; but how well is that soul provided for them all, that hath the sealings of the Spirit unto the day of redemption? Yea, though the soul that was sealed should for the present be under new darkness, new temptations and fears, yet the former sealing will give establishment and relief, when the thoughts run back to the sealing day, and a man remembers how clear God once made his title to Christ.[92]

In the midst of life's darkest days and trials, this sealing work of the Spirit is an anchor to the soul, which solidifies its joy amidst the roughest seas. Nothing, not even death, can wreck the believers delight in Christ. For "he hath sealed them to his glory by the Holy Spirit. So that their hopes are too firmly built to be destroyed by death; and if it cannot destroy their souls, nor overthrow their hopes, they need not fear all that it can do besides."[93] The sealing work of the Spirit brings to the Christian the rarest of all joys—a foretaste of heaven itself, which is so substantial that nothing can finally thwart it.

Flavel's Call to Discern the Spirit

To know that we are truly in Christ is the most comforting truth to be experienced in this life. There is no greater delight than knowing that Christ is ours. For this reason, Flavel proposes that "our sincerity and interest in Christ are matters of the deepest concernment to us in all the world."[94] Such sincerity, though, comes only through the work of the Spirit. As Flavel affirms, "None but the Spirit of God can clear and confirm our title to Christ, for he only searcheth the deep things

---

91. Flavel, *Pneumatologia*, 2:575.
92. Flavel, *England's Duty*, 4:220.
93. Flavel, *Pneumatologia*, 3:119.
94. Flavel, *Twelve Sacramental Meditations*, 6:402.

of God, and it is his office, to witness with our spirits."[95] It is for this reason that Flavel so adamantly calls his readers to discern the Spirit and thereby pursue the sealing work of the Spirit.

Flavel is clear that the assurance is the work of the Spirit because He alone is the author of assurance. Thus, in describing how we discern the Spirit, Flavel first reminds us that "it is nothing else but the Spirit's shining upon his own work, in the hearts of believers, thereby enabling them sensibly to see and feel it to their own satisfaction."[96] While it is the Spirit's work, such a reality does not mean that we are passive in the process. We ought to strive with all rigor to attain, increase, keep, and enjoy the comforting assurance given by the Spirit. As Flavel exhorts, "Full assurance is possible, else it had not been put into the command (2 Peter 1:10). The sealing graces are in you, the sealing Spirit is ready to do it for you, the sealing promises belong to you; but we give not all diligence, and therefore go without the comfort of it."[97] It is the Spirit who seals, but it is the believer who pursues such sealing. Such a pursuit is our responsibility: "Have you not earnests, pledges, and firstfruits of it? Tis your own fault, if every day you feed not upon such blessed comforts of the Spirit."[98]

According to Flavel, the ordinary method of discerning the Spirit is by "searching the scriptures, examining our own hearts, and waiting on the Lord in prayer."[99] Crucial to this endeavor is the examining of our heart for the evidences of the Spirit. Thus, Flavel urges Christians to "the search and study of their own hearts; calls them to reflect upon the effects and operations of the Spirit of God wrought within their own souls, assuring them, that these gracious effects, and the fruits of the Spirit in their hearts, will be a solid evidence of their union with Jesus Christ."[100] Prior to such examination, we must first understand what are the evidences of the Spirit's work. Here, then, it is essential that we search and know the Scriptures, for not only will our hearts

---

95. Flavel, *Twelve Sacramental Meditations*, 6:402.
96. Flavel, *Preparations for Suffering*, 6:37.
97. Flavel, *Practical Treatise*, 3:304.
98. Flavel, *Husbandry Spiritualized*, 5:106.
99. Flavel, *Twelve Sacramental Meditations*, 6:405–6.
100. Flavel, *Method*, 2:328.

be drawn in by the glory of Christ at the center of the Scriptures but we will also come to know better the genuine effects and fruits of the Spirit and how to distinguish them from false evidences.

It is this scriptural knowledge that Flavel seeks to convey in his *The Method of Grace* as he lays out the way in which the Spirit applies the redemptive work of Christ to the people of God. He does so with the aim of aiding his readers in the pursuit of the joy of assurance. Flavel concludes the preface of this work as follows:

> O that you would dwell more in your closets, and be more frequently and fervently upon your knees. O that you would search your hearts more narrowly, and sift them more thoroughly than ever, before the day pass as the chaff, and the Lord's fierce anger come upon you: look into your Bibles, then into your hearts, and then to heaven, for a true discovery of your conditions; and if this poor mite can contribute anything to that end, it will be a great reward of the unworthy labours of thy servant in Christ, John Flavel.[101]

To discern the evidences of the Spirit, we must examine both the Scripture and the soul while prayerfully seeking the Spirit's help.

Flavel guides his readers in this endeavor by repeatedly highlighting these evidences. In his sermon on 1 John 3:24, he presents "the particular marks and trials by which we may discern whether God has given us his Spirit or no, by which grown Christians…may, by the assistance of the Spirit of God (for which therefore they are bound to pray), discern his indwelling and working in themselves."[102] Flavel lists seven genuine evidences of the Spirit's indwelling: (1) the conviction of sin; (2) the quickening of the Spirit resulting in a hunger and thirst for Christ; (3) the sharing in Christ's interests and concerns; (4) the mortification of sin; (5) the strengthening of the desires for, and sincerity of, prayer; (6) the focusing of the mind on God, Christ, heaven, and the world to come; and (7) the giving of ourselves to the government and conduct of the Spirit.[103] Each of these evidences, rightly understood, can be found only in the one in whom the Spirit is

---

101. Flavel, *Method*, 2:14.
102. Flavel, *Method*, 2:336.
103. Flavel, *Method*, 2:336–40.

at work. To have any of them gives some measure of assurance, especially to the struggling Christian. For this reason, Flavel is quick to remind his people that they do not need to find all these evidences in order to experience the joy and comfort of assurance.

While the call to examine oneself for the evidences of the Spirit's work is primary, Flavel also reminds his readers of two other biblical exhortations for experiencing the joy of the Spirit's sealing work. First, Flavel exhorts his readers to beware of grieving the Spirit: "O grieve not the Holy Spirit of God by which you are sealed, to the day of redemption."[104] To grieve the Spirit is to work against his designs and aids. Therefore, as Flavel explains, "There is nothing [that] grieves him more than impure practices, for he is a holy Spirit.... He feels the least touch of sin, and is grieved when thy corruptions within are stirred by temptations, and break out to the defiling of thy life; then is the holy Spirit of God, as it were, made sad and heavy within thee."[105] Such sin includes not only the external acts of unrighteousness but also the internal impulses of the self-centered heart. Pride is certain to grieve the Spirit, for "nothing more provoketh the Lord to withdraw his Spirit, and let you fall, than this sin of self-confidence doth."[106] For Flavel, unrighteousness and self-righteousness grieve the Spirit and, therefore, ultimately grieve the believer.

There is, then, little comfort for those who grieve the Spirit. As Flavel explains, "And when thou thus forsakest his conduct, and crossest his design in thy soul, then doth he usually withdraw as a man that is grieved by the unkindness of his friend. He draws in the beams of his evidencing and quickening grace [and] withholds all divine cordials."[107] When we grieve the Spirit, we struggle to see His work in our hearts, and we lose the confidence of our salvation. Flavel, in desiring his people's joy, is quick to warn them of the dangers and foolishness of grieving the Spirit.

Lastly, Flavel encourages his readers to discern the Spirit through actively pursuing the evidences of the Spirit. If these evidences are being

---

104. Flavel, *Fountain*, 1:542.
105. Flavel, *Fountain*, 1:542–43.
106. Flavel, *Preparations for Suffering*, 6:71.
107. Flavel, *Fountain*, 1:543.

worked into our soul by the Spirit's sanctifying work, then we are to join with the Spirit in these efforts. For "it is both easy and successful striving when the Spirit of God strives in you, and with you."[108] Scripture displays to Christians the effects of the Spirit in their hearts and reminds them that these fruits will only help establish their joy. Thus, as they pursue these evidences, they are also pursuing their own joy with the powerful aid and promises of the Spirit. Flavel, therefore, entreats us to do so: "Would we pray more, and strive more, would we keep our hearts with a stricter watch, mortify sin more thoroughly, and walk before God more accurately; how soon may we attain this blessed assurance, and in it an excellent cure for our distracting and slavish fears."[109] It is the work of the Spirit to seal and assure believers. This ought to persuade and empower us all the more to actively pursue the joy of assurance.

Conclusion

One of the foremost legacies of the Puritan movement is the attention they gave to the person and work of the Spirit. As they sought to see Reformation theology lived out in the worship of the church and the life of the believer, the Puritans emphasized the important role of the Spirit. Flavel is an exemplar of this movement. The Spirit is at the center of his spirituality and, therefore, the center of his joy. While Christ is the object of our joy, it is the Spirit who is its author. As the third person of the triune God, it is His role to apply the redemptive work of Christ to the elect. In so doing, He sanctifies and seals them. He changes their hearts and empowers them to see His handiwork, so that they are assured of their position in Christ. It is this comforting presence that brings believers their greatest joy in life. For Flavel, then, it is of utmost importance that we discern the Spirit's work by prayerfully examining both the Scriptures and our souls in order to rightly identify the fruits of sanctification. The Spirit aids our endeavors as He testifies with our spirits that we are truly the children of God. This sealing work of the Spirit is our joy now and for all eternity. It is this joy of assurance that informs Flavel's understanding of true spirituality.

---

108. Flavel, *Pneumatologia*, 3:232.
109. Flavel, *Practical Treatise*, 3:304.

Chapter 6

Joy in Obeying the Law

Central to Flavel's understanding of the joy of assurance is the necessity of obeying the law.[1] Such obedience is needed for the experience of both assurance and joy. As Flavel exhorts, "Assurance is unattainable without obedience; we can never be comfortable Christians except we be strict and regular Christians…true peace, and consolation is only to be expected and found here."[2] Obedience demonstrates believers' union with Christ and brings considerable delight to their lives. Grounded in the work of Christ and empowered by the work of the Spirit, the Christian's obedience is imperative for joy. Brian Cosby maintains, "The Christian life, according to Flavel, was to reflect this divine grace in an ever-increasing pursuit of holiness and assurance."[3] For Flavel, the pursuit of holiness and assurance are not separate pursuits but one and the same, and both lead to greater joy.

This pursuit of holiness was a hallmark of English Puritan piety. As Kelly Kapic and Randall Gleason assert, "The fundamental nature of spirituality within Puritanism is found in its insistence that the converted soul must go beyond conversion to actual holiness of life."[4] Such concern for holiness was a "preoccupation" for the Puritans and "cannot be overstated."[5] Their emphasis on the pursuit of holiness arose out of their belief that the triune God intended not simply

---

1. For more on Flavel's understanding of the law, see Cosby, *John Flavel: Puritan Life*, 107–19; and Chang, "John Flavel," 101–16.

2. Flavel, *Method*, 2:401.

3. Cosby, *John Flavel: Puritan Life*, 116.

4. Kapic and Gleason, *Devoted Life*, 24.

5. Kapic and Gleason, *Devoted Life*, 25.

to justify the elect but to sanctify them. Those whom God justifies He sanctifies. Thus, holiness is essential to the life of the Christian; believers are created in Christ unto good works (see Eph. 2:10). The Westminster Confession of Faith states,

> These good works, done in obedience to God's commandments, are the fruits and evidences of a true and lively faith; and by them believers manifest their thankfulness, strengthen their assurance, edify their brethren, adorn the profession of the gospel, stop the mouths of adversaries, and glorify God, whose workmanship they are, created in Christ Jesus thereunto, that, having their fruit unto holiness, they may have the end, eternal life.[6]

For the Puritans, it is impossible to live the Christian life without good works. To strive for holiness and good works is the natural outflow of the regenerate heart.

Flavel, and his Puritan contemporaries, understood this pursuit to coincide in large part with obedience to the law of God. Without such obedience, there was no holiness, assurance, or joy. Ernest Kevan explains, "A fundamental principle of Puritanism was the recognition of the exclusive authority of Scripture for all things, a recognition which, in turn, drew attention to the significance of the Law of God."[7] With a robust doctrine of the sufficiency of Scripture for the Christian life, the Puritans returned again and again to the moral law. Kevan continues, "Sin is the transgression of Law, the death of Christ is the satisfaction of Law, justification is the verdict of Law, and sanctification is the believer's fulfillment of the Law."[8] It was the moral law of God, seen most clearly in the Ten Commandments, which guided the believer's obedience and pursuit of holiness. It was, as Calvin writes, "the true and eternal rule of righteousness, prescribed for men of all nations and times, who wish to conform their lives to God's will."[9] To obey the law, then, is to live according to God's design for His people and to experience the joy of God's saving work.

---

6. WCF 16.2.

7. Ernest F. Kevan, *The Grace of Law: A Study in Puritan Theology* (Ligonier, Pa.: Soli Deo Gloria, 1993), 21.

8. Kevan, *Grace of Law*, 21.

9. Calvin, *Institutes*, 2:1503.

Flavel and the Law

To understand Flavel's emphasis on obedience as essential to the believer's joy, it is important to grasp his understanding of the law. Flavel has much in common with the position of the Westminster Assembly. He shares the Assembly's division of the law into moral, ceremonial, and civil.[10] The moral law was identified primarily with the Ten Commandments, the ceremonial consisted mostly of ordinances to inform Israel's worship, and the civil was made up of those judicial laws that guided the nation's political affairs. Of these three categories, only the moral law was understood to be binding for the Christian. As the Westminster Confession of Faith explains, the ceremonial law was voided in the new covenant:

> Beside this law, commonly called moral, God was pleased to give to the people of Israel, as a Church under age, ceremonial laws, containing several typical ordinances, partly of worship, prefiguring Christ, his graces, actions, sufferings, and benefits; and partly holding forth divers instructions of moral duties. All which ceremonial laws are now abrogated under the New Testament.[11]

These ceremonial laws foreshadowed the coming of Christ and were, therefore, fulfilled in Him. Flavel asserts that "the ceremonial law many ways prefigured Christ, his death and satisfaction, by blood, in our room, and so led men to Christ their true propitiation; and all its types were fulfilled and ended in Christ."[12] Such laws, while no longer possessing authority over the lives of believers, are an excellent aid for understanding the person and work of Christ. As Flavel describes, "The ceremonial law is full of Christ, and the gospel is full of Christ: the blessed lines of both Testaments meet in him; and how they both harmonize, and sweetly concentre in Jesus Christ, is the chief scope of that excellent epistle to the Hebrews."[13] No believer should be ignorant of the ceremonial law, as it has much to teach about Christ.

Additionally, the Westminster Confession states that the civil law, like the ceremonial, is no longer in force under the new covenant:

---

10. See WCF 19.
11. WCF 19.3.
12. Flavel, *Vindiciae Legis et Foederis*, 6:337.
13. Flavel, *Fountain*, 1:34.

"To them also, as a body politic, he gave sundry judicial laws, which expired together with the state of that people, not obliging any other, now, further than the general equity thereof may require."[14] Robert Letham writes, "Once Israel as such ceased to be the particular vehicle for God's saving purposes, these laws expired. Therefore, the function they had in the Old Testament no longer exists."[15] Flavel, for his part, says very little about the civil law in his writings.

The dominant focus of Flavel, especially as it relates to the Christian life, is that of the moral law. This is "the rule which God at first revealed to man for his obedience," and it is "summarily comprehended in the ten commandments."[16] The moral law, unlike the ceremonial and civil, is for all people at all times. It is, therefore, binding under the new covenant. As the Westminster Confession stipulates, "The moral law doth forever bind all, as well justified persons as others, to the obedience thereof; and that not only in regard of the matter contained in it, but also in respect of the authority of God the Creator who gave it."[17] This law, while constituted most clearly at Sinai, has bound all humanity since creation. Flavel explains, "Before the law was given at Sinai, all the race of Adam had a law written in their hearts, viz. the light of reason, and dictates of natural conscience; Rom. 2:14."[18] He adds, "The matter of the moral law is unchangeable, as the nature of good and evil is, and cannot be abolished except that distinction could be destroyed, Matt. 5:17–18." If the law could change, it would cease to be binding. This would render the nature of good and evil subjective, and arguably impugn upon the nature of God Himself. For Flavel, such a notion is absurd. The moral law is a sure reflection of the character of God and is, therefore, critical for all people, especially those who claim allegiance to Christ.

Three Uses

Concerning the moral law, many English Puritans held that it had

---

14. WCF 19.4.

15. Letham, *Westminster Assembly*, 296.

16. Flavel, *Exposition*, 6:219.

17. WCF 19.5.

18. Flavel, *Exposition*, 6:219. For more on this understanding among the Puritans, see Kevan, *Grace of Law*, 52–54.

three specific uses or applications. These include the civil, evangelical, and directive.[19] While the first two uses are found explicitly in Martin Luther's writings, it is Calvin who provides the most comprehensive treatment of all three.[20] Regarding its civil use, Calvin explains that it functions "by fear of punishment to restrain certain men who are untouched by any care for what is just and right unless compelled by hearing the dire threats in the law."[21] In this case, the law guides the civil government in establishing rewards and threats of punishment, in order to establish peace and lawfulness among citizens. This function of the law is necessary for civil order. Flavel explains,

> It is law and fear of punishment that keeps the world in order: men are afraid to do evil, because they are afraid to suffer it; they see that law hath inseparably linked penal and moral evils together; if they will presume upon the one, they must necessarily pull the other upon them too; and this keeps them in some order and decorum: there would be no order or security without law.[22]

This first use of the law, as a restraint of wickedness, was universally held among the Reformers and the Puritans.[23]

The second application of the law, its evangelical use, was especially significant to Flavel and his Reformed tradition. In this use, the moral law functions to turn humanity away from self-righteousness to Christ's righteousness. It is evangelical in that it helps people see their need for the gospel. As Calvin describes, "While it shows God's righteousness, that is, the righteousness alone acceptable to God, it

---

19. Beeke and Jones, *Puritan Theology*, 556–57. W. R. Godfrey uses the phrases *usus civilis* or *politicus* (civil or political use), *usus spiritualis* or *theologicus* (spiritual or theological use), and *usus in renatis* (regenerate use). See W. R. Godfrey, "Law and Gospel," in *New Dictionary of Theology*, ed. S. B. Ferguson, D. F. Wright, and J. I. Packer (Downers Grove, Ill.: InterVarsity, 1988), 379.

20. Thus, Beeke and Jones assert, "On this [first] use of the law, the Protestant Reformers were in complete accord." Beeke and Jones, *Puritan Theology*, 556. Concerning the second use of the law, "Here, too, Luther and Calvin were in accord" (556).

21. Calvin, *Institutes*, 1:358.

22. Flavel, *Practical Treatise*, 3:254.

23. For the agreement between Calvin and Luther, see Donald MacLeod, "Luther and Calvin on the Place of the Law," in *Living the Christian Life: Papers Read at the 1974 Westminster Conference* (London: Westminster Conference, 1974), 5.

warns, informs, convicts, and lastly condemns, every man of his own unrighteousness."[24] The law shows God's standard for holiness, which makes explicit our own failure to meet that standard.

Due to his evangelistic fervor, Flavel spends much time on this use of the law.[25] He asserts, "It is utterly useless, as a covenant, to justify us; but exceedingly useful to convince and humble us; it cannot relieve or ease us, but it can and doth awaken and rouse us."[26] The law operates as an alarm to awaken us to our insufficiency and thus our need for grace. In his typical illustrative way, Flavel compares the law to the fiery serpents God's people faced in the wilderness: "The law, like the fiery serpent, smites, stings, and torments the conscience; this drives us to the Lord Jesus, lifted up in the gospel, like the brazen serpent in the wilderness, to heal us. The use of the law is to make us feel our sickness; this makes us look out for a Physician."[27] It is for this reason that Flavel speaks of the law as "wounding" and the gospel as "curing."[28] This wounding is necessary for all humanity, for we are ignorant of our sin and its seriousness.

Thus Flavel, like Calvin, describes the law as a mirror or glass that shows us the depths of our sinfulness.[29] Flavel states, "Sin is but a trifle, till God shews us the face of it in the glass of the law, and then it appears exceedingly sinful."[30] Blind to our sin, we need the law to show us our faults. The depth of our sinfulness means the law is never too demanding, for "the hard, vain, proud hearts of men require such an hammer to break them to pieces."[31] So strongly does Flavel advocate for the significance of this use of the law that he concludes, "No man can come to Christ without the application of the law."[32] The

---

24. Calvin, *Institutes*, 1:354.

25. For a full treatment of Flavel's practice of evangelism, see Boone, *Puritan Evangelism*.

26. Flavel, *Method*, 2:180–81.

27. Flavel, *Method*, 2:181.

28. Flavel, *Method*, 2:297.

29. Calvin writes, "The law is like a mirror. In it we contemplate our weakness, then the iniquity arising from this, and finally the curse coming from both—just as a mirror shows us the spots on our face." Calvin, *Institutes*, 1:354.

30. Flavel, *Method*, 2:320.

31. Flavel, *Method*, 2:181.

32. Flavel, *Method*, 2:327.

law is a necessary tool in the gracious hands of the Spirit to reveal our sinfulness and our desperate need for a Savior.

Finally, it is the third use of the law, as a rule to guide believers, that has occasioned the most controversy. Calvin sees this use of the law as most central, arguing, "The third and principal use, which pertains more closely to the proper use of the law, finds its place among believers in whose hearts the Spirit of God already lives and reigns."[33] This means the law "is the best instrument for them to learn more thoroughly each day the nature of the Lord's will to which they aspire, and to confirm them in the understanding of it."[34] In this third application of the law, believers are both instructed and enabled to obey and live out God's will. For this reason, Calvin had a largely positive view of the moral law.

Luther, on the other hand, did not seem to share Calvin's positive view of the law, though he did give some credence to its use for believers.[35] As John Hesselink notes, "Luther…following the negative strictures of the apostle Paul in his controversies against the Judaizers, saw the law primarily as a corollary of sin, death, and the devil."[36] For Luther, the law was predominately negative because it undermined the gracious promises of the gospel. This contrast, however, is less of a conflict with Calvin's understanding of the law, as it is a consequence of "talking about a different law."[37] Calvin's emphasis is on the goodness of the law within the context of the covenant of grace, whereas

---

33. Calvin, *Institutes*, 1:360.

34. Calvin, *Institutes*, 1:360.

35. There is much discussion concerning Luther's view of the third use of the law. As Beeke and Jones note, "Luther never explicitly developed this concept in his theology, leaving scholars to debate over just what he believed. But he did implicitly endorse the third use of the law by including the Ten Commandments in the Smaller Catechism (1529), explaining how each commandment teaches us to 'fear and love God.' Luther said that prior to conversion the law is a beating stick in God's hand against our sins, but after our conversion the law is the walking stick in our hands to helps us walk with God. The law thus drives sinners to Christ through whom they become 'doers of the law.'" Beeke and Jones, *Puritan Theology*, 557.

36. I. John Hesselink, *Calvin's Concept of the Law* (Allison Park, Pa.: Pickwick, 1992), 255. For more on Luther and Calvin on the law, see MacLeod, "Luther and Calvin," 5–13; and E. A. Downey, "Law in Luther and Calvin," *Theology Today* 41 (1984): 146–53.

37. Hesselink, *Calvin's Concept*, 255.

Luther is focused on its condemning nature and inability to justify the sinner.[38] The difference, therefore, is not one of outright disagreement but one of contrasting emphases.

The majority of English Puritans, however, followed Calvin's lead, and emphasized this third use, placing great prominence on the function of the law in the life of the believer. Question 97 of the Westminster Larger Catechism demonstrates this priority:

> Although they that are regenerate, and believe in Christ, be delivered from the moral law as a covenant of works, so as thereby they are neither justified nor condemned; yet, besides the general uses thereof common to them with all men, it is of special use, to shew them how much they are bound to Christ for his fulfilling it, and enduring the curse thereof in their stead, and for their good; and thereby to provoke them to more thankfulness, and to express the same in their greater care to conform themselves thereunto as the rule of their obedience.

It is evident that the focus here is on Christ's obedience, and that the believer's obedience is to flow out of Christ's obedience. The Christian, then, is called to obey the law, not for justification but because of justification. As Samuel Bolton (1606–1654) writes, "[Papists] preach obedience as a means to justification; we preach justification as a means to obedience. We cry down works in opposition to grace in justification, and we cry up obedience as the fruits of grace in sanctification."[39] For the Puritans, then, the moral law served primarily as a rule of life that was to be obeyed carefully and cheerfully in the power of the Spirit.

A Rule of Life

Flavel agrees with Calvin and the Westminster Assembly on the function of the law for Christians. While believers are set free in Christ, they are not set free from obeying the moral law. Flavel explains, "Christ doth not free believers from obedience to the moral law: It is true that we are no more under it as a covenant for our justification;

---

38. Hesselink, *Calvin's Concept*, 255.

39. Samuel Bolton, *The True Bounds of Christian Freedom* (1645; repr: Edinburgh: Banner of Truth Trust, 2020), 69.

but we are, and must still be under it, as a rule for our direction."[40] This clarification—that obedience to the law is not for justification but rather for sanctification—was essential for Flavel. He is adamant that while Christians are not justified in any way by works, they are justified in order to obey. Their justification by the work of Christ frees them, not *from* obedience to the law but *to* obedience to the law. Thus, he writes, "It is excellent when Christians begin to obey the law *from* life, which others obey *for* life; because they *are* justified, not that they *may be* justified."[41] Again, this distinct context of grace is crucial for Flavel's exposition of the goodness of the law for the people of God.

Such a distinction does not mean, however, that there is not a sense in which believers are freed from the law. Flavel is consistent in pointing out that Christians are no longer under the affliction of the law's demands. He writes, "This is a sure truth, that they who are freed from its penalties are still under its precepts. Though believers are no more under its curse, yet they are still under its conduct."[42] The law, for the Christian, is no longer a burdensome duty but a cherished delight. The weighty condemnations of the law have been removed for those who are in Christ, while only the blessings of obedience remain. Flavel comments, "I say not, they are free from the law as a rule of life; such a freedom were no privilege to them at all: but free from the rigorous exactions, and terrible maledictions of it; to hear our liberty proclaimed from this bondage, is the joyful sound indeed, the most blessed voice that ever our ear heard."[43] It is significant to note that Flavel does not see a conflict between the law and grace in the Christian's life. It is possible to be under the law (as a rule for life) and still be under grace.

Many of Flavel's peers agreed with him. The Westminster Confession states, "Neither are the forementioned uses of the law contrary to the grace of the gospel, but do sweetly comply with it: the Spirit of Christ subduing and enabling the will of man to do that freely and cheerfully which the will of God, revealed in the law, requireth

---

40. Flavel, *Method*, 2:271.
41. Flavel, *Method*, 2:271.
42. Flavel, *Method*, 2:271.
43. Flavel, *Fountain*, 1:206.

to be done."[44] The moral law still reveals what God requires for His creatures, but the gospel of Christ, applied by the Spirit, enables and empowers believers to increasingly live in light of this law. The gospel, therefore, does not negate the law as God's will for His subjects but acts as an encouragement to obey and enjoy it.

It is for this reason that the third use of the law is indispensable to Flavel's ministry and his understanding of the Christian life. All true believers are to "prize the moral law highly, as a rule of life."[45] For Flavel, the law is not simply a standard to endure but a rule of life that is to be valued and treasured. It is not just a requirement from God but God's gracious gift. It is, therefore, to be celebrated. It is for this reason that Flavel often speaks of the "excellency and perfection of the law of God," adding, "we are highly to honour and magnify it as a rule of duty, though we must utterly renounce it as the way of our justification."[46] The law tells believers what they must do, and, by the Spirit, what they can do. To live the Christian life well, believers need the moral law as a rule and guide.

The obligation of the law on believers, as well as its graciousness, is clearly evident in Flavel's discussion of Christ's kingly office. He notes that Christ's authority implies that His people are under His rule. All believers, therefore, are under the law. They "must not be any longer without law to God; but under law to Christ."[47] As king, Christ binds His people to His authority and is the rightful lawgiver. As such, He gives the law in a new way. As Flavel explains, "Here is much strictness, but no bondage; for the law is not only written in Christ's statute-book, the Bible, but copied out by his Spirit upon the hearts of his subjects, in correspondent principles; which makes obedience a pleasure, and self-denial easy."[48] The content of Christ's law is not unique—it is that which is written in Scripture—but its administration is novel, as the Spirit writes it on the hearts of His people. Kevan writes, "It implies no change in the demands of the Law, nor in the

---

44. WCF 19.7.

45. Flavel, *Exposition*, 6:221.

46. Flavel, *Exposition*, 6:222.

47. Flavel, *Fountain*, 1:203.

48. Flavel, *Fountain*, 1:203.

obligation of the believer to recognize its binding authority, but signifies a different administration of it, with a different and deeper motive than is found outside of the experience of Christ."[49] To have Christ as king does not negate the Christian's commitment to the law—rather, it heightens it.

Thus, the idea of law "in the hands of Christ" is especially helpful for grasping Flavel's understanding of the right relationship between the law and the gospel.[50] He argues, "The precepts of the law are still urged under the gospel to enforce duties upon us, Matt. 5:17–18."[51] The work of the law is necessary for those under the gospel, for the law and the gospel, within the covenant of grace, do not only coexist but are coworkers. It is in light of this relationship that Flavel proclaims, "The law sends us to Christ to be justified, and Christ sends us to the law to be regulated."[52] The law, therefore, is not only required to drive us to Christ as the only hope of justification but to serve as a faithful guide for sanctification once we have found Christ.

For Flavel, the law is central to the believer's life. While many in his day saw hostility between the two, Flavel, following the tradition of Calvin and Westminster, saw harmony. Kevan summarizes,

> The Puritan view of the relation of believer to the Law of God is well expressed by Thomas Taylor, who argues that the regenerate are never *sine lege*, nor are they *sub lege* in respect to justification, but they are nevertheless *in lege*, that is, within the compass of the Law for instruction, for subjection, and in so far as it is written within in their hearts.[53]

Freed from the curse and condemnation of the law, believers delight in the law as the revealed will of their heavenly Father.

---

49. Kevan, *Grace of Law*, 187. Kevan states elsewhere, "Christ gave no new laws, but expounded and cleared the old, as a painter who works over an old picture and recovers its glory" (159).

50. For more on this, see Kevan, *Grace of Law*, 184–87.

51. Flavel, *Method*, 2:271.

52. Flavel, *Method*, 2:271.

53. Kevan, *Grace of Law*, 185.

Antinomianism

Many of Flavel's contemporaries did not agree with his position regarding the use of the law in the believer's life. They were among the Antinomians.[54] According to Kevan, they held that the "believer was completely free from all obligation to the Law, and…that any concession to legal duty was an infringement of free grace."[55] Their repudiation of the law's role in the life of the believer arose from the belief that the law belonged to the covenant of works and was, therefore, antithetical to the grace of the gospel. For this reason, most Antinomians denounced the notion of a third use of the law.[56]

Flavel responded by insisting that the law belongs to the covenant of grace. He articulated this conviction in his disputation with the Baptist Philip Cary (d. 1710) over the validity of paedobaptism.[57] Flavel believed that Antinomianism lurked at the heart of Cary's view.[58] For Flavel, the law (as given at Sinai) is not part of the covenant of works. It "was not set up by God as in Adam's covenant, to open the old way of righteousness and life by works; but was added to the promise, as subservient to Christ in its design and use, and consequently can never be a pure Adam's covenant of works."[59] God gave the law at Sinai, not as a revival of the covenant of Adam but as an appendix to the Abrahamic covenant, the covenant of grace.

---

54. For more on Antinomianism, see Beeke and Jones, *Puritan Theology*, 323–29, 556–59; Kevan, *Grace of Law*, 22–28; Mark Jones, *Antinomianism: Reformed Theology's Unwelcome Guest?* (Phillipsburg, N.J.: P&R, 2013); John Von Rohr, *Covenant of Grace*; David Como, *Blown by the Spirit: Puritanism and the Emergence of an Antinomian Underground in Pre-Civil-War England* (Stanford, Calif.: Stanford University Press, 2004); and David D. Hall, *The Antinomian Controversy 1636–1638: A Documentary History* (Durham, N.C.: Duke University Press, 1990).

55. Kevan, *Grace of Law*, 22.

56. For Flavel's most pointed critique of Antinomianism, see Flavel, *Brief Account*, 3:551–91.

57. For a detailed explanation of this debate, see Beeke and Jones, *Puritan Theology*, 729–39.

58. Flavel writes, "Finding my adversary (Cary), in the pursuit of his design, running into many Antinomian delirations, to the reproach and damage of the cause he contends for, I thought it necessary to take the principal errors of Antinomianism into examination, especially at such a time as this, when they seem to spring afresh, to the hazard of God's truth, and the church's peace." Flavel, *Occasions*, 3:419–20.

59. Flavel, *Vindiciae Legis et Foederis*, 6:326.

If the law were part of the covenant of works, then "it regularly and necessarily follows, that either Moses and all Israel were damned, there being no salvation possible to be attained by that first covenant; or else, that there was a covenant of grace at the same time running parallel with that covenant of works."[60] For Flavel, the first option is unthinkable and the second is contradictory. The elect of Israel were not lost to hell, nor were they justified and condemned at the same time. Thus, the law must be related to the covenant of grace. Flavel argues,

> What then can be clearer, than that the law at Sinai was published with gracious gospel-ends and purposes, to lead men to Christ, which Adam's covenant had no respect or reference to? And therefore it can never be a pure Adam's covenant, as you falsely call it, neither is it capable of becoming a pure covenant of works to any man, but by his own fault, in rejecting the righteousness of Christ, and seeking justification by the works of the law, as the mistaken carnal Jews did, Romans 10:3, and other legal judiciaries now do.[61]

The law, according to Flavel, must be part of the covenant of grace if it is to be part of God's intent and purposes.

To understand the law as part of the covenant of works, as a means through which humanity might be justified, is to misunderstand it. As Flavel explains, "This design and intention of God was fatally mistaken by the Jews, ever since God promulgated that law at Sinai, and was by them notoriously perverted to a quite contrary end to that which God promulged it for, even to give righteousness and life, in the way of personal and perfect obedience."[62] The right way to read the law is not to divorce it from Christ, as both the Judaizers and the Antinomians did but to regard it in Christ. Flavel maintains that in this way,

> the Sinai covenant was neither repugnant to the new covenant in its scope and aim; nor yet set up as co-ordinate with it, with a design to open two different ways of salvation to fallen

---

60. Flavel, *Vindiciae Legis et Foederis*, 6:331.
61. Flavel, *Vindiciae Legis et Foederis*, 6:336.
62. Flavel, *Vindiciae Legis et Foederis*, 6:339.

man; but was added to the promise in respect of its evangelical purposes and designs…which shews [its] consistency and sub-ordination with, and to the method of salvation by Christ in the new covenant.[63]

It was this logic that led Flavel to insist on the cogency of the third use of the law and its importance for the Christian life. Flavel was insistent that the law drives us to Christ for justification, and that Christ sends us back to the law for the purpose of sanctification. Believers, therefore, stand in need of both the law and the gospel. This realization is of utmost importance for those who desire to obey.

Flavel and Obedience

Obedience is not an optional add-on to the believer's life but a necessary component of what it means to be faithful. This emphasis in no way undermines Christ's work—rather, it serves to accentuate it. Flavel asserts, "Nothing of that work which Christ did, remains for you to do.… You must work as well as Christ, though not for the same ends Christ did."[64] It is wrong to confuse Christ's work with our work, but it is equally wrong to conclude that His work negates our work. Christ alone "wrought hard to satisfy the law, by fulfilling all righteousness. He wrought all his life long, to work out a righteousness to justify you before God."[65]

Flavel is adamant that believers contribute nothing to their justification in Christ: "This work falls to no hand but Christ's," and yet, "you must work, to obey the commands of Christ into whose right you are come by redemption: you must testify your thankfulness to Christ, for the work finished for you: you must work, to glorify God by your obedience."[66] Such obedience is not optional. It demonstrates our thankfulness to Christ, and it glorifies God. It is unthinkable that the true Christian would not desire to pursue obedience to Christ. This is part of the reason Flavel has little patience for Antinomians:

---

63. Flavel, *Vindiciae Legis et Foederis*, 6:339.
64. Flavel, *Fountain*, 1:439.
65. Flavel, *Fountain*, 1:439.
66. Flavel, *Fountain*, 1:439.

For these, and other divers reasons, your life must be a working life. God preserve all his people from the gross and vile opinions of Antinomian libertines, who cry up grace and decry obedience: who under specious pretences of exalting a naked Christ upon the throne, do indeed strip him naked of a great part of his glory, and vilely dethrone him.[67]

To abandon the significance of obedience hurts the Christian and compromises Christ.

Obedience is a powerful proclamation of the rule and reign of Christ. It is to honor Christ as king, for obedience is precisely what Christ demands as king. As Flavel explains, Christ's kingship over His people is evidenced by His imposing "a new law upon them, and [enjoining] them to be severe and punctual in their obedience to it."[68] As noted earlier, this "new law" is not new in kind but in administration, as God's people are now under Christ's authority. He exhorts his people to follow closely all of His commands, for "the soul that comes under Christ's government, must receive law from Christ; and under law every thought of the heart must come."[69] Thus, the demand to obey is total—it includes the whole being at all times in all places. If Christ is our king, then it is necessary that we obey Him.

Flavel is quick to add, however, that Christ not only demands our obedience but enables it. Here, we see again how Christ's work relates to His people's work. The reason our obedience points to Christ's obedience is because ours is made possible by His. Flavel remarks, "It is true Christ came to be a sacrifice for sin, but not a cloak for sin; to set us at liberty from the bondage of our lusts, not from the ties and duties of our obedience."[70] To neglect obedience undermines Christ's kingly rule and diminishes His priestly work. Christ came to free us from sin and for righteousness. Our obedience, therefore, is the wondrous fruit of His redemptive work.

---

67. Flavel, *Fountain*, 1:439.
68. Flavel, *Fountain*, 1:203.
69. Flavel, *Fountain*, 1:204.
70. Flavel, *Occasions*, 3:477.

The Joy of Obedience

Flavel reminds his readers that while their obedience is indeed for God's glory, it is also for their joy. What God demands, He rewards. As Flavel explains, "Hast thou not found inward peace and comfort flowing into thy soul, upon every piece of sincere obedience!"[71] God is a gracious and generous master, whose remunerations to His servants are abundant in number and kind. They are so extraordinary that Flavel asks, "What service didst thou perform for him, for which he hath not paid thee a thousand times more than it is worth. Didst thou seek him diligently, and not find him a bountiful rewarder?"[72] It is clear that Flavel believes that the Christian's obedience is never in vain but always proves worthwhile. Flavel is insistent that believers will never regret their obedience to Christ in their last days:

> Suppose yourselves now upon your death-bed, all earthly comforts insipid things to you, conscience presaging the wrath to come, time and hope ending together; would you not then wish, O that we had been ruled and governed by Christ's laws and Spirit, and not by Satan, and our own lusts![73]

At death, unbelievers will wish they had lived under the gracious government of Christ. There will be no joy in that season for the disobedient. True believers, however, will be filled with gratitude. As Flavel explains, "The work of obedience faithfully finished, or a steady course of holiness throughout our life, is that which usually yields much peace and joy in death, Acts 20:24."[74] To pursue a life of obedience is to pursue joy in the hour of death.

The path of obedience not only issues in delight at the end of life but also brings joy throughout life: "Obedience to conviction will not only produce peace at death, but it will give you present ease, present relief and refreshment in hand."[75] For Flavel, it is through continued

---

71. Flavel, *Fountain*, 1:538–39.

72. Flavel, *Fountain*, 1:538.

73. John Flavel, *A Coronation Sermon: Preached at Dartmouth to Celebrate the Coronation of William III and Mary II on 11 April, 1689*, in *Works of John Flavel* (1820; repr., Edinburgh: Banner of Truth Trust, 2015), 6:561.

74. Flavel, *Pneumatologia*, 3:65.

75. Flavel, *England's Duty*, 4:297. Flavel notes, "Certainly it will appear to be so

and consistent obedience that we experience the greatest joys in Christ. Thus, he advises his readers, "Improve every spiritual comfort you have from Christ unto greater cheerfulness in the paths of obedience to Christ."[76] Believers increase their joy in Christ by their obedience to Christ. The Bible is replete with God's promises of care to His people, especially as they strive to be holy and faithful before Him. Flavel summarizes these promises as follows: "Let it be thy care to walk exactly in the paths of obedience before me, and I will take care to supply all thy wants from the never-failing fountain of my all-sufficiency."[77] Walking in obedience is to proclaim our trust and confidence in God's goodness and grace. It is to know that our joy is found in Him alone.

To obey God is also to denounce the false joys and empty delights of sin and the world. Such obedience requires believers to fight one of the greatest wiles of the devil—namely, his attempts to convince us that obedience is a drain on the soul. According to Flavel, the devil attempts to convince people that "they shall never laugh more, never be merry more after they have embraced and espoused the ways of holiness."[78] What is needed, then, is to get an example of the truly good life, a life lived in obedience to Christ. Flavel explains, "Well, their own experience shall now confute it, for they now taste that pleasure in Christ, in faith and obedience, which they never tasted in the ways of sin."[79] This pleasure in Christ is to be tasted in faith and obedience. It is obedience to Christ that brings delight in Christ. In fact, so great is the joy of obedience that even the most difficult demands of Christ are better than the sum of sin's promises. The life of obedience brings about a full and lasting joy that sin cannot counterfeit.

---

whether we respect our present comfort or future happiness, both which we may see daily exposed by departure from duty, and secured by keeping close to it" (4:420).

76. Flavel, *England's Duty*, 4:235.

77. John Flavel, *The Righteous Man's Refuge*, in *Works of John Flavel* (1820; repr., Edinburgh: Banner of Truth Trust, 2015), 3:389. Flavel here is speaking specifically of the promise God makes to Abraham in Gen. 17:1. He also references 2 Cor. 6:18 in this same section.

78. Flavel, *England's Duty*, 4:225.

79. Flavel, *England's Duty*, 4:225.

This joy is evidenced by the effects of obedience in our hearts and relationships. Flavel notes that obedience actually changes believers, for "diligence in the work of God is an excellent help to the improvement of grace… [and] diligence in obedience is a great security against backsliding."[80] Obeying Christ furthers our sanctification and protects our perseverance. It also endears us to others, as "it is a comfortable thing to walk with them that walk after the example of Christ.… They are the best and sweetest company this world affords."[81] And lastly, much of the world's difficulties and distresses decrease as the law of Christ reigns in our hearts. Flavel asserts, "O if men were once brought under the power of religion indeed, to walk after Christ in holiness, obedience, meekness, and self-denial; no such miseries as these would be heard of among us, Isa. 11:8–9."[82] All of these benefits further confirm that there is considerable joy in faithfully obeying the law of Christ.

Obedience and Assurance
Fundamental to the joy of obedience is the role it plays in the believer's experience of assurance. Following the argument of 1 John 2:3, Flavel contends that obedience is crucial to assurance: "We perceive and discern ourselves to be sincere believers, and consequently that Christ is our propitiation, when obedience to his commands is become habitual and easy to us."[83] Where there is no obedience to Christ, there is no assurance, and where there is little obedience to Christ, there is little assurance. Obedience to Christ is not possible outside of union with Christ. It is, therefore, a critical piece of evidence that one is a disciple of Christ. This does not mean that Flavel makes obedience a ground of justification. He explains,

> We do not affirm that any of these his works to be meritorious causes of our justification; or that, considered abstractly from the Spirit, they can of themselves seal, or evidence our interest in

---

80. Flavel, *Method*, 2:408.
81. Flavel, *Method*, 2:417.
82. Flavel, *Method*, 2:417.
83. Flavel, *Vindiciae Legis et Foederis*, 6:354. Flavel cites 1 John 2:3: "Hereby we do know that we know him, if we keep his commandments."

> Christ; Neither do we affirm, that any of them are complete and perfect works; but this we say, that they being true and sincere, though imperfect graces, they are our usual and standing evidence, to make out our interest in Christ by.[84]

This statement provides a helpful summary of Flavel's understanding of the relationship between a believer's good works and assurance. Works of obedience, produced by the Spirit, though incomplete and imperfect, give credibility to our confession, thereby strengthening our assurance.

Flavel's logic is simple: true believers are sanctified by the Spirit who increases their desire for holiness and their hatred of sin. "Sanctified souls give themselves up to the government and conduct of the Spirit," says Flavel. "They obey his voice, beg his direction, follow his motions, deny the solicitations of flesh and blood, in obedience to him, Gal. 1:16."[85] The chief evidence of the Spirit's sanctifying work in the believer is obedience to the Spirit's direction. Such obedience is observable, for "all the effects and fruits of interest in Christ are found in the new creature; there are all the fruits of obedience, for we are created in Christ Jesus unto good works."[86] In short, union with Christ produces both inward and outward effects in believers.

Flavel makes it clear that these internal and external effects go together. It is not possible to be changed internally without producing external effects. All those who exhibit the fruit of the Spirit outwardly have been changed inwardly. Flavel maintains,

> The imitation of Christ implies the necessity of sanctification in all his followers; forasmuch as it is impossible there should be a practical conformity in point of obedience, where there is not a conformity in spirit and principle; all external conformity to

---

84. Flavel, *Vindiciae Legis et Foederis*, 6:354.

85. Flavel, *Method*, 2:340. Flavel gives "the particular marks and trials by which grown Christians, when they are in a due composed frame, may, by the assistance of the Spirit of God, (for which they are bound to pray), discern his indwelling and working in themselves" (2:336). These "marks" include conviction of sin, hungering and thirsting for Christ, a sympathy with Christ, a desire to mortify sin, a pleasure in and affection for prayer, thoughts that often run to Christ, and obedience to the direction of the Spirit (2:336–40).

86. Flavel, *Method*, 2:358.

> Christ's practice, depends upon an internal conformity to Christ
> in the principle and Spirit of holiness.[87]

Because they are being sanctified by the Spirit, believers must imitate Christ. Those who do not strive to obey Christ and live for Him have no cause to assume that they are genuine believers. Flavel exhorts, "Let him either put on the life of Christ, or put off the name of Christ; let him shew the hand of a Christian, in works of holiness and obedience, or else the tongue and language of a Christian must gain no belief or credit."[88]

As believers practice obedience they experience assurance. Here, again, Flavel seeks to counter Antinomianism, which disputes his understanding of the relationship between obedience and assurance. At the heart of the debate is the relationship between justification and sanctification. Whereas Flavel distinguished between the two, Antinomians struggled to maintain a distinction, which led them to contest the idea that justification is evidenced by sanctification.[89] Antinomians also objected to Flavel's understanding of the law. As Mark Jones notes, "Their aversion to the necessity of good works, as well as their rejection of the orthodox view of the moral law, caused them to understand assurance of salvation in a manner that was essentially opposed to the Reformed view."[90] For Antinomians, assurance was gained through trusting exclusively in their justification.[91] They ruled out any notion that obedience has a role to play. As Kevan explains, "The believer must therefore obtain his assurance from the testimony of the Spirit who 'giveth full and clear evidence' of his good estate, that he has 'no need to be tried by the fruits of sanctification.'"[92]

Flavel opposed the Antinomian understanding of assurance. While he did not deny that assurance comes by the Spirit's witness,

---

87. Flavel, *Method*, 2:400.

88. Flavel, *Method*, 2:400.

89. As Kevan writes, "Another difficulty to the Antinomians was their inability to make a clear enough distinction between justification and sanctification." Kevan, *Grace of Law*, 24.

90. Jones, *Antinomianism*, 98.

91. Jones, *Antinomianism*, 99.

92. Kevan, *Grace of Law*, 210.

he argued that there was more to it: "I will not deny but there may be an immediate testimony of the Spirit; but sure I am his mediate testimony by his graces in us, is his usual way of sealing believers."[93] Flavel argues that the Scriptures "frequently call the people of God to the examination and trial of their interest in Christ by marks and signs: and accordingly furnish them with variety of such marks from the divers parts or branches of sanctification in themselves."[94] This has been the normal practice of the saints throughout history:

> The experience and practice of the saints recorded in scripture, as well as our contemporaries, or those whose lives are recorded for our imitation, do greatly secure us from the spreading malignancy of Antinomianism. Converse with the living, or read the histories of dead saints, and you will find…[they] are therefore frequent and serious in the trial and examination of their own states by scripture marks and signs.[95]

While Flavel affirms that obedience plays a pivotal role in the cultivation of joyful assurance, he is careful to note that obedience is never perfect or complete in this life. He teaches, "The imitation of Christ necessarily implies the defectiveness and imperfection of the best of men in this life; for if the life of Christ be our pattern, the best and holiest of men must confess they come short in every thing of the rule of their duty."[96] A failure to obey should not undermine assurance nor lead to despair. On the contrary, distress over one's disobedience is a likely indicator of the sincerity of one's faith. Flavel reminds his hearers, "Such defects in obedience make no flaw in your justification; for your justification is not built upon your obedience, but upon Christ's…. Your deep troubles for the defectiveness of your obedience, do not argue you to be less, but more sanctified than those who make no such complaints."[97] The importance of the role of obedience in assurance must be set in the context of Christ's redemptive work on

---

93. Flavel, *Vindiciae Legis et Foederis*, 6:354.
94. Flavel, *Occasions*, 3:557.
95. Flavel, *Occasions*, 3:558.
96. Flavel, *Method*, 2:400.
97. Flavel, *Method*, 2:420.

behalf of His people. While obedience strengthens assurance, it does so only as believers look to Christ.

Flavel's Call to Obey the Law

Throughout his writings, Flavel affirms that obedience is necessary for both the glory of God and the good of the believer. "The duty which God requireth of man is obedience to his revealed will,"[98] he asserts. This revealed will, as has been demonstrated, is the moral law, "which is summarily comprehended in the ten commandments."[99] Believers must strive to obey the law. This pursuit in no way undermines the gospel but rather displays it. When believers obey the law, they honor the Father who loves them, the Christ who redeems them, and the Spirit who empowers them. They demonstrate the goodness of their God and His rule. Such obedience has a certain character and shape to it. As Flavel makes clear, it is obedience of a certain kind, one that uniquely glorifies the character and work of God.

First, it is a faith-filled obedience. There is no true obedience that does not arise from faith. Flavel explains that faith is primary because it "is the principle from whence all obedience flows; and no man can perform any duty aright in the estate of unbelief (Heb. 11:6)."[100] As significant as obedience is for the Christian, it is both impossible and ineffectual outside of faith in the work of Christ. Thus, as Flavel describes, "If a man be in Christ, sorrow for sin is something, and renewed obedience is something; God looks upon them favourably, and accepts them graciously in Christ: but out of him they signify no more than the intreaties and cries of a condemned malefactor, to reverse the legal sentence of the judge."[101]

For this reason, Flavel proclaims "that one act of faith in the Lord Jesus pleases God more than all the obedience, repentance, and strivings to obey the law, through thy whole life, can do."[102] It is essential to understand that the obedience that gives life and joy is that which

---

98. Flavel, *Exposition*, 6:217.
99. Flavel, *Exposition*, 6:219.
100. Flavel, *Exposition*, 6:144.
101. Flavel, *Fountain*, 1:187.
102. Flavel, *Fountain*, 1:187.

proceeds from faith in Christ's work. The Christian's obedience always stems from Christ's obedience. This reminder not only protects believers from legalism but also keeps them from despair. "Happy were it," Flavel writes, "if puzzled and perplexed Christians would turn their eyes from the defects that are in their obedience, to the fulness and completeness of Christ's obedience; and see themselves complete in him, when most lame and defective in themselves."[103] Faith-filled obedience, then, flows from salvation in Christ.

This central truth leads to the second mark of obedience: it is joy-filled. According to Flavel, believers should "do nothing begrudgingly for God," for they have great reason "to obey with cheerfulness."[104] In fact, the knowledge that they have been freed from condemnation, and transferred from death to life, ought to produce thankful obedience to Christ. Flavel comments, "Let them that are so delivered, spend their days on earth in praise and cheerful obedience."[105] The thankful life is the obedient life, for "obedience and service are the only real manifestations of gratitude."[106] Obedience ought never be drudgery but delight. This does not mean that obedience is always easy and enjoyable but that it is a joy because it honors Christ. Given God's mercy in Christ, obedience is a pleasure.

Lastly, Flavel states that obedience is comprehensive. If Christ is our king, then we are His servants. Such service must be a reality. Flavel writes,

It is but a mockery to give Christ the empty titles of Lord and King, whilst ye give your real service to sin and Satan.... Christ doth not compliment with you; his pardons, promises, and salvation are real; O let your obedience be so too! Let it be sincere and universal obedience; this will evidence your unfeigned subjection to Christ.[107]

---

103. Flavel, *Fountain*, 1:59.

104. Flavel, *Method*, 2:405.

105. Flavel, *Method*, 2:440.

106. John Flavel, *The Seaman's Companion: Six Sermons on the Mysteries of Providence as Relating to Seamen; and the Sins, Dangers, Duties and Troubles of Seamen*, in *Works of John Flavel* (1820; repr., Edinburgh: Banner of Truth Trust, 2015), 5:410.

107. Flavel, *Fountain*, 1:209.

The call to obey Christ is universal, meaning it is a recognition of His authority in every sphere and every moment of life. It also implies that the whole self is engaged in serving Christ. For this reason, Flavel pleads with believers to "employ all the power [they] have for God in the duties of obedience."[108] Thankfully, the Lord encourages His people to such obedience as He continually comforts them in their duties. Flavel reminds that God uses these comforts "to glue souls fast by them to the way of holiness," for "these enjoyments of God, which you have met with in prayer and hearing, in meditation, sacraments, &c. should engage your hearts for ever in the ways of obedience."[109] Here, again, we observe the way in which Flavel unites duty and delight, as obedience to Christ brings about joy in Christ which, in turn, leads to the service of Christ.

Conclusion

This union of duty and delight is a fundamental component of Flavel's spirituality. He holds that obedience to Christ is a means of enjoying Christ. This joy in Christ increases as the Spirit enables believers to see that obedience is the fruit of His work and, therefore, a significant sign of their interest in Christ. All believers must strive to obey the law with their whole hearts and lives, not to obtain salvation but to experience the joy of God's work of salvation. Flavel's biblical spirituality highlights the importance of obedience:

> Converse with the living, or read the histories of dead saints, and you shall find.... They find cause enough to suspect their own sincerity, doubt the truth of their faith, and of their graces; and are therefore frequent and serious in the trial and examination of their own states by scripture marks and signs. They urge the commands and threatenings, as well as the promises, upon their own hearts to promote sanctification; excite themselves to duty and watchfulness against sin; they also encourage themselves by the rewards of obedience, knowing their labour is not in vain in the Lord: and all this while they look not for that in themselves, which is only to be found in Christ; nor for that in the law, which

---

108. Flavel, *Method*, 2:84.
109. Flavel, *England's Duty*, 4:233.

is only to be found in the gospel; nor for that on earth which is only to be found in heaven: this is the way they take. And he that shall tell them their sins can do them no hurt, or their duties do them no good, speaks to them not only as a Barbarian, in a language they understand not, but in such a language as their souls detest and abhor.[110]

For Flavel, there is no contradiction between our work and Christ's work, between the law and the gospel, between duty and delight. All of these work together for God's glory and our good.

---

110. Flavel, *Occasions*, 3:558.

Chapter 7

Joy in Keeping the Heart

How can believers strengthen the joy of assurance? For Flavel, the answer is keeping the heart. This is the chief work of those who desire to know their standing in Christ and experience the resultant joy. Flavel explains, "The greatest difficulty in conversion is to win the heart to God; and the greatest difficulty after conversion is to keep the heart with God. Here lies the very pinch and stress of religion; here is what makes the way to life a narrow way, and the gate to heaven a strait gate."[1] Flavel's emphasis was not unusual among the Puritans.[2] Based on Proverbs 4:23, they held that keeping the heart is central to the cultivation of personal piety.[3] As J. I. Packer claims, "This is because Puritanism was essentially an experimental faith, a religion of 'heart-work,' a sustained practice of seeking the face of God."[4] It was of chief importance for the Puritans that believers know, guard, and encourage their hearts.

Puritan spirituality is, therefore, primarily focused on the heart. As Daniel Webber confirms, "Whether we think in terms of those

---

1. Flavel, *Saint Indeed*, 5:423.

2. To better understand the Puritans' emphasis on keeping the heart, see Richard Webber, "Sanctifying the Inner Life," in *Aspects of Sanctification: The Westminster Conference 1981* (Hertfordshire, England: Evangelical Press, 1982), 41–61; and Brian G. Hedges, *Watchfulness: Recovering a Lost Spiritual Discipline* (Grand Rapids: Reformation Heritage Books, 2018). For more on Flavel's understanding of keeping the heart, see Allen, "Theologian as Pastor," 56–68; Embry, *Honest*, 13–17; and Yuille, *Inner Sanctum*, 35–38, 95–96.

3. "Keep thy heart with all diligence; for out of it are the issues of life" (Prov. 4:23), quoted in Flavel, *Saint Indeed*, 5:423.

4. Packer, *Quest*, 215.

who occupied the pulpits, or those who sat in the pews, the common consensus was that the heart is the primary concern of the Christian."[5] By way of confirmation, Richard Baxter asserts,

> See that your chief study be about the heart, that there God's image may be planted, and his interest advanced, and the interest of the world and flesh subdued, and the love of every sin cast out, and the love of holiness succeed: and that you content not yourselves with seeming to do good in outward acts, when you are bad yourselves, and strangers to the great internal duties. The first and great work of a Christian is about his heart.[6]

This "great work" is what Flavel calls "keeping the heart." Often described as watchfulness, the Puritans viewed this work as primary among the spiritual duties. Brian Hedges describes it as "the whetstone of the spiritual disciplines, the one practice that keeps the other habits sharp."[7] As the heart is the source of words, thoughts, and actions, so the discipline of keeping the heart is that from which all other spiritual habits flow. It is, as Flavel writes, "the great business of the Christian's life."[8] To neglect this practice is to undermine our joyful assurance in Christ.

The Nature of Keeping the Heart

Fundamental to Flavel's instruction on this essential duty is his understanding of the heart. While Scripture sometimes points to "some particular noble faculty of the soul," it is best to take the heart "more generally for the whole soul, the inner man; for look what the heart is to the body, that the soul is to the man."[9] Thus, to keep the heart is to keep the soul; it is to keep the whole inner person. At the center of the Puritans' understanding of the nature of the soul is the notion that it consists of three faculties.[10] Clifford Boone explains, "Those who

---

5. Webber, "Sanctifying the Inner Life," 43.

6. Richard Baxter, *The Practical Works of the Rev. Richard Baxter* (London: James Duncan, 1830), 2:531.

7. Hedges, *Watchfulness*, 4.

8. Flavel, *Saint Indeed*, 5:425.

9. Flavel, *Saint Indeed*, 5:423.

10. Pivotal to this discussion of "faculty psychology" is Perry Miller, *The New*

examine the faculty psychology of Puritan writers mention the intellect (sometimes referred to as the mind, or the understanding), the will and the affections (sometimes referred to as the passions or the emotions)."[11] These three categories, even if not specifically expressed, are generally assumed in any discussion of the soul by seventeenth-century Puritans.[12]

Standing in this tradition, Flavel clearly articulates a tripartite view of the soul.[13] He writes, "The soul of man is a vital, spiritual, and immortal substance, endowed with an understanding, will, and various affections; created with an inclination to the body, and infused thereinto by the Lord."[14] These three faculties are critical to grasping Flavel's concept of the heart and how to keep it. First, he speaks of the soul as being equipped with the understanding. Boone explains, "Flavel sees the human intellect as the highest natural excellency of man, the superior and most noble power of the soul, the leading faculty of the soul, and that which differentiates man from animal."[15] Flavel considers it the leading faculty "because the will follows its practical

---

England Mind: The Seventeenth Century (Cambridge, Mass.: Belknap Press, 1982), 42–45. For more, see Yuille, *Puritan Spirituality*, 32–34; and Boone, *Puritan Evangelism*, 68–97.

11. Boone, *Puritan Evangelism*, 69.

12. Boone states, "The majority of scholarship maintains that the faculty psychology of seventeenth-century Puritanism counted the faculties of the soul to be three—the intellect, the will, and the affection." Boone, *Puritan Evangelism*, 71.

13. Yuille notes that "Flavel seems to fluctuate between a bi-partite and tripartite division. In the final analysis, the difference is unimportant, given the fact that the function of the affections remains the same in both paradigms." Yuille, *Inner Sanctum*, 35n14. While this may be true in his presentation, Boone argues well that "a careful examination of the places in which Flavel emphasizes the intellect and will to the exclusion of the affections, in the light of the places in which he is trying to be comprehensive in his definitions, reveals that he indeed holds to a 'tri-partite division.'" Boone, *Puritan Evangelism*, 72.

14. Flavel, *Pneumatologia*, 2:495. He mentions these three faculties again later in this treatise, stating, "I find that God hath, answerably, endued and furnished it with an understanding, will, and affections, whereby it is capable of being wrought upon by the Spirit in the way of grace and sanctification in this world in order to the enjoyment of God, its chief happiness in the world to come" (2:523).

15. Boone, *Puritan Evangelism*, 74. This priority of the mind among the faculties was consistent with Flavel's Puritan contemporaries. See Yuille, *Puritan Spirituality*, 45–46.

dictates. It sits at the helm, and guides the course of the soul."[16] In addition to directing the will, the intellect also includes the individual's conscience and judgment—a "faculty of the reasonable soul by which a man apprehends and judges all intelligible things."[17]

The soul also includes the will. It possesses the ability "to govern, moderate, and over-rule the actions of life."[18] For Flavel, "The will is a faculty of the rational soul, whereby a man either chuseth or refuseth the things which the understanding discerns and knows."[19] Thus, both the understanding and will are influencing faculties and, though distinct, they relate closely to one another. Flavel comments, "The understanding seems to bear the same relation to the will, as a grave counsellor doth to a great prince."[20] It is the will, much like a powerful ruler, that is characterized by freedom and dominion. It is free in that "it cannot be compelled and forced," and it has dominion for "it rules over the body…by way of absolute command," and "over the other powers and passions of the soul…by way of suasion."[21] The power of the will, as Boone points out, "is not absolute. It can persuade the mind. It can restrain the affections. But it can do neither absolutely."[22] Even so, it is clear that the will is a faculty of much consequence in the soul.

The third faculty of the soul is the "various affections and passions, which are of great use and service to it, and speak the excellency of its nature."[23] These affections comprise the core of the soul, enabling believers to enjoy God. "They are," as Stephen Yuille describes, "the

---

16. Flavel, *Pneumatologia*, 2:503. Flavel is quick to note that while the understanding guides the will, it is "not impelling, or rigorously enforcing its dictates upon the will; for the will cannot be so imposed upon; but by giving it a directive light, or point, as it were, with its finger, what it ought to chuse, and what to refuse" (2:503). For more on this, see Yuille, *Inner Sanctum*, 36n16.

17. Flavel, *Pneumatologia*, 2:503.

18. Flavel, *Pneumatologia*, 2:505.

19. Flavel, *Pneumatologia*, 2:506.

20. Flavel, *Pneumatologia*, 2:506.

21. Flavel, *Pneumatologia*, 2:506–7. It is important to note Flavel holds that the "liberty of the will must be understood to be in things natural, which are within its own proper sphere, not in things supernatural" (2:506). Therefore, the will "cannot move towards Christ, in the way of faith," unless it is "determined and drawn to Christ" (2:506). See Boone, *Puritan Evangelism*, 81–83.

22. Boone, *Puritan Evangelism*, 83.

23. Flavel, *Pneumatologia*, 2:509.

inclination or disinclination of the soul to a particular object. The soul loves that which it perceives to be good. This love is manifested in desire (when the object is absent) and delight (when the object is present). This hatred is manifested in fear (when the object is absent) and sorrow (when the object is present)."[24] For Flavel, the greatest good is God Himself: "The soul considered in full union with and fruition of God, its supreme happiness, is accordingly furnished with affections of love, delight, and joy, whereby it rests in him and enjoys its proper blessedness in his presence for ever."[25] It is clear, therefore, that the affections were created to delight in their Creator.

Due to sin, the affections do not operate according to their good design. Flavel is quick to remind his readers that their affections are now "corrupted and inverted by sin! The concupiscible appetite greedily fastens upon the creature, not upon God; and the irascible appetite is turned against holiness, not sin."[26] What is true of the affections is true of the other faculties, for sin corrupts the whole soul. Flavel writes, "When sin is in dominion, the soul is in a very sad condition; for it darkens the understanding, depraves the conscience, stiffens the will, hardens the heart, misplaces and disorders all the affections; and thus every faculty is wounded by the power and dominion of sin over the soul."[27] This devastation is not final for believers, for Christ sends the Spirit to regenerate the soul.

> By regeneration this disordered soul is set aright again: sanctification being…the renovation of the soul after the image of God.… The darkened understanding is again illuminated (Eph. 1:18), the refractory will sweetly subdued (Ps. 110:3), the rebellious appetite, or concupiscence gradually conquered (Rom. 5:7). And thus the soul which sin had universally depraved is again by grace restored and rectified.[28]

---

24. Yuille, *Inner Sanctum*, 37. Yuille ties this conception of the affections to Augustine, especially seen in his work *The City of God*. Yuille, *Inner Sanctum*, 37n20.

25. Flavel, *Pneumatologia*, 2:510.

26. Flavel, *Pneumatologia*, 2:510.

27. Flavel, *Method*, 2:192.

28. Flavel, *Saint Indeed*, 5:426.

It is this view of the renewed faculties that fuels Flavel's commitment to keeping the heart.

By "keeping the heart," Flavel means "the diligent and constant use and improvement of all holy means and duties, to preserve the soul from sin, and maintain its sweet and free communion with God."[29] Again, the aim is to preserve the heart "from sin, which disorders it; and maintain that spiritual and gracious frame, which fits it for a life of communion with God."[30] As to the means, Flavel identifies six key acts:

> (1) Frequent observation of the frame of the heart, turning in and examining how the case stands with it; (2) Deep humiliation for heart-evils and disorders; (3) Earnest supplications and instant prayer for heart-purifying and rectifying grace; (4) The imposing of strong engagements and bonds upon ourselves to walk more accurately with God, and avoid the occasions whereby the heart may be induced to sin; (5) A constant holy jealously over our own hearts; (6) The realizing of God's presence with us, and setting the Lord always before us.[31]

This list highlights the difficulty of keeping the heart. Flavel instructs, "This is the work, and of all works in religion it is the most difficult, constant, and important work. It is the hardest work; heart-work is hard work indeed."[32] Given its difficulty, believers are incapable of fulfilling this work on their own. Flavel maintains, "We are as able to stop the sun in its course, or make the rivers run backward, as by our own skill and power to rule and order our hearts: we may as well be our own saviours, as our own keepers."[33] However, believers are not alone in this work but rather receive the Spirit's assistance: "A natural man hath no power, a gracious man hath some, though not sufficient; and that power he hath, depends upon the exciting and assisting strength

---

29. Flavel, *Saint Indeed*, 5:423.
30. Flavel, *Saint Indeed*, 5:426.
31. Flavel, *Saint Indeed*, 5:426–28.
32. Flavel, *Saint Indeed*, 5:428.
33. Flavel, *Saint Indeed*, 5:424.

of Christ."[34] Thus, the "duty is ours though the power be God's."[35] Keeping the heart is required by God and made possible in Him.

The Reason for Keeping the Heart

Having considered Flavel's understanding of the heart, and what it means to keep it, it is evident why he placed such importance on it. Lewis James Greenwood Allen notes, "Flavel makes no attempt to soften the demands of the life dedicated to heart-keeping, but labours to give clear and compelling motives as to why this work should be done."[36] Flavel puts forth six reasons why believers should endeavor to keep the heart: "(1) The honour of God; (2) The sincerity of our profession; (3) The beauty of our conversation; (4) The comfort of our souls; (5) The improvement of our graces; and (6) Our stability in the hour of temptation."[37] All these are "dependent on our sincerity and care in the management of this work."[38] Thus, Christians should keep their hearts for the honor of God (see reason 1), the health of their soul (reasons 3, 5, and 6), and the happiness of their heart (reasons 2 and 4).

The Honor of God

Flavel's primary motivation for keeping the heart is the honor of God. He explains, "The glory of God is much concerned therein; heart-evils are very provoking evils to the Lord."[39] God's glory is especially provoked by sins of the heart, for they lie at a person's core and are easily hidden. These "heart-evils" are easy to ignore, yet far more dangerous in nature. As Flavel asserts, "Outward sins are sins *majoris infamice*, of greater scandal; but heart-sins are oftentimes *majoris reatus*, sins of greater guilt. To be troubled for grosser sins, and have not trouble for ordinary sins daily incurred, is an ill sign of a bad heart."[40] While external sins may be easier to recognize and confess, God is most glorified as believers dig out the very root of sin in the soul. It

---

34. Flavel, *Saint Indeed*, 5:424.

35. Flavel, *Saint Indeed*, 5:424.

36. Allen, "Theologian as Pastor," 60.

37. Flavel, *Saint Indeed*, 5:429.

38. Flavel, *Saint Indeed*, 5:429.

39. Flavel, *Saint Indeed*, 5:429.

40. Flavel, *Touchstone*, 5:556–57.

demonstrates a true hatred of sin as it is an insult to God's glory rather than demonstrating a mere aversion to the consequences of sin. Flavel concludes, "O then, never slight heart-evils; for by these God is highly wronged and provoked; and for this reason let every Christian make it his work to keep his heart with all diligence."[41] The primary reason for keeping the heart is that which motivates all of life: the glory of God.

The Health of the Soul

Keeping the heart is also for our good. For Flavel, it brings spiritual health and happiness. It produces spiritual health by "improving our graces," "beautifying our conversation," and solidifying our perseverance.[42] Like a well-cultivated garden, a kept heart is fruitful ground for the graces of God to flourish. Flavel writes, "The improvement of our graces depends upon the keeping our hearts; I never knew grace thrive in a negligent and careless soul: the habits and roots of grace are planted in the heart; and the deeper they are radicated there, the more thriving and flourishing grace is."[43] Without a well-kept heart, our best duties fall on hard soil and, therefore, fail to produce lasting fruit. Flavel counsels, "A man may go with a heedless spirit from ordinance to ordinance, abide all his days under the choicest teaching, and yet never be improved by them; for heart-neglect is a leak in the bottom, no heavenly influences, how rich soever, abide in that soul."[44] Flavel places such a high priority on the diligent keeping of the heart, for neglecting it subverts all other disciplines of the Christian life. Yuille comments,

> Keeping watch over the soul is foundational to other spiritual duties, because their effectiveness depends in large part upon the removal of those encumbrances that dampen the affections. Unconfessed sin, unchecked pride, and undisciplined thoughts tend to render the soul insensible to any "influences" that God sets forth in duties.[45]

41. Flavel, *Saint Indeed*, 5:430.
42. Flavel, *Saint Indeed*, 5:429.
43. Flavel, *Saint Indeed*, 5:435.
44. Flavel, *Saint Indeed*, 5:436.
45. Yuille, *Inner Sanctum*, 96

Keeping the heart, therefore, is vital to spiritual health; without it, all other labors will be barren.

Additionally, when believers keep watch over their hearts, stripping them of sinful inclinations and stirring them toward biblical ones, their conduct will change. As Flavel explains, "It is impossible that a disordered and neglected heart should ever produce well-ordered conversation; and since (as this text observes) the issues or streams of life flow out of the heart as their fountain, it must needs follow, that such as the heart is, the life will be."[46] For Flavel, it is the nature of a person's discourse that is one of most useful indicators of the nature of their heart. Believers who are diligent in keeping their hearts, then, will be noticeably unique in the graciousness of their speech. As he writes, "Take a Christian in a good frame, and how serious, heavenly, and profitable, will his converses and duties be! what a lovely companion is he during the continuance of it!"[47] The increasing health of our hearts, then, will result in the increasing health of our discourse. Such comeliness of communication, however, greatly lacks when heart-work is unappreciated. As Flavel describes,

> And what else can be the reason why the discourses and duties of many Christians, are become so frothy and unprofitable, their communion both with God, and one another, becomes as a dry stalk, but because their hearts are neglected? Surely this must be the reason of it, and verily it is an evil greatly to be bewailed…so the attracting beauty that was wont to shine from the conversation of the saints upon the faces and consciences of the world…this is in great measure lost, to the unspeakable detriment of religion.[48]

Keeping a close watch on the heart, therefore, provides fertile ground for God's grace, in addition to enriching our conduct.

Lastly, keeping the heart protects believers against the many temptations that seek to disrupt and destroy their communion with

---

46. Flavel, *Saint Indeed*, 5:432. Flavel is speaking of the text that undergirds this entire work: Prov. 4:23.

47. Flavel, *Saint Indeed*, 5:433.

48. Flavel, *Saint Indeed*, 5:433.

God.[49] To neglect the heart is to leave ourselves open to the schemes of Satan. Flavel contends, "How easy a conquest is a neglected heart? It is no more difficult to surprize it, than for an enemy to enter that city whose gates are open and unguarded."[50] The best defense against sin is to keep the heart at all times. Flavel writes, "The motions of sin are weakest at first, a little care and watchfulness may prevent much mischief now, which the careless heart not heeding, is brought within the power of temptation."[51] Subverting the first "motions" of sin at the outset of temptation is necessary to guard against the more calamitous effects of sin at its climax. A consistent watch over the heart is essential for persevering in the faith, for if the heart is lost, the whole person is lost: "The careless heart is an easy prey to Satan in the hour of temptation, his main batteries are raised against that fort-royal, the heart; if he wins that, he wins all; for it commands the whole man."[52] There is sufficient cause to keep the heart, for God uses it to grow, beautify, and sustain our faithfulness in Christ.

The Happiness of the Heart

Flavel's exhortation to keep the heart is related directly to the pursuit of joy. This is due in large part to the relationship that exists between joy and assurance. These two are inseparable, meaning there is no true joy without true assurance. The inference, for Flavel, is obvious: those who fail to keep the heart will experience little assurance and, therefore, little joy. He states, "The comfort of our souls doth much depend upon the keeping of our hearts; for he that is negligent in attending his own heart, is (ordinarily) a great stranger to assurance, and the sweet comforts flowing from it."[53]

Keeping the heart is pivotal to assurance because it is an indicator of the genuineness of faith. Flavel teaches, "The sincerity of our profession much depends upon the care and conscience we have in keeping our hearts; for it is most certain, that a man is but an hypocrite in his

---

49. For more on how watchfulness helps believers fight temptation, see Hedges, *Watchfulness*, 50–56.

50. Flavel, *Saint Indeed*, 5:436.

51. Flavel, *Saint Indeed*, 5:437.

52. Flavel, *Saint Indeed*, 5:436.

53. Flavel, *Saint Indeed*, 5:433.

profession, how curious soever he be in the externals of religion, that is heedless and careless of the frame of his heart."[54] A lack of concern for the heart says a great deal about the authenticity of one's confession. As Webber explains, a failure to keep the heart "was the mark of a hypocrite, no matter what a man's profession, gifts, or the externals of religion to which he gave himself."[55] The opposite case is also true—namely, diligently keeping the heart is a sign of sincere faith.[56] Flavel would agree with Thomas Brooks, who writes, "He that makes it his work, his daily work, his greatest work, his work of works, to keep a continual guard upon his heart, he certainly is in a blessed state."[57]

For Flavel, diligence in keeping the heart is not just an evidence of sincere faith but a means by which believers obtain assurance. "I deny not but it is the work and office of the Spirit, to assure you," he explains, "and yet do confidently affirm, that if ever you attain assurance, in the ordinary way wherein God dispenses it, you must take pains with your own hearts."[58] Keeping the heart is the way in which believers discern the Spirit's work in their lives. While it is certainly the Spirit who works His graces in us, and it is the Spirit who enables us to see such work, it is our responsibility to look for the presence of that work. We must earnestly care for our hearts so that we can both recognize and encourage this grace in us. Flavel asserts,

> A neglected heart is so confused and dark, that the little grace which is in it, is not ordinarily discernible: the most accurate and laborious Christians, that take most pains, and spend most time about their hearts, do yet find it very difficult to discover the pure and genuine works of the Spirit there: how then shall the Christian who is (comparatively) negligent and remiss about heart-work, be ever able to discover it?[59]

A failure to keep the heart suppresses the work of God's grace and allows sin to flourish. When this happens, it cripples assurance. Flavel

---

54. Flavel, *Saint Indeed*, 5:430.
55. Webber, "Sanctifying the Inner Life," 55.
56. See Flavel, *Method*, 2:395, 420.
57. Brooks, *Complete Works*, 3:389.
58. Flavel, *Saint Indeed*, 5:434.
59. Flavel, *Saint Indeed*, 5:434.

warns, "It is corruption unmortified which clouds the face of God, and breaks the peace of his people, and consequently imbitters the life of a Christian."[60] Thus, keeping the heart strengthens our assurance by rooting out that sin which obscures it. As Hedges explains, "When believers lose assurance because of sin, renewing their watch is one of the means of getting back in the way of holiness and assurance."[61] A close watch of the heart awakens believers from their laziness and aids them in mortifying sin. This watchfulness, then, is necessary in sustaining assurance and joy. Flavel remarks, "Suppose it possible for a careless Christian to attain assurance, yet it is impossible he should long retain it…. For a little pride, vanity, carelessness, will dash to pieces all that for which they have been labouring a long time, in many a weary duty."[62]

What is true of assurance is also true of joy. Neglecting the heart undermines assurance and happiness. Flavel declares, "A negligent and careless heart must of necessity produce a disorderly and scandalous life."[63] Such a life means God will "inwardly excommunicate their souls from all comfortable fellowship with himself, and the joys of his salvation."[64] Keeping of the heart, however, protects joy as it helps prevent the rising and flourishing of sin. Flavel asks, "What is the true cause and reason of all this, but the neglecting of their hearts? Were our hearts better kept, all this would be prevented."[65] Delight is sustained by maintaining watchfulness over the heart.

There is, then, much happiness for those who keep the heart. It helps the "comfort of ordinances be sweet."[66] Flavel declares, "O what precious communion might you have with God every time you approach him, if your hearts were but in frame!"[67] An earnest keeping of the heart proves our sincerity, strengthens our assurance, and invigorates our joy. Thus, Flavel exhorts, "Since, then, the joy of our

---

60. Flavel, *Method*, 2:386.
61. Hedges, *Watchfulness*, 57.
62. Flavel, *Saint Indeed*, 5:435.
63. Flavel, *Saint Indeed*, 5:501.
64. Flavel, *Saint Indeed*, 5:501.
65. Flavel, *Saint Indeed*, 5:501.
66. Flavel, *Saint Indeed*, 5:500.
67. Flavel, *Saint Indeed*, 5:499.

life, the comfort of our souls, rises and falls with our diligence in this work, keep your hearts with all diligence."[68]

It is easy to see why Flavel viewed keeping the heart as the most important duty in the believer's life. He maintains, "I hope thou art fully satisfied how consequential and necessary a work the keeping of the heart is, it being a duty that wraps up so many dear interests of the soul in it."[69] The centrality of our heart to our person is matched by the centrality of watchfulness to our duties. Keeping the heart is the one duty that cannot be ignored.

The Means of Keeping the Heart

While Flavel spends many pages discussing what it looks like to keep the heart in different seasons of life, he summarizes his teaching by focusing on six essential means: (1) keeping the Word, (2) examining the heart, (3) contemplating heaven, (4) mortifying sin, (5) enjoying God, and (6) meditating.[70] In order to better grasp the duty of keeping the heart, it is important to make sense of these means. It is here that the practical nature of Flavel's spirituality is most clearly evident.

Keeping the Word

The first of Flavel's exhortations highlights the role of Scripture in keeping the heart. He asks, "Would you thus keep your hearts as hath been persuaded? Then furnish your hearts richly with the word of God, which is their best preservation against sin."[71] It is no accident that Flavel begins with Scripture, for there is no keeping the heart without keeping Scripture. Believers must be diligent to abide in God's Word.[72] Flavel asserts, "Keep the word, and the word will keep you: as

---

68. Flavel, *Saint Indeed*, 5:435

69. Flavel, *Saint Indeed*, 5:437.

70. Flavel, *Saint Indeed*, 5:504–7. I have personally summarized these six ways in a manner that hopefully gives credence to Flavel's understanding. The rest of this chapter seeks to explain these practices and demonstrate that while Flavel only briefly touches on them in this work, they are found throughout his writings.

71. Flavel, *Saint Indeed*, 5:504.

72. This theme is prevalent among the Puritans. As Webber notes, "Thomas Goodwin lists as his first remedy against vain thoughts, 'to get the heart furnished and enriched with good stock of sanctified and heavenly knowledge in spiritual and heavenly truths.'" Webber, "Sanctifying the Inner Life," 47. For another example of the

the first receiving of the word regenerated your hearts, so the keeping of the word within you will preserve your hearts."[73] It is the Word of God that protects believers from sin, as it is the Word that reveals their sin and points them to their Savior.

The Word "makes the soul, upon which it works, to forego and quit the dearest interests it hath in this world for Jesus Christ."[74] It does this work through the following acts:

> First, It hath an awakening efficacy upon secure and sleepy sinners; it rouses the conscience, and brings a man to a sense and feeling apprehension…. Secondly, The law of God hath an enlightening efficacy upon the minds of men: It is eye-salve to the blinded eye…. Thirdly, The word of God hath a convincing efficacy: It sets sin in order before the soul…. Fourthly, The law of God hath a soul-wounding, an heart-cutting efficacy; It pierces into the very soul and spirit of man…. Fifthly, The word hath a heart-turning, a soul-converting efficacy in it: It is a regenerating, as well as a convincing word.[75]

Thus, the Word of God is essential for restoring and keeping the heart. Those who drift from the Word of God will drift from God. Webber affirms, "It was inconceivable to the Puritan that a man could make progress in any part of his Christian life apart from the Bible. It was his only sure guide to a proper understanding of the requirements that God has placed upon him, and the condition of his own heart."[76] Flavel and the Puritans believed that Scripture is efficacious because it is the very word of the Holy Spirit.[77] Flavel explains, "And it is most

---

centrality of Scripture in the piety of the Puritans, see J. Stephen Yuille, "A String of Pearls (Psalm 119): The Biblical Piety of Thomas Manton," in *Puritan Piety: Writings in Honor of Joel R. Beeke*, ed. Michael A. G. Haykin, and Paul M. Smalley (Fearn, Scotland: Christian Focus, 2018), 215–34.

73. Flavel, *Saint Indeed*, 5:504.

74. Flavel, *Method*, 2:296.

75. Flavel, *Method*, 2:296–97.

76. Webber, "Sanctifying the Inner Life," 47.

77. J. I. Packer explains that John Owen defined inspiration "as the inbreathing of the Holy Spirit, whereby revelations are given, received, and transmitted, both orally and in writing." Packer, *Quest*, 86. As Owen himself writes, "As to the doctrine contained in it [Scripture], and the words wherein that doctrine is delivered, it is wholly his [God's]; what that speaks, he speaks himself. He speaks in it and by it." John

certain, that it is not a power inherent in itself, nor derived from the instrument by which it is managed, but from the Spirit of the Lord, who communicates to it all that power and efficacy which it hath upon our souls."[78] It is for this reason that we must give such diligence to keeping the Word.

We keep the Word when it dwells in the heart. Flavel exhorts, "Let it dwell, not tarry with you for a night, and let it dwell richly and plentifully; in all that is of it, in its commands, promises, threats; in all that is in you, in your understanding, memories, consciences, affections, and then it will preserve your hearts."[79] To keep the heart is to let the entirety of the Word dwell in the entirety of our person. This is not a passive endeavor. As Flavel makes clear, the love of the Word "manifests itself in our longing after it" and "our diligent attendance to it."[80] We attend to it "by preserving it carefully in our hearts and memories," and when we labor "to get an high esteem of it, and an experimental feeling of it, and frequently meditate on it."[81] Keeping the Word means we "study the word more, and the concerns and interests of the world less."[82] It is to "treasure up its rules in your hearts."[83] We actively keep our hearts by actively keeping the Word in our hearts.

This emphasis on Scripture as the first means of keeping the heart is a reminder that the focus of the heart must be first and foremost outside itself. As Hedges notes, "A watchful heart is not a heart preoccupied with itself, but with Christ and the great things of the gospel."[84] There is a time for self-examination, but the first priority is always to look to God and His Word.[85]

Owen, quoted in Packer, *Quest*, 87. This understanding is also confirmed by the WCF 1.4, "The authority of holy Scripture, for which it ought to be believed and obeyed, dependeth not upon the testimony of any man or church, but wholly upon God (who is truth itself), the Author thereof; and therefore it is to be received, because it is the Word of God."

78. Flavel, *Method*, 2:298.
79. Flavel, *Saint Indeed*, 5:504.
80. Flavel, *Exposition*, 6:275.
81. Flavel, *Exposition*, 6:275.
82. Flavel, *Divine Conduct*, 4:470.
83. Flavel, *Divine Conduct*, 4:470.
84. Hedges, *Watchfulness*, 82.
85. Significant for Flavel and the Puritans in this endeavor is to sit regularly under

Examining the Heart

To keep the heart, we must know the heart. "Call your hearts frequently to an account," declares Flavel, "if ever you mean to keep them with God."[86] He encourages his readers to examine their hearts, to exhort them to reject sin and pursue Christ: "We should call our hearts to account every evening, and say, O my heart! Where has thou been to-day? What an account canst thou give of them? O naughty heart! vain heart! couldst thou not abide by the fountain of delights? Is there better entertainment with the creature than with God?"[87] Those who diligently keep their hearts are those who review their hearts consistently and honestly, asking the difficult questions that lead to life and godliness.

This practice is often referred to as self-examination.[88] Webber explains that it has two components. The first has to do with our "standing before God," whether or not we are Christians.[89] The second

---

the preaching of the Word. For more on the "life-giving power" of the preached Word, see Packer, *Quest*, 282–83.

86. Flavel, *Saint Indeed*, 5:505.

87. Flavel, *Saint Indeed*, 5:505.

88. The priority of self-examination among the Puritans finds its source in John Calvin and his insistence on the necessity of this practice for Christians. Calvin writes, "In the meantime, believers are taught to examine themselves carefully and humbly, lest the confidence of the flesh creep in and replace assurance of faith." Calvin, *Institutes*, 3.2.11. Such sentiment was not minor in Calvin—rather, as Beeke notes, "Foxgrover has shown scores of quotations that Calvin firmly believed in the necessity of self-examination and in searching the conscience. Calvin has related the need for self-examination to a great variety of topics: knowledge of God and ourselves, judgment, repentance, confession, affliction, the Lord's Supper, providence, duty, and the kingdom of God, etc." Joel Beeke, *Assurance of Faith*, 67. The Puritans, following Calvin, would make the practice of self-examination central to their piety. As Webber explains, "Our Puritan forefathers believed that the Scriptures encouraged self-examination. In support of such practice they cited verses like 1 Cor 11:28 and 2 Cor 13:5. It was their belief that the deceitfulness of the heart, the cunning of Satan, and the world in which we live, all furnished evidence of its necessity." Webber, "Sanctifying the Inner Life," 50. Thomas Watson provides an example of such a call to examination, giving twenty-four marks by which godly men ought to examine themselves. He writes, "Look at the saints' characteristics here, and never leave off till you have got them stamped upon your soul. This is the grand business that should swallow up your time and thoughts." Thomas Watson, *The Godly Man's Picture* (1666; repr., Edinburgh: Banner of Truth, 1992), 8.

89. Webber, "Sanctifying the Inner Life," 50.

has to do with our "present condition" as Christians, whether we are in a "thriving or languishing" state.[90] When Flavel speaks of keeping the heart, he has the second in view. It is the work of believers. Flavel clarifies, "Carnal and formal persons take no heed to this, they cannot be brought to confer with their own hearts.... But saints know those soliloquies and self-conferences to be of excellent use and advantage."[91] True Christians, though cognizant of the difficulty, long to converse with their own hearts.

This conversing with the heart encapsulates what Flavel means by self-examination. It is to "bring your hearts and the word together by solemn self-examination; confer with your reins, and commune with your own hearts."[92] It is important to note the priority of Scripture in this endeavor, for it is the truth of the Word of God that we bring to our hearts. To do so, we must search the Word and search our hearts. As Flavel exhorts, "It is the slipperiness of our hearts in reference to the word, that causes so many slips in our lives. Conscience cannot be urged or awed with forgotten truths; but keep it in the heart, and it will keep both heart and life upright."[93] As we consider the state of our heart by means of the Word, we learn how it has gone astray. We confront its disobedience and call it back from continuing down the destructive path of sin. In this way, we keep our hearts. Flavel maintains,

> The oftener the heart meets with rebukes and checks for wandering, the less it will wander: If every vain thought were retracted with a sigh, every excursion of the heart from God with a severe check, it would not dare so boldly and frequently to digress and step aside: those actions which are committed with reluctancy, are not committed with frequency.[94]

Such examination "is as necessary as sweet," for it secures the believer's joy by means of keeping the heart from sin.[95]

---

90. Webber, "Sanctifying the Inner Life," 50.
91. Flavel, *Saint Indeed*, 5:426.
92. Flavel, *Touchstone*, 5:536.
93. Flavel, *Saint Indeed*, 5:504.
94. Flavel, *Saint Indeed*, 5:505.
95. Flavel, *Saint Indeed*, 5:505.

Contemplating Heaven

A prime hindrance to keeping the heart is its susceptibility to distraction. Many believers spend little time examining the heart because their focus is elsewhere. We will only keep the heart when we understand it to be the primary concern of life. Flavel observes, "He that will keep his heart, must take heed of plunging himself into such a multiplicity of earthly business, as he cannot manage without neglecting his main business."[96] This statement exemplifies a core feature of Puritan piety—namely, an emphasis on heavenly-mindedness.[97] Dewey Wallace notes, "The holy and spiritually minded person was to think much of heaven, for he or she already lived there within the soul. Accordingly, 'heavenly mindedness' was one of the most prominent themes of Puritan spirituality in this era."[98] Zeal in keeping the heart arises in those who have weighed the glory of heaven as exceedingly rich. Those who fix their gaze on heaven will find the effort required to watch their hearts.

Those who neglect their hearts value the things of earth more than the things of heaven. They have filled their lives with so much of the world that their hearts have followed suit. Believers must take heed "lest thy shop steal away from thy closet; God never intended earthly employments for a stop, but rather a step to heavenly ones."[99] Flavel does not call us out of this world but exhorts us to engage this world for the purposes of the next. The issue is one of priority. Flavel states, "Our hearts are narrow, and know not how to manage two businesses

---

96. Flavel, *Saint Indeed*, 5:505.

97. Such an emphasis, though present in medieval monasticism, became most prominent in Calvin and the Puritans. Tom Schwanda asserts, "While earlier Christians, including Bernard, desired heaven, there does not appear to be the same degree of emphasis upon meditating on heaven as practiced by Calvin and the Puritans." Tom Schwanda, *Soul Recreation*, 137. Thus, Calvin writes, "Therefore, believers ascribe to God's grace the fact that, illumined by his Spirit, they enjoy through faith the contemplation of heavenly life." Calvin, *Institutes*, 3.2.40. But it was the Puritans, according to Schwanda, that "greatly expanded the connection between heavenly-mindedness and meditation on heaven with contemplation." Schwanda, *Soul Recreation*, 136. The classic example of Puritan heavenly-mindedness is Richard Baxter's *Saints' Everlasting Rest*.

98. Wallace, *Spirituality*, xvi–xvii.

99. Flavel, *Saint Indeed*, 5:505

of such different natures, as earthly and heavenly matters without detriment to one."[100] The heart will inevitably center on that which most commands our time and attention. We must be careful, then, not to become too busy in earthly endeavors. As Flavel explains, "If thy ship is overladen, thou must cast some overboard: More business than thou canst well manage, is like more meat than thou canst well digest, which will quickly make a sickly soul."[101] A life encumbered by worldly pursuits reflects an ailing heart in drastic need of recalibrating.

A heart that indulges earthly things is in grave danger. For this reason, Flavel exhorts, "Though the world be in your hands, let it not justle Christ out of your hearts."[102] In keeping the heart, believers seek to be single-minded in their focus on the kingdom of God, not the kingdom of man. They cannot let "Christ and the world share and divide [their] hearts in two halves betwixt them."[103] Rather, they must "exercise heavenly-mindedness, and keep [their] hearts upon things eternal, under all the providences with which the Lord exercises [them] in this world."[104] No matter what God may bring into our lives, we are to care for our hearts by keeping our focus on the things of heaven, not the things of earth. This heavenly-mindedness, argues Flavel, encourages our heart to both health and happiness, for "when the salt of heavenly-mindedness is cast into the spring, the streams will run clearer, and sweeter."[105]

Mortifying Sin

A significant feature of keeping the heart is eliminating sin from all of life.[106] This must be a zealous pursuit, in order to kill sin in its very

---

100. Flavel, *Divine Conduct*, 4:430.

101. Flavel, *Saint Indeed*, 5:505.

102. Flavel, *Saint Indeed*, 5:505.

103. Flavel, *Fountain*, 1:102.

104. Flavel, *Divine Conduct*, 4:430.

105. Flavel, *Saint Indeed*, 5:433.

106. For the Puritans, this concept of eradicating sin was known as mortification. Along with vivification, it was one of the two key aspects of sanctification. As Beeke and Jones explain, "The complement of mortification is vivification…. We must not only seek to kill sin; we must also seek to do the will of God…. We need both killing and quickening, ceasing to evil and learning to do well (Isa. 1:16–17)." Beeke and Jones, *Puritan Theology*, 532. This emphasis on mortification was present in Calvin's

beginning. Flavel explains, "He that will find his house in good repair, must stop every chink as soon as discovered; and he that will keep his heart, must not let a vain thought be long neglected; the serpent of heart-apostasy is best killed in the egg of a small remission of care."[107] Those who are truly concerned about the heart are keen to mortify sin when it first appears. Furthermore, Flavel argues,

> So it is in the mortification of sin; it is not this or that particular member or act, but the whole body of sin that is to be destroyed, and accordingly the conflict is in every faculty of the soul; for the Spirit of God, by whose hand sin is mortified, doth not combat with this or that particular lust only, but with sin, as sin; and for that reason with every sin, in every faculty of the soul.[108]

The battle against sin is not occasional—rather, it demands the believer's active, constant, and careful attention. This is due to sin's grip on the soul. Prior to the regenerating work of the Spirit, the individual was under the command and control of sin. "The crucifixion of sin," says Flavel, "necessarily implies the subversion of its dominion in the soul: A mortified sin cannot be a reigning sin."[109] Sin's reign in the heart is due to its power to deceive us into believing that it is most natural and delightful. Its power "rises from the suitableness it hath, and pleasure it gives to the corrupt heart of man: It seems to be as necessary as the right hand, and as useful and pleasant as the right-eye."[110] To mortify sin is to attack its assumed power and pleasure, for "the mortified heart is dead to all pleasures and profits of sin; it hath no

---

thinking as well: "On this account, in my judgment, repentance can thus be well defined: it is the true turning of our life to God, a turning that arises from a pure and earnest fear of him; and it consists in the mortification of our flesh and of the old man, and in the vivification of the Spirit." Calvin, *Institutes*, 3.3.5; see also 3.5.8. Arguably the most prominent example of the Puritan understanding of mortification is found in John Owen, *On the Mortification of Sin in Believers*, in *Works of John Owen*, ed. Richard Rushing (Edinburgh: Banner of Truth Trust, 1968), 6:5–87. For a more in-depth treatment of mortification in Calvin and Owen, see Randall C. Gleason, *John Calvin and John Owen on Mortification: A Comparative Study in Reformed Spirituality* (New York: Peter Lang, 1995).

107. Flavel, *Saint Indeed*, 5:505–6.
108. Flavel, *Method*, 2:374.
109. Flavel, *Method*, 2:372.
110. Flavel, *Method*, 2:372.

delight or pleasure in it; it becomes its burden and daily complaint."[111] The heart that is kept, then, is that which sees sin as alien and antagonistic to its own flourishing.

This all-encompassing hatred of sin comes only from the work of the Spirit in the heart. Flavel is adamant that it is the Spirit who is the fundamental basis of any true mortification of sin: "The sanctifying Spirit is the only effectual principle of mortification; and without him, no resolutions, vows, abstinences, castigations of the body, or any other external endeavours, can ever avail to the mortification of one sin."[112] The Spirit's work does not negate the believer's responsibility to work. We are to make use of every means given by the Spirit to kill sin. While the means are many, Flavel focuses on five remedies in particular:

> Daily watching against the occasions of sin…Earnest cries to heaven for preventing grace…Deep humblings of soul for sins past, which is an excellent preventive unto future sins…Care to give no furtherance or advantage to the design of sin by making provision for the flesh to fulfil the lusts thereof…Willingness to bear due reproofs for sin.[113]

As these means highlight, the work of mortifying sin centers upon an active dependence on grace and an attentive watch over the heart.

Basic to this whole enterprise is a profound realization of the seriousness of sin's strength and spread. Without this awareness, it is likely that we will ignore little sins, especially those that are internal. The danger, as Flavel points out, is that "little sins neglected, will quickly become great and masterless: The greatest crocodile once lay in an egg; the greatest oak was once but an acorn.… Men little think what a proud, vain, wanton, or worldly thought may grow to: Behold how great a matter a little fire kindles!"[114] The diligent keeping of the heart requires that we decisively mortify our sin in its every occurrence. An apathy toward sin is too perilous for the heart to endure.

The result of such mortification is joy. Flavel states, "There is a wonderful sweetness in mortification, for dost thou not feel a blessed

---

111. Flavel, *Method*, 2:372.
112. Flavel, *Method*, 2:377.
113. Flavel, *Method*, 2:373.
114. Flavel, *Saint Indeed*, 5:506.

calmness, cheeriness, and tranquility in thy conscience, when thou hast faithfully repelled temptations, successfully resisted and overcome thy corruptions?"[115] It is this "comfort and sweetness resulting from mortification [that] should effectually persuade every believer to more diligence about it."[116]

Enjoying God

Flavel's penchant for the significance of joy in the Christian life is evident as he stresses how necessary communion with God is for keeping the heart.[117] He exhorts, "Take heed of losing the liveliness and sweetness of your communion with God, lest thereby your hearts be loosed off from God."[118] Though Christians can keep their hearts out of mere duty, it is far better if they keep them out of great delight. Joy will always have more power to drive the heart than obligation. As Flavel explains, "It is true, conscience of duty may keep the heart from neglecting it; but when there is no higher motive, it drives on deadly, and is filled with distractions."[119] It is clear that Flavel is not minimizing the importance of duty but rather emphasizing the greater rule of joy, for "nothing more engages the heart to a constancy and evenness in walking with God, than the sweetness which it tastes therein."[120] Such sweetness is experienced most keenly in the believer's communion with God.[121] There is no greater earthly joy: "I must tell you Christians,

---

115. Flavel, *Method*, 2:386.

116. Flavel, *Method*, 2:385.

117. For the Puritans, to commune with God was to enjoy God and to enjoy God was to commune with God. As J. D. Williams explains, "Enjoyment of God was not only the greatest delight of believers, but also their goal and duty, to be earnestly and actively sought by diligently exploring the pleasures of communion with God." Williams, "Puritan Quest," 95. Beeke and Jones root this emphasis on the joy of communing with God in the writing of Augustine. They write, "Owen picked up on a theme found in Augustine, namely, communion as the 'enjoyment,' or possession of and delighting in the triune God." Beeke and Jones, *Puritan Theology*, 103; cf. Augustine, *On Christian Doctrine* 1.5, in *Works of Aurelius Augustine*, ed. Marcus Dods (Edinburgh: T&T Clark, 1892), 9:10. For more on Flavel's concept of joy, see chapter 3 of the present volume.

118. Flavel, *Saint Indeed*, 5:506.

119. Flavel, *Saint Indeed*, 5:506.

120. Flavel, *Saint Indeed*, 5:506.

121. Thus, Williams expresses, "The experience which lay at the heart of Puritan

you must look for no such delights as these, in any earthly enjoyment, none better than these, till you come home to glory; communion with God then appears most excellent in as much as it is found to be the desire and delight of all gracious souls."[122] Thus, believers must continually seek the satisfaction of communing with God.

Central to Flavel's understanding is the distinction between a state of communion and actual communion.[123] The second flows from the first. The state of communion "is nothing else but the joint interest that Christ and the saints have in the same things…a koinonia, i.e. a fellowship or joint interest between them, upon which ground they are called co-heirs with Christ."[124] We commune with Christ as we are in union with Him, which is possible only through His redeeming work as the God-man. According to Flavel, it "depends upon the hypostatical union of our nature, and the mystical union of our persons with the Son of God; in the first he partakes with us, in the second we partake with him."[125] For Flavel, the prerequisite of experiencing actual communion with God is union with Christ, which brings forth the graces of the Spirit in the heart of the believer. He asserts, "Where there is no union, there can be no communion."[126] And this "communion with God pre-supposes the habits of grace implanted in the

---

devotion was that of *communion with God,* the mutual exchange of love and delight between God and the believing soul." Williams, "Puritan Quest," 89.

122. Flavel, *England's Duty,* 4:252.

123. For Flavel's most in-depth presentation of communion with God, see Flavel, *England's Duty,* 4:235–68. Packer summarizes the broader Puritan notion of communion with God, especially as seen in the work of Owen, in five propositions: (1) "a relationship of mutual interchange between God and man"; (2) "a relationship in which the initiative and power are with God"; (3) "a relationship in which Christians receive love from, and respond in love to, all three persons of the Trinity"; (4) "a relation of active, forward-looking friendship between God and man"; (5) "enjoyed in a special way at the Lord's Table." Packer, *Quest,* 203–15. Thus, Owen writes, "Now, communion is the mutual communication of such good things as wherein the persons holding that communion are delighted, bottomed upon some union between them…. Our communion, then, with God consisteth in his communication of himself to us, with our returnal unto him of that which he requireth and accepteth, flowing from that union which in Jesus Christ we have with him." Owen, *Of Communion,* 2:9.

124. Flavel, *Method,* 2:145.

125. Flavel, *Method,* 2:145.

126. Flavel, *England's Duty,* 4:239.

soul by sanctification; a sound and sincere change of heart. No sanctification, no communion."[127] For this reason, "we must be put into a state of fellowship before ever we can have actual communion with God."[128] Our communion with God depends on God's gracious work for us and in us.

It is this work of God, whereby we enter into a state of communion, that enables us to experience actual communion with Him. This "is an actual fellowship or communion the saints have with Christ in holy duties, wherein Christians let forth their hearts to God by desires, and God lets forth his comforts and refreshments again into their hearts; they open their mouths wide, and he fill them."[129] To commune with God in an actual sense is to participate in fellowship with Him. It is to dine with Christ and He with us.[130] This supping with Christ, while incorporating the duties and the affections, is not to be equated with them. As Flavel explains, "This is what I say, that communion with God consisteth not in the mere performance of duties.... Neither do all stirrings and workings of the affections infallibly evidence and prove communion betwixt Christ and that soul."[131] Communing with God is not simply engaging in spiritual duties in a way that captures our affections. It is not less than this but rather more.

Flavel lays out three primary ways (or methods) by which we may commune with God: "(1) In the contemplation of his attributes; (2) In the exercises of our graces in religious duties; and (3) In his various providences."[132] To begin with, we commune with God through meditating on His attributes: "There is a sweet and sensible communion betwixt God and his people, in the contemplation of the Divine attributes, and the impressions God makes by them upon our souls, whilst we meditate on them."[133] When we consider who God is, we gain a greater awareness of ourselves and Him, and the Spirit impresses these realities upon the heart. In so doing, we commune with Him. As God's

---

127. Flavel, *England's Duty*, 4:239.
128. Flavel, *England's Duty*, 4:237.
129. Flavel, *Method*, 2:144.
130. Flavel, *England's Duty*, 4:238.
131. Flavel, *England's Duty*, 4:238.
132. Flavel, *England's Duty*, 4:240.
133. Flavel, *England's Duty*, 4:240.

"immense greatness," "purity and holiness," "goodness and mercy," "veracity and faithfulness," "anger and displeasure," and "omniscience" situate themselves into our minds, the Spirit works them into our soul, and we come to know Him more and more.[134]

Second, we experience communion with God through "the exercises of our graces in the various duties of religion; in prayer, hearing, sacraments, &c."[135] Flavel expounds, "As God hath planted various graces in regenerate souls, so he hath appointed various duties to exercise and draw forth those graces; and when they do so, then have his people sweet actual communion with him."[136] The spiritual duties are means by which God intends to bring forth the graces He has given us in Christ. As we pray, hear the Word of God, and participate in the sacraments, we are encouraged to repent, believe, love, and exhibit the fruit of the Spirit. God makes Himself known to us through these duties and we respond to Him in the grace He has given us. As God comes near to us, we draw ever nearer to Him.

Third, Flavel notes that "there is another method of communion with God in the way of his providences, for therein also his people walk with him."[137] At times, God will draw His people to Himself by bringing them into a season or situation where they will especially sense their need for Him. Flavel gives three such providences; God might bring believers into a season of discipline, want, or danger. Flavel explains,

> There are times when providence straitens the people of God; when the waters of comfort ebb and run very low, wants pinch; if then the soul returns filial dependence upon fatherly care, saying with David, Ps 23:1, 'The Lord is my shepherd, I shall not want;' it belongs to him to provide, and to me to depend: I will trust my

---

134. Flavel describes such communion in more detail in Flavel, *England's Duty*, 4:240–44. For more on the nature of communion with God through knowing Him, see J. I. Packer, *Knowing God* (Downers Grove, Ill.: InterVarsity, 1973), 24–32.

135. Flavel, *England's Duty*, 4:244.

136. Flavel, *England's Duty*, 4:244.

137. Flavel, *England's Duty*, 4:245.

Father's care and love. Here now is sweet communion with God under pinching wants.[138]

As believers consider God in His attributes and pursue God through His means, they must also seek to draw near to Him in His providences.

The vitality of our communion with God will greatly aid us in keeping the heart. It will incline the heart to God and disincline the heart from sin. "The heart is an hungry and restless thing; it will have something to feed upon; if it enjoy nothing from God, it will hunt for something among the creatures, and there it often loses itself, as well as its end."[139] Flavel reminds us that the more the heart tastes the goodness of fellowship with God, the more it will lose its appetite for sin. To enjoy communion with God, then, is a necessary way of ensuring that we do not lose the heart.

Meditating

Flavel concludes his discussion of keeping the heart with an exhortation to meditate: "Habituate thy heart to spiritual meditations, if thou wouldst have it free from those burdensome diversions."[140] To keep the heart inclined to God, believers must keep the heart thinking on God. The Puritans referred to such thinking as meditation.[141] Beeke and Jones explain, "For the Puritans, meditation was a daily duty that enhanced every other duty of the Christian life. As oil lubricates an engine, so meditation facilitates the diligent use of means of grace, deepens the marks of grace, and strengthens one's relationships to others."[142] The daily practice of meditation encourages the heart

---

138. Flavel, *England's Duty*, 4:245.

139. Flavel, *Saint Indeed*, 5:506.

140. Flavel, *Saint Indeed*, 5:506.

141. Definitions of Puritan meditation abound, but Yuille's summary exemplifies its basic concepts: "It is a dwelling or reflecting upon Scripture, a musing or mulling over the biblical text, whereby the truth of God's Word grips the three main faculties of the soul: the understanding, the affections, and the will." Yuille, "Conversing with God's Word: Scripture Meditation in the Piety of George Swinnock," *Journal of Spiritual Formation & Soul Care* 5, no. 1 (2012): 37. Packer agrees, "In meditation the Puritan would seek and challenge his heart, stir his affections to hate sin and love righteousness, and encourage himself with God's promises, just as preachers would do from the pulpit." Packer, *Quest*, 24.

142. Beeke and Jones, *Puritan Theology*, 891.

toward greater faithfulness to God. Flavel affirms, "By this mean you will get a facility and dexterity in heart-work."[143]

For Flavel, meditation was to be the believer's consistent and constant practice.[144] He exhorts, "Redeem some time every day for meditation; [to] get out of the noise and clamour of the world."[145] This was Flavel's practice. According to his anonymous biographer, "He was very thoughtful, and when not discoursing or reading, much taken up in meditation, which made him digest his notions well."[146] Through constancy in meditation, believers impress the truths of God, by the aid of the Spirit, into their hearts and lives. It is vital, therefore, to "meditate upon what you hear; for, without meditation, it is not like to have any effectual operation upon you."[147] The heart is kept by God's Word only when the Word is digested by means of meditation.

The practice of meditation not only encourages the assimilation of truth but also empowers believers to take truth with them. As Webber describes, "It was generally thought that the best time of the day for concentrated meditation was the morning, as this would not only put us in a good frame of mind for the day, but also provide food for further thought for what Flavel called 'the time between times.'"[148] These times of fixed meditation train us to meditate throughout the whole day, especially in those seemingly insignificant junctures of life.[149] As we learn to redeem every moment by being "good husbands

---

143. Flavel, *Saint Indeed*, 5:506.

144. Such prominence given to meditation was typical for most Puritans. As Beeke writes, "The Puritans stressed the need for meditation.... One cannot be a solid Christian without meditating." Joel Beeke, *Puritan Reformed Spirituality: A Practical Theological Study from Our Reformed and Puritan Heritage* (Webster, N.Y.: Evangelical Press, 2006), 78. For example, Beeke quotes Watson's exhortation, "A Christian without meditation is like a soldier without arms, or a workman without tools. Without meditation the truths of God will not stay with us; the heart is hard, and the memory slippery, and without meditation all is lost." Thomas Watson, quoted in Beeke, *Puritan Reformed Spirituality*, 79.

145. Flavel, *Method*, 2:234.

146. "Life of the Late," 1:xvi.

147. Flavel, *Method*, 2:302.

148. Webber, "Sanctifying the Inner Life," 48.

149. Thus, Flavel saw the importance of both deliberate and occasional meditation, though he placed priority on the deliberate. For a more detailed explanation of

upon [our] thoughts," we ensure that our hearts do not wander and our time is not wasted.[150]

Like his Puritan contemporaries, Flavel spent much time instructing his hearers on the proper subjects of meditation. Beeke and Jones note, "The Puritans never tired of saying that biblical meditation involves thinking upon the triune God and His Word."[151] To meditate rightly is to think on God: His attributes, character, and works. Such knowledge of God is found primarily in His Word, and secondarily in His works. Flavel explains, "The object of meditation is twofold. First, the word. Secondly, the works of God. The works of God are twofold. First, internal. Secondly, external. The external works of God are twofold. First, of creation. Secondly, of providence."[152] There is, then, no lack of inspiration for the believer's meditation, as God's Word and works abound in declaring who He is and what He has done.[153] While the Word of God ought to be our chief object of meditation, we should also marvel at God's works in the heart and the world.[154]

Finally, meditation on God is not simply a thinking on the things of God but an active speaking of His truth to our hearts. As Flavel asserts,

> It is observable that the Hebrew word *suach*, which is used for meditation, or thinking, signifies both to think and to speak in the mind. When the understanding, or mind resolves, and meditates the things that come into it, that very meditation is an inward speaking, or hidden word in the heart, Deut. 15:9.[155]

---

these two types of meditation, see Beeke and Jones, *Puritan Theology*, 891–93; and Schwanda, *Soul Recreation*, 124–29.

150. Flavel, *Saint Indeed*, 5:506.

151. Beeke and Jones, *Puritan Theology*, 890.

152. Flavel, *Husbandry Spiritualized*, 5:8.

153. To get a better sense of the range of topics on which the Puritans meditated, see sample lists of such subjects in Beeke, *Puritan Reformed Spirituality*, 87–92.

154. For an example, see Flavel, *Twelve Sacramental Meditations*, 6:378–460. Flavel's meditation on God's external works can be seen in Flavel, *Husbandry Spiritualized*, 5:3–205. To better understand the Puritans on meditation, see Beeke and Jones, *Puritan Theology*, 899–903.

155. Flavel, *Pneumatologia*, 2:503.

As they read and hear God's Word, believers are to think on it throughout the day, as though they "are the companions with whom our hearts talk and converse."[156] This ongoing conversing will greatly aid our endeavor to keep the heart and to walk in joy with God.

Conclusion

Flavel's understanding of what it means to keep the heart reveals the main contours of his spirituality. It is by the keeping of the heart that "Christ distinguishes the formal and serious Christian."[157] Given the centrality of the heart, Flavel believes that an unkept heart is an unkept life. While there is no more difficult work, it yields the greatest reward. As Flavel posits, "As for those whose hearts are filled with the joys of assurance, if extraordinary care be not used, it is a thousand to one if they ever long enjoy it."[158] The diligent keeping of the heart greatly strengthens and sustains our assurance in Christ, which only heightens our experience of the joy of Christ. This theme of the joy of assurance is woven throughout Flavel's exhortations to keep the heart. It is the joy of assurance that drives his call for Christians to keep the heart.

---

156. Flavel, *Pneumatologia*, 2:504.
157. Flavel, *Saint Indeed*, 5:507.
158. Flavel, *Saint Indeed*, 5:435.

Chapter 8

Joy in Carrying the Cross

Flavel's joy of assurance is on full display in his approach to suffering. As Brian Cosby notes, "[Flavel] did not write about suffering from an ivory tower, but as one who was well acquainted with a variety of afflictions."[1] He lost his parents after they contracted the plague while imprisoned for nonconformity. He lost his first wife and son in childbirth and buried two other wives before his own death at age sixty-one. Additionally, he underwent persistent persecution throughout his ministry, being expelled from the Church of England due to the Act of Uniformity in 1662, and further separated from his church a few years later on account of the Five Mile Act. Much of his ministry was spent on the run, gathering with his people under the cover of darkness. It was not until the very end of his life that he experienced any substantial freedom as a pastor.

In light of his personal suffering, it is unsurprising that Flavel wrote so much on the topic. Cosby argues that "the theme of suffering permeates Flavel's *Works*."[2] This emphasis was not unique to Flavel. As Dewey Wallace confirms, "Puritan spiritual writers, especially after 1660 with the failure of Puritan hopes, devoted considerable attention to the affliction of the godly."[3] In fact, says Wallace, "The theme of the suffering of the godly is thus common in Puritan spiritual writers. Far from prosperity being equated with godliness in this literature, the

---

1. Cosby, *Suffering and Sovereignty*, 4.

2. Cosby, *Suffering and Sovereignty*, 6. As Cosby notes, such a theme is seen most prominently in the following writings: Flavel, *Token*, 5:604; Flavel, *Preparations for Sufferings*, 6:3–83.

3. Wallace, *Spirituality*, xxiv.

opposite is the case: affliction is the lot of the godly while prosperity often accompanies the ungodly."[4] Flavel's writings prove Wallace's assertion. He writes, "[God] had rather their hearts be heavy under adversity, than vain and careless under prosperity; the choicest spirits have been exercised with the sharpest suffering, and those that now shine as stars in heaven, have been trod under foot as dung on the earth."[5] For Flavel, suffering does not imply God's absence but His presence. All affliction is under God's great and good control.

It is this formidable faith in God's providence that enables Flavel to see all the trials of life as serving the twin purposes of God's glory and His people's good. Thus, Flavel understands suffering to be an occasion of joy for believers, as God is always faithful to use it for their benefit. He comments, "Possibly we cannot discern this at present, but rather pre-judge the works of God, and say all these things are against us; but hereafter we shall see, and with joy acknowledge them to be the happy instruments of our salvation."[6] Affliction, in the hands of a loving heavenly Father, is the means by which He sanctifies His people. This is most evident in the way in which suffering deepens the believer's assurance. "The time of greatest sufferings for Christ," asserts Flavel, "is the usual season of assurance."[7] It is by means of trial that God strengthens our assurance and, in so doing, establishes our joy. Joy "unspeakable amidst outward troubles" is "the fruit of assurance."[8] To faithfully carry the cross, then, is to pursue this joy of assurance in Christ.

Flavel's Theology of Suffering

To grasp the place of suffering in Flavel's spirituality, it is essential to comprehend its place in his theology. For Flavel, suffering is that misery and evil which has its origin in sin. He explains, "Afflictions in themselves are evil (Amos 2:6), very bitter and unpleasant.... It is

---

4. Wallace, *Spirituality*, xxv.

5. Flavel, *Preparations for Suffering*, 6:7–8.

6. John Flavel, *The Balm of the Covenant Applied to the Bleeding Wounds of Afflicted Saints: II Samuel 23.5*, in *Works of John Flavel* (1820; repr., Edinburgh: Banner of Truth Trust, 2015), 6:99.

7. Flavel, *Exposition*, 6:201.

8. Flavel, *Exposition*, 6:201.

evil, as it is the fruit of sin, and grievous unto sense (Heb 12:11)."[9] Afflictions are, says Flavel, the effects of God's vindictive wrath against the wickedness of sin.[10] Such misery, therefore, began in Eden, when Adam and Eve ate of the forbidden fruit. In this act of disobedience, "there was a twofold evil, the evil of sin, and the evil of punishment, both very great."[11] This evil of punishment includes the "loss of God's image," "horror of conscience," "sorrow of female sex," "curse on the creature," "expulsion from paradise," and "death both of body and soul."[12] It is clear that Flavel understands all human suffering to be both an evil and an effect of sin.

Yet, Flavel also maintains that there is a sense in which suffering is not evil, for it comes from the hand of God. As he clarifies, afflictions are "not morally and intrinsically evil, as sin is; for if so, the holy God would never own it for his own act as he doth (Mic 3:2), but always disclaimeth sin (James 1:3)."[13] Thus, suffering is an evil, in that it brings misery, but not a sinful evil. It is the result of sin, not sin itself. For this reason, Flavel can affirm that suffering comes from God's command, without God being responsible for evil. In response to the claim that God's judgment of the wicked and affliction of the righteous undermine His goodness, Flavel asserts, "No; it is the property of goodness to hate and punish evil in the impenitent.... And the affliction of the saints flow from his goodness, and end in their true and eternal good."[14] God, in both His judgment and discipline, is completely just and good. It is right that He judges the wicked and trains the righteous. In such actions, as Cosby points out, "Flavel understood God to be the author of suffering, but not the author of sin."[15] It is crucial, therefore, to understand Flavel's conception of suffering as arising both from humanity's sinfulness and God's providence.

---

9. Flavel, *Navigation Spiritualized*, 5:251.

10. Flavel, *Navigation Spiritualized*, 5:252.

11. Flavel, *Exposition*, 6:170.

12. Flavel, *Exposition*, 6:170.

13. Flavel, *Navigation Spiritualized*, 5:251.

14. Flavel, *Exposition*, 6:156.

15. Cosby, *Suffering and Sovereignty*, 19.

Suffering and Sin

As noted above, Flavel ties all suffering to the entrance of sin into the world. Before the fall, humanity lived in a blessed relationship with God, and "enjoyed the gracious presence and favour of God…which was better than life."[16] However, Flavel points to Adam's disobedience: "All mankind by their fall lost communion with God, are under his wrath and curse; and so made liable to all the miseries in this life, to death itself, and to the pains of hell for ever."[17] All human suffering results from this sin. If there were no sin, there would be no suffering. This does not mean that suffering is always the direct result of our actual sins. Flavel maintains "that all the sufferings of believers in this world are not for their sins; but some of them are for the prevention of sin."[18] Therefore, at times, affliction is due to sin. At other times, it arises from God's providential care and design.

According to Flavel, it is possible to distinguish between the sufferings of this world and the sufferings of the world to come.[19] Those of this world are "the miseries of life, as sickness, pain, poverty on the body; fear, trouble, sorrow on the mind, and at last death itself."[20] Such misery includes the body and the soul, or outward and inward affliction. The miseries of the world to come, however, are far worse. These, notes Flavel, are the "pains and torments of hell for ever," which include both the "pain of loss and pain of sense."[21] Those who are outside Christ are "miserable here, and miserable to eternity."[22] Flavel does not want anyone to neglect the great salvation we have in Christ.[23] Believers are saved from all misery in the world to come, and their suffering in this world always works for their good.

Focusing on the sufferings of this world, Flavel repeatedly demonstrates that they are both inward and outward, physical and spiritual. This understanding is seen most clearly in his presentation of the

---

16. Flavel, *Exposition*, 6:173.
17. Flavel, *Exposition*, 6:173.
18. Flavel, *Occasions*, 3:575.
19. Flavel, *Exposition*, 6:174.
20. Flavel, *Exposition*, 6:174.
21. Flavel, *Exposition*, 6:174.
22. Flavel, *Exposition*, 6:174.
23. Flavel, *Exposition*, 6:174.

sufferings of Christ on the cross. Here, Flavel acknowledges that "the sufferings of our Lord Jesus Christ upon the cross were two-fold, viz. His corporeal, and spiritual sufferings."[24] Christ suffered immensely, both in body and soul. According to Flavel, "His corporeal and more external sufferings were exceeding great, acute, and extreme sufferings; for they were sharp, universal, continual, and unrelieved by any inward comfort."[25] These physical miseries were as great as any human being could possibly experience and were only surpassed by that which He suffered inwardly. As Flavel contends, "His soul was filled up with grief, and had an heavier burden of its own to bear than that of the body; so that instead of relieving, it increased unspeakably the burden of its inward man."[26] For Flavel, the inward suffering of the soul far outweighs outward suffering of the body. "Consider what mere inward troubles of the soul can do upon the strongest body: they spend its strength, and devour the spirits."[27] When these two sufferings meet together, as they did in Christ, the misery of affliction is felt most deeply.

Inward suffering is most dangerous when it affects the believer's faith. Flavel exhorts, "By fretting and discontent, you do yourselves more injury than all afflictions you lie under could do; your own discontent is that which arms your troubles with a sting; it is you that make your burden heavy, by struggling under it."[28] The greatest misery is that which exacerbates the burden and cuts off all opportunities for comfort. The discontent, bitterness, and despair, arising from faithlessness, is far worse than any other hardship of life. It is this sinful suffering of the soul that Flavel finds most appalling:

> Sure then thou has more reason to lament thy dead heart, than thy dead friend. Divert the stream of thy troubles speedily, and labour to recover thyself out of this temper quickly; lest sad experience shortly tell thee, that what thou now mournest for is but a trifle to what thou shalt mourn for hereafter. To lose

---

24. Flavel, *Fountain*, 1:421.
25. Flavel, *Fountain*, 1:421.
26. Flavel, *Fountain*, 1:422.
27. Flavel, *Fountain*, 1:424.
28. Flavel, *Saint Indeed*, 5:444.

the heavenly warmth and spiritual liveliness of thy affections, is undoubtedly a far more considerable loss, than to lose the wife of thy bosom, or the sweetest child that ever a tender parent laid in the grave.[29]

There is, according to Flavel, no worse fate than to be left with the anguish of sin. Sin not only causes suffering but fuels anguish.

Suffering and God

Central to Flavel's understanding of suffering is the belief that it comes by God's command. Cosby explains, "All suffering—though stemming from Adam's fall in the garden—is ultimately decreed from all eternity and brought forth into time and space by God's providential ordering."[30] In order to appreciate Flavel's conception of suffering, it is first necessary to grasp his doctrine of God's providence. It is in this doctrine that God's sovereign power and merciful provision meet, for it asserts that He works all things for His glory and the good of His people (Rom. 8:28).

God's providence is a significant tenet of Puritan theology and spirituality. As Sinclair Ferguson writes, "The doctrine of divine providence occupies a major place in classical Puritan practical theology and interpretation of the Christian life."[31] Of Puritan treatments on the subject, it is Flavel's *Divine Conduct, or The Mystery of Providence* that is widely recognized as preeminent. John Murray contends that "the best known writer on the subject of providence is John Flavel with his work entitled *The Divine Conduct* or *The Mystery of Providence*, first published 1678 and reprinted many times in the course of the centuries."[32] In this work, Flavel reflects in detail upon the truth of

---

29. Flavel, *Token*, 5:619. It is important to note, here, that Flavel is not unsympathetically calling for believers to quickly move past their emotions. Rather, the emotions should not "become sinful and exorbitant, when they divert us from, or distract us in our duties, so that our intercourse with heaven is stopt and interrupted by them" (5:618). Thus, Flavel warns of allowing our sorrow to so overcome us that we block the one stream of true comfort we have.

30. Cosby, *Suffering and Sovereignty*, 30.

31. Sinclair Ferguson, "The Mystery of Providence," in Kapic and Gleason, *The Devoted Life*, 211.

32. John J. Murray, "John Flavel and the Problem of Providence," in *Triumph*

Psalm 57:2, which says, "I will cry unto God most high; unto God that performeth all things for me."[33] This verse, then, effectively presents the heart of God's providence.

While Flavel focuses mostly on the second half of the verse, it is the first phrase that grounds his doctrine of providence. Here, David cries out to "God most high." As Flavel explains, "Saul is high, but God the Most High; and, without his permission, [David] is assured Saul cannot touch him."[34] Flavel's articulation of God's providence is built upon the assumption of God's complete sovereignty. His convictions align closely with those of his contemporaries in the Westminster Assembly:

> God the great Creator of all things doth uphold, direct, dispose, and govern all creatures, actions, and things, from the greatest even to the least, by His most wise and holy providence, according to His infallible foreknowledge and the free and immutable counsel of His own will, to the praise of the glory of His wisdom, power, justice, goodness, and mercy.[35]

As Alexandra Walsham points out, the Puritans understood providence to have a "dual definition: it comprised both knowledge and power."[36] God not only foresees all things past, present, and future but by His power He ordains it. All that comes to pass does so according to His will and pleasure. Christ "hath an universal empire over all things" and is "the head of the whole world by way of dominion."[37]

Christ is not, however, only sovereign over the world, He is "an head to the church by way of union and special influence."[38] Though He rules all creation, He uniquely governs His church. In fact, His rule of creation is for the benefit of His church. As Flavel explains, "The church is his special care and charge; he rules the world for her

---

through Tribulation: Papers Read at the 1998 Westminster Conference (London: Westminster Conference, 1998), 100.

33. See Flavel, *Divine Conduct*, 4:342.

34. Flavel, *Divine Conduct*, 4:345.

35. WCF 5.1.

36. Alexandra Walsham, *Providence in Early Modern England* (Oxford: Oxford University Press, 1999), 9.

37. Flavel, *Divine Conduct*, 4:350.

38. Flavel, *Divine Conduct*, 4:350.

good, as an head consulting the welfare of the body."[39] Thus, God's sovereignty always works toward His good purposes for His people. It is in this employment of God's sovereignty for the church's good that Flavel sees the doctrine of God's providence. Cosby notes that Flavel "stresses providence as the personal outworking of sovereignty in everyday life."[40] Or, as the Westminster Confession confirms, "As the providence of God doth, in general, reach to all creatures, so, after a most special manner, it taketh care of his Church, and disposeth all things to the good thereof."[41]

The essence of God's providence is found in the phrase "who performeth all things." This statement, according to Flavel, identifies "the most strict and proper notion of providence, which is nothing else but the performance of God's gracious purposes and promises to his people."[42] Providence is God's work of fulfilling His Word. It is God's payment of what He has pledged. As Flavel declares, "Payment is the performance of promises. Grace makes the promise, and providence the payment."[43] Thus, it is God's providential works that supply the most prominent witness to the truthfulness of His words. They give tangible evidence to His faithfulness. In so doing, they provide tremendous encouragement to the Christian. Such a heartening influence is seen in Flavel's exposition of providence as "universal, effectual, beneficial, and encouraging."[44]

First, God's providence is universal in the following way:

> It hath not only its hand in this or that, but *in all* that concerns them: it hath its eyes upon every thing that relates to them throughout their lives, from first to last; not only great and more important, but the most minute and ordinary affairs of our lives are transacted and managed by it: it touches all things that touch us, whether more nearly or remotely.[45]

---

39. Flavel, *Divine Conduct*, 4:350.
40. Cosby, *Suffering and Sovereignty*, 42.
41. WCF 5.7.
42. Flavel, *Divine Conduct*, 4:345.
43. Flavel, *Divine Conduct*, 4:345.
44. Flavel, *Divine Conduct*, 4:346.
45. Flavel, *Divine Conduct*, 4:346.

There is nothing in all the universe that God does not sovereignly control, and this includes every detail of the believer's life. He is at work in every one of our affairs. Furthermore, Flavel asserts, God's work is not only universal but effectual. Flavel teaches, "Providence doth not only undertake, but [performs] and perfects what concerns us: it goes through with its designs, and accomplishes what it begins: no difficulty clogs it, no cross accidents so falls in its way, but it carries its design through it."[46] God completes every undertaking of His will. None of His purposes can fail.

These truths encourage the heart because they confirm that God's providence is always beneficial to us. "Indeed," says Flavel, "providence neither doth, nor can do anything that is really against the true interest and good of the saints."[47] It is no wonder, therefore, that Flavel sees God's providence as such an encouragement to the soul. He asks, "And if so, how cheering, supporting, and encouraging, must the consideration of these things be, in a day of distress and trouble? What life and hope will it inspire in our hearts and prayers withal, when great pressures lie upon us?"[48] It is this glorious scope of God's providence that frames Flavel's understanding of suffering.

Flavel's all-encompassing view of God's providence leads him to identify God as the ultimate source of suffering. If God has decreed "all things whatsoever come to pass, even the smallest," then "God's hand is to be acknowledged in the greatest afflictions."[49] All afflictions come by the order of God. Flavel submits, "The rod of affliction goes round, and visits all sorts of persons, without difference; it is upon the tabernacles of the just and the unjust, the righteous and the wicked; both are mourning under the rod."[50] While both the just and unjust experience affliction, their sufferings are not equal. The believer's suffering is unique, for its hardship never rises to the heights of God's

---

46. Flavel, *Divine Conduct*, 4:346.
47. Flavel, *Divine Conduct*, 4:346.
48. Flavel, *Divine Conduct*, 4:346.
49. Flavel, *Exposition*, 6:160–61.
50. Flavel, *Token*, 5:623.

goodness in it.[51] It is for this reason that Flavel often refers to these troubles as "afflictive providences."[52]

An afflictive providence, as Cosby explains, is how Flavel affirms "God's sovereignty over affliction" and His "providential design for affliction."[53] It is Flavel's preferred expression for describing how God uses suffering for His sanctifying designs in the believer. "The design and aim of these afflictive providences, is to purge and cleanse them from that pollution into which temptations have plunged them."[54] God ordains these hardships to weaken and suppress the believer's love of the flesh and the world. These "afflictive providences will drive us to the feet of God, and there make us to judge and condemn ourselves."[55] In midst of hardship, believers will desire to draw closer to God and, in so doing, will draw further away from sin. Such communion with God is one end of these afflictive providences. Flavel writes,

> Let not Christians mistake themselves, if when God is smiting, they are humbled, searching their hearts, and blessing God for the discoveries of sin made by their afflictions; admiring his wisdom in timing, moderating, and chusing the rod; kissing it with a childlike submission, and saying, it is good for me that I have been afflicted: That soul hath real communion with God, though it may be for a time without joy. [56]

---

51. It is important to note that Flavel does offer some hope for the unregenerate: "Poor creature! thy case is sad, but yet do not wholly sink and suffer thyself to be swallowed up of grief: thou hast laid thy dear one in the grave, yet throw not thyself headlong into the grave after him; that will not be the way to remedy thy misery: but then sit down a while, and ponder these three things." Flavel, *Token*, 5:624. The last of these considerations is important, for Flavel asserts that "this affliction for which thou mournest, may be the greatest mercy to thee that ever yet befel thee in this world. God hath now made thy heart soft by trouble, shewed thee the vanity of this world, and what a poor trifle it is which thou madest thy happiness: there is now a dark cloud spread over all thy worldly comforts. Now, O now! if the Lord would but strike in this affliction, and by it open thine eyes to see thy deplorable state, and take off thy heart for ever from the vain world, which thou now seest hath nothing in it; and cause thee to chuse Christ, the only abiding good for thy portion" (5:625).

52. For more, see Cosby, *Suffering and Sovereignty*, 48–51.

53. Cosby, *Suffering and Sovereignty*, 48.

54. Flavel, *Divine Conduct*, 4:407.

55. Flavel, *Divine Conduct*, 4:461.

56. Flavel, *England's Duty*, 4:245.

God brings afflictions into the lives of His people, not to hurt them but to help them. In His hands, the most difficult tribulation becomes a means of gain for His people.

Summary

Flavel's theology of suffering recognizes both the reality of sin and its consequences, as well as the certainty of God's control and care. Though all suffering has its root in sin, it is God alone who directs it. This means that, when in the midst of affliction, believers do not look merely at their sin but to their God. Ultimately, it is God who rules over all that comes to pass, and He governs all things for the good of His people. For those who are in Christ, suffering is ultimately good. In fact, such afflictive providences are necessary for believers, given their sin. Flavel exhorts,

> Consider that afflictive providences are of great use to the people of God; they cannot live without them. The earth doth not more need chastening frosts and mellowing snows, than our hearts do nipping providences. Let the best Christian be but a few years without them, and he will be sensible of the want of them; he will find a sad *remission* and declining upon all his graces.[57]

Thus, our sinfulness and God's providence demand that we not despair in suffering but rather rejoice. It is through our suffering that God draws us near to Him and makes His grace sweet to us. We, therefore, should find great joy in carrying the cross.

Flavel's Joy in Suffering

For Flavel, joy in the midst of trial is not only a possibility but an expectation. In view of God's providential care, believers are called to rejoice even in the most difficult afflictions. Flavel declares, "How sad and dismal soever the face of Providence be, yet still maintain spiritual joy and comfort in God under all."[58] Such joy does not imply the absence of pain and sorrow in suffering—rather, believers rejoice

---

57. Flavel, *Divine Conduct*, 4:487–88. Italics in the original.
58. Flavel, *Divine Conduct*, 4:428.

in the midst of the pain and sorrow.[59] Flavel notes, "There is no season wherein spiritual joy and comfort in God is unseasonable."[60] Echoing the apostle Paul's conviction in Philippians 4, Flavel believes that a right understanding of God and our relation to Him is the secret to contentment in all circumstances. He notes, "Spiritual joy or comfort is nothing but the cheerfulness of our heart in God, and the sense of our interest in him, and in his promises."[61] Such cheerfulness is possible in suffering when we remember the promises of God in Christ and reflect upon our standing in Him.

Remember the Promises of God in Christ
Flavel's repeated admonition for suffering Christians is to remember what they have in Christ. They have a Savior whose suffering for them far exceeds any earthly affliction they will ever know. Additionally, it is through His suffering that all of their hardship has been tempered and transformed. Flavel explains, "If Christ died the cursed death of the cross for us, how cheerfully should we submit to, and bear any cross for Jesus Christ?"[62] When we consider the cross of Christ and all that He accomplished for us, we receive strength to rejoice in suffering. To Flavel, such strength arises from three key truths: "First, that we shall carry it but a little way. Secondly, Christ bears the heaviest end of it. Thirdly, innumerable blessings and mercies grow upon the cross of Christ."[63]

Due to Christ's work on the cross, suffering is significantly diminished. The believer's suffering is only earthly. A glorious eternity awaits them. Flavel observes, "Sorrow and the saints are not married together! or suppose it so, heaven shall make a divorce. Our sufferings are but for a while.... They are but the sufferings of the present

---

59. In fact, in this same section, Flavel commends, "When the providences of God are sad and afflictive, either upon the church in general, or your families and persons in particular; then it is seasonable for you to exercise godly sorrow and humility of spirit." Flavel, *Divine Conduct*, 4:428.

60. Flavel, *Divine Conduct*, 4:428.

61. Flavel, *Divine Conduct*, 4:429.

62. Flavel, *Fountain*, 1:329.

63. Flavel, *Fountain*, 1:329

time."[64] Christians will undoubtedly endure affliction with greater fortitude and felicity if they remember the eternal misery from which Christ has delivered them. Flavel exhorts, "What comparison is there betwixt the intermitting sorrows and sufferings of this life, and the continued uninterrupted wrath to come? Our troubles here are not constant, there are gracious relaxations, lucid intervals here; but the wrath to come allows not a moment's ease or mitigation."[65] In Christ, the hardships of this world are bearable, for they are momentary and miniscule in light of the glory that is to come.[66]

According to Flavel, it is the glory of heaven that removes the sting from suffering. First, it reminds us that there is an end to affliction: "That which daunts and amazes men in times of trouble is, that they can see no end of them. Hence the heart faints, and hands hang down through discouragement: but now faith brings the joyful tidings of the end of troubles."[67] A perspective that sees the end with eyes of faith is a great comfort in the darkest trials. "The sweetness of the end," writes Flavel, "will infinitely more than recompense the sorrows and troubles of the way."[68] We rejoice in hardship as we are reminded that Christ's suffering will one day end our suffering.

Christ's suffering for us not only shortens the duration of our suffering but also reduces its intensity, for He "himself bears the heaviest end of it."[69] It is Christ who "divideth sufferings with [us], and takes the largest share to himself."[70] All earthly distress pales in comparison to Christ's. Flavel remarks, "By comparing our sufferings with the sufferings of others, which exceedingly diminisheth and shrinks them up; sometimes the believer compares his sufferings with Christ's, and then he is ashamed that ever he should complain or droop under them."[71] It is difficult to fold under the pressure of our afflictions when considering what Christ endured.

---

64. Flavel, *Fountain*, 1:330.
65. Flavel, *Fountain*, 1:472.
66. Flavel, *Preparations for Suffering*, 6:44.
67. Flavel, *Preparations for Suffering*, 6:44.
68. Flavel, *Method*, 2:286.
69. Flavel, *Fountain*, 1:330.
70. Flavel, *Fountain*, 1:330.
71. Flavel, *Preparations for Suffering*, 6:44.

Christ's suffering is most apparent to believers in their participation in the Lord's Supper. Here, our gaze is set firmly on His suffering for us. Such contemplation emboldens the afflicted believer. Flavel exhorts,

> Is there any among you that are faint-hearted, and ready to shrink away from any sufferings for Christ, as unable to bear and endure any thing for his sake? To such I would say in the words of this text, *Behold the Lamb of God!* Did Christ suffer such grievous things for you! and cannot you suffer small matters for him?… Nothing is found to fortify a man's spirit for suffering, as the meditation of Christ's for us doth.[72]

There is great encouragement in recognizing how and why Christ suffered. In sum, He suffered in our place. Flavel argues, "What are our sufferings to Christ's? Alas, there is no compare; there was more bitterness in one drop of his sufferings than in a sea of ours."[73] So great is the discrepancy between His suffering and ours that it is right to say that He has taken all our sorrows. Flavel proclaims, "So speak as the thing is, Christ doth not only bear half, or the better part, but the whole of our cross and burden. Yea, he bears all, and more than all; for he bears us and our burden too, or else we would quickly sink, and faint under it."[74] Our joy in suffering is made possible in the light of the cross of Christ because it gives us the vantage point to understand God's kindness.

Lastly, Christ's work on the cross transforms our suffering into blessing. Flavel explains, "It is reviving to think what an innumerable multitude of blessings and mercies are the fruit and offspring of a sanc-tified cross."[75] God uses affliction to create and cultivate holiness and happiness in His people. According to Flavel, this is accomplished in five ways. First, God uses suffering to mortify sin: "These troubles are ordered as so many occasions and means to mortify the corruptions that are in their hearts; there are rank weeds springing up in the best soil, which need winter weather to rot them.… Adversity kills those

---

72. Flavel, *Twelve Sacramental Meditations*, 6:416.

73. Flavel, *Twelve Sacramental Meditations*, 6:440.

74. Flavel, *Fountain*, 1:330.

75. Flavel, *Fountain*, 1:331.

corruptions which prosperity bred."[76] These "sanctified providences" are designed to make His people more holy by showing them sin's presence and sin's destruction in their hearts. They are, then, means to greater joy in God. Flavel notes, "Those that have seen and felt the evil of sin in the deep troubles of their spirits for it, will account all reproaches, all losses, all sufferings from men, to be but as nothing to the burthen of sin."[77] Our suffering becomes a joy to us when we realize how God uses it to extinguish the more substantial burden of our sin.

Second, as God uses these trials for our holiness, it becomes more and more apparent that we are indeed children of God. This clearing of our interest in Christ is critical to our rejoicing in suffering. Flavel also reminds his readers that suffering helps to move God's people toward greater communion with Him through spiritual duties. He writes, "By these troubles and distresses, they are awakened to their duties, and taught to pray more frequently, spiritually, and fervently."[78] Our afflictions often aid us to see the insecurity of the world compared with the steadfastness of heaven. This reminds us where our true hope lies and intensifies our desire for God and His grace. Flavel exclaims, "Ah! What drowsiness and formality is apt to creep in upon the best hearts, in the time of prosperity; but when the storm rises, and the sea grows turbulent and raging, now they cry as the disciples to Christ, *Lord, save us, we perish.*"[79] Suffering awakens people to their need of God, exhorting them to draw near to Him, and produces the happiness that can only come from fellowship with Him. It indeed brings blessing after blessing to the believer.

Third, God's mercies through suffering are seen not only in the lives of individual Christians but also in the life of the church. Flavel highlights how suffering promotes the church's good: "These sufferings and trials of the church, are ordained to free it of abundance of hypocrites, which were its reproach, as well as burden."[80] Adversity, while taxing, greatly benefits the church as it acts like a sieve, straining

---

76. Flavel, *Preparations for Suffering*, 6:10.
77. Flavel, *Method*, 2:457.
78. Flavel, *Preparations for Suffering*, 6:11.
79. Flavel, *Preparations for Suffering*, 6:11.
80. Flavel, *Preparations for Suffering*, 6:11.

out those who are not genuine believers, those who are often known only to siphon the life out of God's people. Such winnowing, argues Flavel, occurs only in seasons of difficulty: "Multitudes of hypocrites, like flies in a hot summer, are generated by the church's prosperity; but this winter weather kills them."[81]

Fourth, suffering does not only draw out pretenders from the church but it draws true believers closer to one another. Flavel says, "The church's sufferings are ordered and sanctified, to endear them to each other. Times of common suffering, are times of reconciliation, and greater endearments among the people of God; never more endeared, than when most persecuted; never more united, than when most scattered."[82]

Fifth, such trials most often send God's people to Him. They are made freshly aware of their need. Flavel asserts, "What drowsiness and formality is apt to creep in upon the best hearts, in the time of prosperity; but when the storm rises, and the sea grows turbulent and raging, now they cry as the disciples to Christ, *Lord, save us, we perish*."[83]

For Flavel, God's goodness is never quite as clear on this earth than when hardship comes. To know joy in suffering, then, is to remind ourselves continually of God's gracious promises to us in Christ. Such promises summon us to remember that God has shortened, abated, and transformed all our suffering. For Flavel, these truths are the source of considerable delight for the suffering believer.

Reflecting on Assurance in Christ

These heartening promises only take hold in those who are assured of their standing in Christ. Assurance, therefore, is vital to knowing joy in suffering. Cosby writes, "According to Flavel, cultivating greater assurance of salvation is an important way to experience comfort and hope in the midst of suffering."[84] By God's design, that which is most needed in suffering is best developed in suffering. Suffering leads to an assurance of salvation that produces a joy that sustains us in the

---

81. Flavel, *Preparations for Suffering*, 6:11.
82. Flavel, *Preparations for Suffering*, 6:11.
83. Flavel, *Preparations for Suffering*, 6:11.
84. Cosby, *Suffering and Sovereignty*, 107.

greatest afflictions. It is important, then, to grasp how assurance is both cultivated by suffering and acts as a comfort in suffering.

Flavel views suffering as one of the chief ways we grow in assurance: "Trials are the high way to assurance."[85] The hardships of life lead us to greater confidence concerning our standing in Christ. It is as if God says, "I will try him by prosperity and by adversity, by persecutions and temptations, and he shall see his heart is better than he suspects it to be. This shall be the day of resolution to his fears and doubts."[86] God uses suffering to aid His children in seeing His work in their lives. Such times of adversity test our faith and give us the opportunity to prove our standing in Christ. Thus, Flavel contends, the usual season for assurance is "the times of greatest sufferings for Christ."[87]

Crucial to the development of assurance is recognizing that suffering arises from following Christ. God has designed such persecution to test the believer. Flavel instructs, "The very design and aim of providence in permitting and ordering them, is to try you. The design of Satan is to destroy you; but God's design is to try you."[88] What Satan intends as persecution to harm us, God uses to help us. Such help comes because "the fire of persecution, or sufferings for religion, may be judged intense, and high enough to separate gold and dross."[89] Intense persecution separates the feigned from the faithful. Flavel explains, "A man may serve many masters, if they all command the same things, or things subordinate to each other; but he cannot serve two masters, if their commands clash and interfere with each other: And such are the commands of Christ and the flesh in a suffering hour."[90] In times of suffering, believers will either stand firm in serving Christ or withdraw to serve themselves. By serving Christ they will show themselves to be of Christ. This, in turn, serves to strengthen their assurance. Flavel writes,

> So the discovery of your sincerity will be full of sweetness and joy unspeakable: It will never repent you that you have prayed

---

85. Flavel, *Touchstone*, 5:581.
86. Flavel, *Touchstone*, 5:581.
87. Flavel, *Exposition*, 6:201.
88. Flavel, *Touchstone*, 5:575.
89. Flavel, *Touchstone*, 5:574.
90. Flavel, *Touchstone*, 5:575.

and mourned, that you have trembled and feared, that you have searched and tried: Nay, it will never repent you, that God hath tried you by thousands of sharp afflictions and deep sufferings, if, after all, your sincerity may be fully cleared up to the satisfaction of your souls; for in the same day your sincerity shall be cleared, your title to Christ will be made as clear to your souls as your sincerity is; you may then go to the promises boldly, and take your own Christ into your arms of faith, and say, "My beloved is mine, and I am his!"[91]

The joy of knowing that we belong to Christ is so rich that it brings hope and help in the most desperate situations.

Flavel mentions many advantages of a sincere faith in times of great suffering. A sincere Christian will not "shrink and flinch from Christ in a day of suffering," because "sincere godliness dethrones that idol, the love of this world, in all true Christians."[92] A strong assurance weakens our love of the world by strengthening our love of heaven. We are given a "discovery of better things in heaven," which "will establish and fix [our] spirits, that it shall not be in the power of creatures to shake [us] off from Christ [our] foundation."[93] Not only does a sincere faith wean us from the things of earth but it also focuses our attention on that which is eternal. Flavel explains, "It sets the heart upon heaven, and things eternal.... Surely nothing is more conducive to our stability than this, in the hour of temptation."[94] The assured heart knows its eternal landing place and rests there continually. As a result, the promises of the next world triumph over the temptations of the present world.

Thus, assurance of our standing in Christ imparts a distinctive perspective of life, according to Flavel: "Sincerity takes its measures of present things by the rules of faith and eternity; it goes not by the same reckoning and account that others do, who judge of things by sense, and the respects they have to the present world."[95] Our sufferings are made lighter by this new outlook, for we are reminded that

---

91. Flavel, *Touchstone*, 5:593.
92. Flavel, *Touchstone*, 5:577.
93. Flavel, *Touchstone*, 5:577.
94. Flavel, *Touchstone*, 5:577.
95. Flavel, *Touchstone*, 5:578.

our afflictions are "not worthy to be compared to the glory which shall be revealed in us."[96] Death itself is transformed by the powerful hope which assurance brings. As Flavel declares, "Assurance will call a bloody death a safe passage to Canaan through the Red sea."[97] Death, for the sincere Christian, is but a "wedding-day" and an escape "out of prison."[98] It is a beginning, not an end; a day of delight, not of disaster. There is, therefore, consolation even in the greatest hardships of this life. Flavel proclaims, "A steady eye upon the other world makes us more than conquerors over the troubles of this world."[99]

Furthermore, our assurance in Christ drives us to submit to God's will and make His aim our chief delight. If we know all that Christ has done, and we trust that He has done it for us, then our greatest honor will be to serve Him. Our confidence in Him will fuel a single-minded desire to live for Him, no matter the earthly consequences. As Flavel states, "A man of one only design, puts to all his strength to carry it; nothing can stand before him."[100] Thus, assurance strengthens our resolve and joy, as it becomes our pleasure to follow Christ. Such tested sincerity "is that holy oil which makes the wheels of the soul run nimbly, even in the difficult paths of obedience."[101] When we have confidence that we are a true follower of Christ, we are set free to pursue His good purposes, knowing that even the deepest troubles will not overtake us.

Lastly, notes Flavel, "sincerity knits the soul to Christ, and union with him secures us in the greatest trials."[102] To know that we are in Christ is to enjoy communion with Him, and this assures us that afflictions can never ultimately harm us. It also reminds us that we are never alone in our trials, and that Christ will continually send "fresh supplies" to care for us.[103] For "sincerity alone hath all the heavenly

---

96. Rom. 8:18, as cited by Flavel, *Touchstone*, 5:578.

97. Flavel, *Practical Treatise*, 3:304.

98. Flavel, *Practical Treatise*, 3:304.

99. Flavel, *Touchstone*, 5:579.

100. Flavel, *Touchstone*, 5:578.

101. Flavel, *Touchstone*, 5:578.

102. Flavel, *Touchstone*, 5:577.

103. Here, Flavel also quotes Col. 1:11: "Strengthened with all might, according

aids and assistances to stability, and perseverance in suffering times."[104] To be assured of our standing in Christ is to be assured that we have "Christ's intercession in heaven," "the Spirit's consolation in all [our] troubles," "the beneficial ministry of angels," "a stock of prayers, going up from them all over the world," and "multitudes of precious promises in the scriptures."[105] In light of all these blessings, our afflictions, even death, are made more acceptable. Flavel writes, "Assurance is a lump of sugar, indeed, in the bitter cup of death; nothing sweetens like it…. This puts roses in the pale cheeks of death, and makes it amiable."[106] There is no comfort in suffering like that of having assurance in Christ.

It is clear that Flavel views assurance as that which emboldens the believer in every affliction. He exhorts, "Give the Lord no rest, till your hearts be at rest by the assurance of his love, and the pardon of your sins; when you can boldly say the Lord *is your help*, you will quickly say what immediately follows, *I will not fear what man can do unto me*."[107] It is assurance that erodes our deepest fears of suffering, for we know that in Christ our afflictions are shortened, lightened, and transfigured. These truths enable us to face hardship with the certainty that God is with us. Flavel concludes this regarding assurance:

> In a word it is a sweet support, in all the troubles and afflictions on this side the grave. Let the assured soul be cast into what condition the Lord pleases; be it upon a bed of sickness; yet this gives his soul such support and comfort, that he shall not say, I am sick. Sin being forgiven, the soul is well, when the body is in pain. Let him be cast into a prison, here is that which will turn a prison into a paradise. Let him be pinched with outward want; this will supply all.[108]

It is this joy of assurance that transforms even the most severe difficulty into delight. It is what secures the promises of God's providence

---

to his glorious power, unto all patience and longsuffering with joyfulness." Flavel, *Touchstone*, 5:577.

104. Flavel, *Touchstone*, 5:579.
105. Flavel, *Touchstone*, 5:579.
106. Flavel, *Pneumatologia*, 3:11.
107. Flavel, *Practical Treatise*, 3:304. Italics in the original.
108. Flavel, *Twelve Sacramental Meditations*, 6:453.

into the Christian's own heart and experience. This is why the doctrine of assurance is central to Flavel's life and ministry.

Conclusion

Flavel is not unaware of, or unsympathetic to, the agony of affliction. He knows firsthand that "the cup of sufferings is a very bitter cup" and that "suffering work [is] some of the Christian's hardest labour and exercise."[109] Such difficulty, however, should never lead us to despair. While suffering in itself is a great evil, it is for our good according to God's kind providence. Flavel declares, "Oh! the Christian's suffering time is commonly his clearest and most comfortable time."[110] It is in these times of affliction that we see most clearly our great need and Christ's gracious provision. When all the world seems to be taken from us, we realize that Christ is enough, and cling all the more to Him. In so doing, our interest in Christ becomes more evident to us. Thus, such "sad and afflictive providences, in what kind or degree soever they befall us, we may warrantably conclude they are blessings to us, and come from the love of God."[111] They are, indeed, the "gifts of Christ."[112]

It is this knowledge of God's providence over—and presence in— the most difficult afflictions that strengthens us to rejoice in suffering. Flavel remarks,

> The devil persuades you, that the ways of obedience and strict godliness are a perfect bondage; but if ever God regenerate you, you will find his ways, 'ways of pleasantness, and all his paths peace: you will rejoice in the way of his commandments as much as in all riches:' you will find the worst work Christ puts you about, even suffering work, sweeter than all the pleasures that ever you found in sin.[113]

God uses suffering to helps us to see that we are in Christ. For this reason, says Flavel, "whatever [we] suffer for God suffer it cheerfully."[114]

---

109. Flavel, *Preparations for Suffering*, 6:4, 52–53.
110. Flavel, *Preparations for Suffering*, 6:41.
111. Flavel, *Divine Conduct*, 4:480.
112. Flavel, *England's Duty*, 4:77.
113. Flavel, *Method*, 2:278.
114. Flavel, *Method*, 2:277.

Chapter 9

Conclusion

John Flavel exhibited an acute desire for God's people to find true joy in Him. According to his view, the "main care of a Christian in this world" is to "maintain his joy in God to the last," for "religion is no melancholy thing, but the fountain of all joy and pleasure."[1] Such joy was not merely a central theme of his ministry but a prime feature of his experience. He had tasted the extraordinary delight of knowing he belonged to Christ. As his biographer confirms, "[Flavel] tried himself by the scripture marks of sincerity and regeneration; by this means he attained a well-grounded assurance, the ravishing comforts of which were many times shed abroad in his soul; this made him a powerful and successful preacher, as one who spoke from his own heart to those of others."[2] Flavel's joy was preeminently rooted in assurance—a profound happiness that flowed from his cleared interest in Christ.

Thus, for Flavel, assurance is the wellspring of Christian joy. He asks, "What is the fruit of assurance?" His response: "Joy unspeakable amidst outward troubles."[3] The assurance that one is in Christ produces a delight which is both unspeakable and unshakable. Such joy is more profound and more permanent than anything the world has to offer. It is, says Flavel, the very joy of heaven:

> All gracious souls are sealed objectively, i.e., they have those works of grace wrought on their souls, which do, (as but now was said), ascertain and evidence their title to glory; and in many are

---

1. Flavel, *Exposition*, 6:204.
2. "Life of the Late," 1:xi–xii.
3. Flavel, *Exposition*, 2:201.

sealed formally; that is, the Spirit helps them clearly to discern their interest in Christ, and all the promises. This both secures heaven to the soul in itself, and becomes also an earnest or pledge of that glory in the unspeakable joys and comforts that it produces in the soul.[4]

Those who are sure they are in Christ are also certain of their eternal joy in heaven. This confidence brings heavenly delight into their present lives.[5]

As demonstrated in this book, it is this joy of assurance that forms both the essence and expression of Flavel's spirituality. It is central to his concept of the Christian life because it enlivens the believer. As Flavel declares, "There is nothing in this world, which true Christians more earnestly desire, than to be well assured and satisfied of the love of Jesus Christ to their souls."[6] Such assurance is "the pleasure of life; yea, the most rational, pure, and transporting pleasure. What is life without pleasure? And what pleasure is there in the world, comparable to this pleasure? For let the sealed and assured believer consider, and compare; and he must needs find a joy and pleasure, beyond the joy of the whole earth."[7] When this joy of assurance animates the believer's life, it strengthens him in every circumstance: "It is a fountain of joy and comfort in the darkest and saddest hour.... [It] is the oil that makes the chariot-wheels of the soul free to follow the Lord."[8] What is most desirable for the Christian is that which is most helpful to the Christian. This makes assurance the believer's chief pursuit. In short, it is "that which will turn a prison into a paradise,"[9] according to Flavel.

For this reason, Flavel repeatedly calls his congregation to pursue the joy of assurance. He exhorts, "You that have received Jesus Christ truly, give yourselves no rest till you are fully satisfied that you have

---

4. Flavel, *Fountain*, 6:201.

5. Flavel is quick to note, however, that such joy, while of the same type as that of heaven, is not of the same degree. He explains, "It hath the very scent and taste of heaven in it, and there is but a gradual difference betwixt it and the joy of heaven." Flavel, *England's Duty*, 4:218.

6. Flavel, *Twelve Sacramental Meditations*, 6:451.

7. Flavel, *Twelve Sacramental Meditations*, 6:452.

8. Flavel, *Preparations for Suffering*, 6:39.

9. Flavel, *Twelve Sacramental Meditations*, 6:453.

done so; acceptance brings you to heaven hereafter, but assurance will bring heaven into your souls now."[10] Such joy of assurance, then, is not only the essence of Flavel's spirituality but it is its expression. It is not only the motivation for the Christian life but its greatest manifestation. Believers, therefore, ought to pursue the joy of God which is only theirs in Christ. According to Flavel, the Christian life ought to be lived in a way that seeks this joy of assurance. Thus, he repeatedly exhorts his people to consider deeply the wonders of the triune God, to obey lovingly the commands of God, and to turn intentionally to the things of God. Here, the primary features of Flavel's spirituality (that is, looking to Christ, discerning the Spirit, obeying the law, keeping the heart, and carrying the cross) are on full display. As Christians engage in these, they grow more confident of their standing in Christ, and thus experience more delight in God. In this way, they arrive at "the very desire of [their] heart[s]."[11] For the sake of his people's joy, Flavel continually called them to seek greater certainty of their interest in Christ, and reminded them again and again of the ordinary means of doing so. He knew of nothing that would bring greater joy, for the joy of assurance is the very marrow of the Christian life well lived.

Before concluding this book, a few remarks concerning the significance of its thesis (namely, the joy of assurance as the essence and expression of Flavel's spirituality) are needed. First, it sheds light on the relationship between joy and assurance in Puritan thought, which in turn contributes to a better understanding of Puritan spirituality. The Puritans' emphasis on the doctrine of assurance is well-documented, but very little attention has been given to why they elevated it to such a prominent position in the Christian life. This study of Flavel exhibits one important reason—namely, the inextricable link between joy and assurance. This observation serves as a corrective to those who see the Puritan pursuit of assurance as an expression of overscrupulous legalism. In his cultivation of assurance, Flavel was not obsessed with law but grace, and he was not compelled by fear but love. In sum, his aim was joy. It was this emphasis, as demonstrated in this book, that informed his spirituality, in that it (1) shaped his approach to the

---

10. Flavel, *Method*, 2:138.
11. Flavel, *Method*, 2:138.

means of grace, (2) compelled him to obey God's law, (3) motivated him to keep his heart with all diligence, and (4) strengthened him amid suffering.

Second, it provides a much-needed glimpse into the life and ministry of one of the most consequential, yet neglected, religious figures of seventeenth-century England. As Sinclair Ferguson observes, "[Flavel] illustrated the Puritan vision of the godly minister and faithful preacher."[12] This work contributes to a better understanding of this influential figure—particularly, what shaped his approach to pastoral ministry. In brief, he labored to bring others to the joy of assurance. Much could be said concerning his polemical engagement and political involvement, but these are secondary to Flavel's concern for his people's spiritual good. He was convinced that the best thing he could do for them was to point them to Christ as the wellspring of assurance and, therefore, of joy. This concern is prevalent throughout his sermon material and led him to focus consistently on the theme of Christ's mediatorial work as the only foundation of peace and comfort. He declares, "To your work, Christian, to your work.… Whatever communion God and the soul maintains, it is in this way. Count all, therefore, but dross in comparison to that excellency which is the knowledge of Jesus Christ."[13]

Third, it speaks to the contemporary church by highlighting Flavel's remarkable ministry, which arose from his supreme delight in knowing that he belonged to Christ. It is this joy-filled spirituality that profoundly influenced Jonathan Edwards, George Whitefield, Charles Spurgeon (1834–1892), Archibald Alexander (1772–1851), and others, thereby ensuring Flavel's legacy.[14] And it is this joy-filled assurance that is still needed today. Given the widespread prevalence of false (or at least inadequate) notions of both joy and assurance in our day, the church stands in need of those who have trodden the path of a biblically informed doctrine of assurance. Flavel is a tremendous exemplar of what it means to cultivate a cheerfulness of heart founded upon a sense of one's interest in Christ. "All the comforts of believers," says he,

---

12. Sinclair Ferguson, "The Mystery of Providence," 212.

13. Flavel, *Fountain*, 1:42.

14. See Cosby, "John Flavel: The Lost Puritan," 124–29.

"are streams from this fountain."[15] Again, "Take away the knowledge of Christ, and a Christian is the most sad and melancholy creature in the world. Let Christ but manifest himself, and dart the beams of his light into their souls, it will make them kiss the stakes, sing in flames, and shout in the pangs of death."[16] Persuaded of this, Flavel emphasized the importance of cultivating the knowledge of Christ in the soul: "All other knowledge, however pleasant and profitable, is not worthy to be named in the same sentence with the knowledge of Christ."[17] Christ is the fountain of assurance and, therefore, the fountain of joy, and it is this joyful assurance that constitutes the essence and expression of John Flavel's spirituality.

---

15. Flavel, *Fountain*, 1:35.
16. Flavel, *Fountain*, 1:35.
17. Flavel, *Fountain*, 1:34.

Bibliography

Primary Sources

Ambrose, Isaac. *Looking unto Jesus: A View of the Everlasting Gospel.* London, 1658.

Arrowsmith, John. *Theanthropos; or, God-Man: Being an Exposition upon the First Eighteen Verses of the First Chapter of the Gospel according to St John.* London, 1660.

Augustine. *On Christian Doctrine.* In *Works of Aurelius Augustine,* edited by Marcus Dods, 9:1–171. Edinburgh: T & T Clark, 1892.

Baxter, Richard. *The Practical Works of the Rev. Richard Baxter.* Vol. 2. London: James Duncan, 1830.

Bolton, Samuel. *The True Bounds of Christian Freedom.* 1645. Reprint, Edinburgh: Banner of Truth Trust, 2020.

Brooks, Thomas. *The Complete Works of Thomas Brooks.* Edited by A. B. Grosart. Vol. 2. London: James Nisbet, 1866.

———. *Heaven on Earth: A Treatise on Christian Assurance.* 1654. Reprint, Edinburgh: Banner of Truth Trust, 2004.

———. *The Works of Thomas Brooks.* Edited by Alexander Balloch Grosart. 1861–1867. Reprint, Edinburgh: Banner of Truth Trust, 1980.

Burgess, Anthony. *Spiritual Refining: or, A Treatise of Grace and Assurance.* London: A. Miller, 1652.

Calamy, Edmund, and Samuel Palmer. *The Nonconformist's Memorial.* Vol. 2. London, 1802.

Calvin, John. *Commentaries on the Epistle of Paul to the Romans.* Edited and translated by John Owen. Vol. 19. *Calvin's Commentaries.* Grand Rapids: Baker, 2003.

———. *Institutes of the Christian Religion.* Edited by John T. McNeill. Translated by Ford Lewis Battles. 2 vols. Louisville: Westminster John Knox Press, 2006.

Cary, Philip. *A Just Reply to Mr. John Flavell's Arguments, by Way of Answer to a Discourse Lately Published, Entitled, A Solemn Call.* London: J. Harris, 1690.

Cheynell, Francis. *The Divine Triunity of the Father, Son, and Holy Spirit.* London, 1650.

Durham, James. *Christ Crucified; or, The Marrow of the Gospel in 72 Sermons on Isaiah 53.* Edinburgh, 1683.

Edwards, Jonathan. *Religious Affections.* In *Works of Jonathan Edwards.* Edited by John E. Smith. Vol. 2. New Haven, Conn.: Yale University Press, 1959.

———. *Sermons and Discourses, 1743–1758.* In *Works of Jonathan Edwards.* Edited by Wilson H. Kimnach. Vol. 25. New Haven, Conn.: Yale University Press, 2006.

———. *Typological Writings.* In *Works of Jonathan Edwards.* Edited by Wallace E. Anderson, Mason I. Lowance Jr., and David H. Walters. Vol. 11. New Haven, Conn.: Yale University Press, 1993.

Elys, Edmond. *Reflections upon Several Passages in a Book Entitled, The Reasonableness of a Personal Reformation, and The Necessity of Conversion, with a Letter to Mr. John Galpine, Concerning His Printed Encomuim to J. F.* London, 1692.

Flavel, John. *Antipharmacum Saluberrimum: A Serious and Seasonable Caveat to All the Saints in This Hour of Temptation.* In *Works of John Flavel,* 4:515–57. 1820. Reprint, Edinburgh: Banner of Truth Trust, 2015.

———. *The Balm of the Covenant Applied to the Bleeding Wounds of Afflicted Saints: II Samuel 23.5.* In *Works of John Flavel,* 6:83–119. 1820. Reprint, Edinburgh: Banner of Truth Trust, 2015.

———. *A Brief Account of the Rise and Growth of Antinomianism, with Reflections upon the Errors of the Sect*. In *Works of John Flavel*, 3:551–91. 1820. Reprint, Edinburgh: Banner of Truth Trust, 2015.

———. *A Caution to Seamen: A Dissuasive against Several Horrid and Detestable Sins*. In *Works of John Flavel*, 5:293–342. 1820. Reprint, Edinburgh: Banner of Truth Trust, 2015.

———. *The Character of an Evangelical Pastor Drawn by Christ*. In *Works of John Flavel*, 6:564–85. 1820. Reprint, Edinburgh: Banner of Truth Trust, 2015.

———. *A Coronation Sermon: Preached at Dartmouth to Celebrate the Coronation of William III and Mary II on 11 April, 1689*. In *Works of John Flavel*, 6:545–63. 1820. Reprint, Edinburgh: Banner of Truth Trust, 2015.

———. *Divine Conduct or the Mystery of Providence: A Treatise upon Psalm 57.2*. In *Works of John Flavel*, 4:336–497. 1820. Reprint, Edinburgh: Banner of Truth Trust, 2015.

———. *England's Duty under the Present Gospel Liberty*. In *Works of John Flavel*, 4:3–306. 1820. Reprint, Edinburgh: Banner of Truth Trust, 2015.

———. *An Exposition of the Assembly's Shorter Catechism*. In *Works of John Flavel*, 6:138–317. 1820. Reprint, Edinburgh: Banner of Truth Trust, 2015.

———. *A Familiar Conference between a Minister and a Doubting Christian Concerning the Sacrament of the Lord's Supper*. In *Works of John Flavel*, 6:460–69. 1820. Reprint, Edinburgh: Banner of Truth Trust, 2015.

———. *The Fountain of Life: A Display of Christ in His Essential and Mediatorial Glory*. In *Works of John Flavel*, 1:17–561. 1820. Reprint, Edinburgh: Banner of Truth Trust, 2015.

———. *Gospel Unity Recommended to the Churches of Christ*. In *Works of John Flavel*, 3:592–608. 1820. Reprint, Edinburgh: Banner of Truth Trust, 2015.

————. *Husbandry Spiritualized: The Heavenly Use of Earthly Things.* In *Works of John Flavel*, 5:3–205. 1820. Reprint, Edinburgh: Banner of Truth Trust, 2015.

————. *A Hymn upon Romans 5.6–11.* In *Works of John Flavel*, 6:469–70. 1820. Reprint, Edinburgh: Banner of Truth Trust, 2015.

————. *The Method of Grace in the Gospel Redemption.* In *Works of John Flavel*, 2:3–474. 1820. Reprint, Edinburgh: Banner of Truth Trust, 2015.

————. *Mount Pisgah: A Sermon Preached at the Public Thanksgiving, February 14, 1688–89, for England's Delivery from Popery.* In *Works of John Flavel*, 4:307–35. 1820. Reprint, Edinburgh: Banner of Truth Trust, 2015.

————. *A Narrative of Some Late and Wonderful Sea Deliveries.* In *Works of John Flavel*, 4:497–515. 1820. Reprint, Edinburgh: Banner of Truth Trust, 2015.

————. *Navigation Spiritualized: A New Compass for Seamen.* In *Works of John Flavel*, 5:206–93. 1820. Reprint, Edinburgh: Banner of Truth Trust, 2015.

————. *The Occasions, Causes, Nature, Rise, Growth and Remedies of Mental Errors.* In *Works of John Flavel*, 3:413–92. 1820. Reprint, Edinburgh: Banner of Truth Trust, 2015.

————. *Pneumatologia: A Treatise of the Soul of Man.* In *Works of John Flavel*, 2:475–3:238. 1820. Reprint, Edinburgh: Banner of Truth Trust, 2015.

————. *A Practical Treatise of Fear.* In *Works of John Flavel*, 3:239–320. 1820. Reprint, Edinburgh: Banner of Truth Trust, 2015.

————. *Preparations for Suffering, or The Best Work in the Worst Times.* In *Works of John Flavel*, 6:3–83. 1820. Reprint, Edinburgh: Banner of Truth Trust, 2015.

————. *The Reasonableness of Personal Reformation and the Necessity of Conversion.* In *Works of John Flavel*, 6:470–545. 1820. Reprint, Edinburgh: Banner of Truth Trust, 2015.

————. *The Righteous Man's Refuge.* In *Works of John Flavel*, 3:321–413. 1820. Reprint, Edinburgh: Banner of Truth Trust, 2015.

————. *A Saint Indeed, or The Great Work of a Christian Explained and Applied.* In *Works of John Flavel,* 5:417–509. 1820. Reprint, Edinburgh: Banner of Truth Trust, 2015.

————. *The Seaman's Companion: Six Sermons on the Mysteries of Providence as Relating to Seamen; and the Sins, Dangers, Duties and Troubles of Seamen.* In *Works of John Flavel,* 5:342–416. 1820. Reprint, Edinburgh: Banner of Truth Trust, 2015.

————. *A Sermon Preached at the Funeral of John Upton, of Lupton (Devon): II Chronicles 35.24–25.* In *Works of John Flavel,* 6:120–37. 1820. Reprint, Edinburgh: Banner of Truth Trust, 2015.

————. *Tidings from Rome or England's Alarm.* In *Works of John Flavel,* 4:557–86. 1820. Reprint, Edinburgh: Banner of Truth Trust, 2015.

————. *A Token for Mourners.* In *Works of John Flavel,* 5:604–66. 1820. Reprint, Edinburgh: Banner of Truth Trust, 2015.

————. *The Touchstone of Sincerity, or The Signs of Grace and the Symptoms of Hypocrisy.* In *Works of John Flavel,* 5:509–604. 1820. Reprint, Edinburgh: Banner of Truth Trust, 2015.

————. *Twelve Sacramental Meditations Upon Select Places of Scripture, to Prepare Believers for the Ordinance of the Lord's Supper.* In *Works of John Flavel,* 6:378–460. 1820. Reprint, Edinburgh: Banner of Truth Trust, 2015.

————. *A Two-Column Table of the Sins and Duties Attaching to Church Membership.* In *Works of John Flavel,* 6:586–89. 1820. Reprint, Edinburgh: Banner of Truth Trust, 2015.

————. *Vindiciae Legis et Foederis, or A Reply to Mr. Philip Cary's Solemn Call in which He Contends Against the Right of Believers' Infants to Baptism.* In *Works of John Flavel,* 6:318–78. 1820. Reprint, Edinburgh: Banner of Truth Trust, 2015.

————. *Vindiciarum Vindex: A Refutation of Mr. Philip Cary's Rejoinder to My Defence of the Right of Believers' Infants to Baptism.* In *Works of John Flavel,* 3:493–550. 1820. Reprint, Edinburgh: Banner of Truth Trust, 2015.

Galpine, John. "A Short Life of John Flavel." In *Flavel, the Quaker, and the Crown: John Flavel, Clement Lake, and Religious Liberty in*

Seventeenth-Century England. Cambridge, Mass.: Rhwhym Books, 2000.

Gillies, John. *Memoirs of the Life of Reverend George Whitefield.* New Haven, Conn.: Joseph Barber, 1812.

Goodwin, Thomas. *The Heart of Christ in Heaven Towards Sinners on Earth.* In *Works of Thomas Goodwin D. D.* Vol. 5. London, 1681–1704.

———. *Of Christ the Mediator.* In *Works of Thomas Goodwin D. D.* Vol. 5. London, 1681–1704.

———. *The Works of Thomas Goodwin, D. D.* Edited by John C. Miller. 12 vols. Edinburgh: James Nichol, 1861–1867.

———. *The Works of Thomas Goodwin.* Vol. 4. Grand Rapids: Reformation Heritage Books, 2006.

Gouge, William. *A Learned and Very Useful Commentary upon the Whole Epistle to the Hebrews.* London, 1655.

Keach, Benjamin. *The Rector Rectified and Corrected, with Some Remarks upon Mr. John Flavel's Last Book in Answer to Mr. Philip Cary by Benjamin Keach.* London: John Harris, 1692.

Lake, Clement. *Something by Way of Testimony concerning Clement Lake of Crediton in Devonshire; with Something He Wrote in His Life Time, by Way of Answer, unto John Flavell, Independent Preacher of Dartmouth.* London: T. Sowle, 1692.

"The Life of the Late Rev. Mr. John Flavel, Minister of Dartmouth." In *Works of John Flavel,* 1:iii–xvi. 1820. Reprint, Edinburgh: Banner of Truth Trust, 2015.

Mather, Increase. *Memoirs of the life of the late reverend Increase Mather, D. D.* London: John Clark, 1725.

———. "Preface to the Reader." In Flavel, *England's Duty under the Present Gospel Liberty.* London: J. R., 1689.

Owen, John. *Christologia, or, A Declaration of the Glorious Mystery of the Person of Christ.* In *Works of John Owen,* 12:3–339. London: Johnstone and Hunter, 1850–1855.

———. *Communion with God.* Edited by R. J. K. Law. 1657. Reprint, Edinburgh: Banner of Truth Trust, 1991.

———. *Meditations and Discourses on the Glory of Christ Applied.* In *Works of John Owen*, 12:343–526. London: Johnstone and Hunter, 1850–1855.

———. *Of Communion with God the Father, Son, and Holy Ghost, Each Person Distinctly, in Love, Grace, and Consolation; or, The Saint's Fellowship with the Father, Son, and Holy Ghost Unfolded.* In *Works of John Owen.* Edited by William H. Gould. Vol. 2. 1850–1853. Reprint, Edinburgh: Banner of Truth Trust, 1980.

———. *On the Mortification of Sin in Believers.* In *Works of John Owen*, edited by Richard Rushing, 6:5–87. Edinburgh: Banner of Truth Trust, 1968.

Perkins, William. *The Works of That Famous and Worthy Minister of Christ, Mr. William Perkins.* Vol. 1. London: John Legatt, 1612.

Rutherford, Samuel. *The Covenant of Life Opened.* Edinburgh: Andro Anderson, 1655.

Sibbes, Richard. *The Complete Works of Richard Sibbes.* Edited by A. B. Grosart. Vol. 3. London: James Nisbet, 1862.

———. *An Exposition of 2nd Corinthians Chapter One.* In *Works of Richard Sibbes.* Edited by Alexander B. Grosart. Vol. 3. 1862–1864. Reprint, Edinburgh: Banner of Truth Trust, 1981.

———. *A Fountain Sealed.* In *Works of Richard Sibbes.* Edited by Alexander B. Grosart. Vol. 6. 1862–1864. Reprint, Edinburgh: Banner of Truth Trust, 1978.

———. *The Witness of Salvation.* In *Works of Richard Sibbes.* Edited by Alexander B. Grosart. Vol. 7. 1862–1864. Reprint, Edinburgh: Banner of Truth Trust, 1982.

———. *Works of Richard Sibbes.* Edited by Alexander B. Grosart. 7 vols. 1862–1864. Reprint, Edinburgh: Banner of Truth Trust, 1973.

———. *Yea and Amen; or, Precious Promises and Privileges.* In *Works of Richard Sibbes.* Edited by Alexander B. Grosart. Vol. 4. 1862–1864. Reprint, Edinburgh: Banner of Truth Trust, 1983.

Watson, Thomas. *The Godly Man's Picture.* 1666. Reprint, Edinburgh: Banner of Truth, 1992.

Wood, Anthony à. *Athenae Oxonienses: An Exact History of all the Writers and Bishops who have had their Education in the University of Oxford.* Vol. 4. London: T. Bennet, 1691–1692.

Secondary Sources

Alexander, Archibald. *Practical Truths.* New York: American Tract Society, 1857.

Allen, Lewis James Greenwood. "The Theologian as Pastor: The Life, Times and Ministry of John Flavel." ThM thesis, Westminster Theological Seminary, 2014.

Beck, Peter. "'The Fountain of Life': The Excellency of Christ in the Preaching of John Flavel." *Puritan Reformed Journal* 5, no. 1 (2013): 43–57.

Beeke, Joel R. *Assurance of Faith: Calvin, English Puritanism, and the Dutch Second Reformation.* American University Studies 89. New York: Peter Lang, 1991.

———. "Does Assurance Belong to the Essence of Faith? Calvin and the Calvinists." *The Master's Seminary Journal* 5, no. 1 (1994): 43–71.

———. *Knowing and Growing in Assurance of Faith.* Fearn, Scotland: Christian Focus, 2017.

———. "Personal Assurance of Faith: The Puritans and Chapter 18.2 of the Westminster Confession." *Westminster Theological Journal* 55, no. 1 (1993): 1–30.

———. *Puritan Evangelism.* Grand Rapids: Reformation Heritage Books, 1999.

———. *Puritan Reformed Spirituality: A Practical Theological Study from Our Reformed and Puritan Heritage.* Webster, N.Y.: Evangelical Press, 2006.

———. *The Quest for Full Assurance: The Legacy of Calvin and His Successors.* Edinburgh: Banner of Truth, 1999.

———. *A Reader's Guide to Reformed Literature: An Annotated Bibliography of Reformed Theology*. Grand Rapids: Reformation Heritage Books, 1999.

Beeke, Joel R., and Mark Jones. *A Puritan Theology: Doctrine for Life*. Grand Rapids: Reformation Heritage Books, 2012.

Beeke, Joel R., and Randall J. Pederson, eds. *Meet the Puritans*. Grand Rapids: Reformation Heritage Books, 2006.

Berkhof, Louis. *The Assurance of Faith*. Grand Rapids: Eerdmans, 1939.

———. *Systematic Theology*. 4th ed. Grand Rapids: Eerdmans, 1996.

Boone, Clifford B. *Puritan Evangelism: Preaching for Conversion in Late Seventeenth-Century English Puritanism as Seen in the Works of John Flavel*. London: Paternoster, 2013.

Bremer, Francis J. *Puritanism: A Very Short Introduction*. Oxford: Oxford University Press, 2009.

Bremer, Francis J., and Tom Webster, eds. *Puritans and Puritanism in Europe and America: A Comprehensive Encyclopedia*. Santa Barbara, Calif.: ABC-CLIO, 2006.

Calamy, Edmund, and A. G. Matthews. *Calamy Revised: Being a Revision of Edmund Calamy's Account of the Ministers and Others Ejected and Silenced, 1660–1662*. Oxford: Oxford University Press, 1988.

Carruthers, S. W., and Westminster Assembly. *The Confession of Faith*. Glasgow: Free Presbyterian Publications, 1958.

Chang, Kwai Sing. "John Flavel of Dartmouth, 1630–1691." PhD diss., University of Edinburgh, 1952.

Coffey, John. *Persecution and Toleration in Protestant England, 1558–1689*. Studies in Modern History. Harlow, England: Longman, 2000.

Coffey, John, and Paul C. H. Lim, eds. *The Cambridge Companion to Puritanism*. Cambridge Companions to Religion. Cambridge: Cambridge University Press, 2008.

Como, David R. *Blown by the Spirit: Puritanism and the Emergence of an Antinomian Underground in Pre–Civil-War England*. Stanford, Calif.: Stanford University Press, 2004.

Cosby, Brian H. "The Christology of John Flavel." *Puritan Reformed Journal* 4, no. 1 (January 2012): 116–34.

———. "John Flavel: The Lost Puritan." *Puritan Reformed Journal* 3, no. 1 (January 2011): 113–32.

———. *John Flavel: Puritan Life and Thought in Stuart England.* Lanham, MD: Lexington Books, 2014.

———. *Suffering and Sovereignty: John Flavel and the Puritans on Afflictive Providence.* Grand Rapids: Reformation Heritage Books, 2012.

———. "The Theology of Suffering and Sovereignty as Seen in the Writings and Ministry of John Flavel, c. 1630–1691." PhD diss., Australian College of Theology, 2012.

———. "Toward a Definition of 'Puritan' and 'Puritanism': A Study in Puritan Historiography." *Churchman* 122, no. 4 (Winter 2008): 297–314.

Dallimore, Arnold A. *George Whitefield: The Life and Times of the Great Evangelist of the Eighteenth-Century Revival.* 2 vols. Edinburgh: Banner of Truth Trust, 1970.

Dandelion, Pink. *An Introduction to Quakerism.* Cambridge: Cambridge University Press, 2007.

de Reuver, Arie. *Sweet Communion: Trajectories of Spirituality from the Middle Ages through the Further Reformation.* Grand Rapids: Reformation Heritage Books, 2007.

Dever, Mark E. "Calvin, Westminster and Assurance." In *The Westminster Confession into the 21st Century*, edited by J. Ligon Duncan III, 303–41. Vol. 1. Fearn, Scotland: Christian Focus, 2003.

———. *Richard Sibbes: Puritanism and Calvinism in Late Elizabethan and Early Stuart England.* Macon, Ga.: Mercer University Press, 2000.

Di Gangi, Mariano, ed. *Great Themes in Puritan Preaching.* Guelph, Ont.: Joshua Press, 2007.

Downey, E. A. "Law in Luther and Calvin." *Theology Today* 41 (1984): 146–53.

Dulles, Avery. *The Assurance of Things Hoped For: A Theology of Christian Faith*. New York: Oxford University Press, 1994.

Duncan, J. Ligon, III, ed. *The Westminster Confession into the 21st Century*. Vol. 1. Fearn, Scotland: Christian Focus, 2003.

Embry, Adam, ed. *An Honest, Well-Experienced Heart: The Piety of John Flavel*. Profiles in Reformed Spirituality. Grand Rapids: Reformation Heritage Books, 2012.

———. "John Flavel's Theology of the Holy Spirit." *The Southern Baptist Journal of Theology* 14, no. 4 (Winter 2010): 84–99.

———. "Keeper of the Great Seal of Heaven: Sealing of the Spirit in the Thought of John Flavel." ThM thesis, The Southern Baptist Theological Seminary, 2008.

———. *Keeper of the Great Seal of Heaven: Sealing of the Spirit in the Thought of John Flavel*. Grand Rapids: Reformation Heritage Books, 2011.

Ferguson, Sinclair. *John Owen on the Christian Life*. Edinburgh: Banner of Truth Trust, 1987.

———. "The Mystery of Providence." In *The Devoted Life: An Invitation to the Puritan Classics*, edited by Kelly M. Kapic and Randall C. Gleason, 211–24. Downers Grove, Ill.: InterVarsity Press, 2004.

———. *The Whole Christ: Legalism, Antinomianism, and Gospel Assurance; Why the Marrow Controversy Still Matters*. Wheaton, Ill.: Crossway, 2016.

Fesko, John. "John Owen on Union with Christ and Justification." *Themelios* 37, no. 1 (2012): 7–19.

———. *The Theology of the Westminster Standards: Historical Context and Theological Insights*. Wheaton, Ill.: Crossway, 2014.

George, Timothy. *Theology of the Reformers*. Nashville: Broadman, 1988.

Gleason, Randall C. *John Calvin and John Owen on Mortification: A Comparative Study in Reformed Spirituality*. New York: Peter Lang, 1995.

Godfrey, W. R. "Law and Gospel." In *New Dictionary of Theology*, edited by S. B. Ferguson, D. F. Wright, and J. I. Packer, 379. Downers Grove, Ill.: InterVarsity, 1988.

Gratsch, Edward J., ed. *Principles of Catholic Theology: A Synthesis of Dogma and Morals*. New York: Alba House, 1981.

Gwyn-Thomas, J. "The Puritan Doctrine of Christian Joy." In *Puritan Papers: Vol. 2, 1960–1962*, edited by J. I. Packer, 119–40. Phillipsburg, N.J.: P&R, 2001.

Hall, David D. *The Antinomian Controversy 1636–1638: A Documentary History*. Durham, N.C.: Duke University Press, 1990.

Hambrick-Stowe, Charles E. *The Practice of Piety: Puritan Devotional Disciplines in Seventeenth-Century New England*. Chapel Hill: University of North Carolina Press, 1982.

Hawkes, R. M. "The Logic of Assurance in English Puritan Theology." *Westminster Theological Journal* 52, no. 2 (September 1990): 247–61.

Hedges, Brian G. *Watchfulness: Recovering a Lost Spiritual Discipline*. Grand Rapids: Reformation Heritage Books, 2018.

Helm, Paul. *Calvin and the Calvinists*. Edinburgh: Banner of Truth Trust, 1982.

Hesselink, I. John. *Calvin's Concept of the Law*. Allison Park, Pa.: Pickwick, 1992.

Hill, Christopher. *The Century of Revolution, 1603–1714*. New York: W. W. Norton, 1980.

———. *Puritanism and Revolution: Studies in Interpretation of the English Revolution of the 17th Century*. New York: St. Martin's Press, 1997.

———. *Society and Puritanism in Pre-Revolutionary England*. New York: St. Martin's Press, 1997.

Horton, Michael Scott, and J. Matthew Pinson, eds. *Four Views on Eternal Security*. Counterpoints. Grand Rapids: Zondervan, 2002.

Howe, John. *A Treatise of Delighting in God*. Edited by C. Matthew McMahon and Therese B. McMahon. Coconut Creek, Fla.: Puritan

Publications, 2012. Google Books. https://books.google.com /books?id=-bFDBQAAQBAJ.

———. *The Works of John Howe: As Published During His Life*. Vol. 1. London: William Tegg, 1848.

Jones, Mark. *Antinomianism: Reformed Theology's Unwelcome Guest?* Phillipsburg, N.J.: P&R, 2013.

———. *Why Heaven Kissed Earth: The Christology of the Puritan Reformed Orthodox Theologian, Thomas Goodwin (1600–1680)*. Gottingen: Vandenhoeck & Ruprecht, 2010.

Kapic, Kelly M., and Randall C. Gleason, eds. *The Devoted Life: An Invitation to the Puritan Classics*. Downers Grove, Ill.: InterVarsity Press, 2004.

Kelly, James William. "Flavell, John (bap. 1630, d. 1691)." In *Oxford Dictionary of National Biography*, edited by H. C. G. Matthew and Brian Harrison. Oxford: Oxford University Press, 2004.

Kevan, Ernest F. *The Grace of Law: A Study in Puritan Theology*. Morgan, Pa.: Soli Deo Gloria, 1997.

Knappen, M. M. *Tudor Puritanism*. Chicago: Chicago University Press, 1939.

Leith, John H. *Assembly at Westminster: Reformed Theology in the Making*. Richmond, Va.: John Knox Press, 1973.

———. *John Calvin's Doctrine of the Christian Life*. Louisville: Westminster John Knox Press, 1989.

Letham, Robert. *The Westminster Assembly: Reading Its Theology in Historical Context*. Phillipsburg, N.J.: P&R, 2009.

Life of Rev. John Flavell, of Dartmouth. Christian Biography. London, 1834.

Lloyd-Jones, Martyn. *The Puritans: Their Origins and Successors*. Edinburgh: Banner of Truth, 1987.

Lovelace, Richard F. *Dynamics of Spiritual Life: An Evangelical Theology of Renewal*. Downers Grove, Ill.: InterVarsity, 1979.

MacLeod, Donald. "Luther and Calvin on the Place of the Law." In *Living the Christian Life: Papers Read at the 1974 Westminster Conference*, 5–13. London: Westminster Conference, 1974.

Macleod, Ian. "True and Nominal Christians Distinguished." *Puritan Reformed Journal* 9, no. 1 (January 2017): 197–214.

Marsden, George. *Jonathan Edwards: A Life*. New Haven, Conn.: Yale University Press, 2003.

Marshall, I. Howard. *Kept by the Power of God: A Study of Perseverance and Falling Away*. 2nd ed. Minneapolis: Bethany Fellowship, 1974.

McCallum, Douglas. "The Christology of John Flavel." ThM thesis, Westminster Theological Seminary, 2017.

McGrath, Alister E. *Christian Spirituality: An Introduction*. Oxford: Blackwell, 1999.

———. *Christian Theology: An Introduction*. 5th ed. Chichester, England: Wiley-Blackwell, 2011.

Miller, Perry. *The New England Mind: From Colony to Province*. Cambridge, Mass.: Harvard University Press, 1953.

Mitchell, Alexander F. *The Westminster Assembly: Its History and Standards; Being the Baird Lectures for 1882*. Philadelphia: Presbyterian Board of Publication and Sabbath-School Work, 1897.

Murray, Iain H. "John Flavel." *Banner of Truth Magazine*, no. 60. September, 1968.

———. *The Puritan Hope: Revival and the Interpretation of Prophecy*. Edinburgh: Banner of Truth Trust, 1971.

Murray, John J. "John Flavel and the Problem of Providence." In *Triumph through Tribulation: Papers Read at the 1998 Westminster Conference*, 99–118. London: Westminster Conference, 1998.

———. *Redemption Accomplished and Applied*. Grand Rapids: William B. Eerdmans, 2015.

Noll, Mark A. "John Wesley and the Doctrine of Assurance." *Bibliotheca Sacra* 132, no. 526 (April 1975): 161–77.

Nuttall, Geoffrey F. *The Holy Spirit in Puritan Faith and Experience*. Chicago: University of Chicago Press, 1992.

———. *Visible Saints: The Congregational Way, 1640–1660*. Oxford: Basil Blackwell, 1957.

Nuttall, Geoffrey F., and Owen Chadwick, eds. *From Uniformity to Unity, 1662–1962*. London: S. P. C. K., 1962.

Nuttall, Geoffrey F., Roger Thomas, R. D. Whitehorn, and H. Lismer Short. *The Beginnings of Nonconformity*. London: James Clarke, 1964.

Packer, J. I. *Knowing God*. Downers Grove, Ill.: InterVarsity Press, 1973.

———, ed. *Puritan Papers: Vol. 2, 1960–1962*. Phillipsburg, N.J.: P&R, 2001.

———. *A Quest for Godliness: The Puritan Vision of the Christian Life*. Wheaton, Ill.: Crossway, 1990.

———. "The Redemption and Restoration of Man in the Thought of Richard Baxter: A Study in Puritan Theology." DPhil diss., Oxford University, 1954.

Parker, Nathan Thomas. "Proselytisation and Apocalypticism in the British Atlantic World: The Theology of John Flavel." PhD diss., Durham University, 2013.

Peterson, Robert A. *Our Secure Salvation: Preservation and Apostasy*. Explorations in Biblical Theology. Phillipsburg, N.J.: P&R, 2009.

Potkay, Adam. "Spenser, Donne, and the Theology of Joy." *Studies in English Literature* 46, no. 1 (Winter 2006): 43–66.

Roberts, S. Bryn. *Puritanism and the Pursuit of Happiness: The Ministry and Theology of Ralph Venning*. Suffolk, England: Boydell Press, 2015.

Robertson, O. Palmer. "The Holy Spirit in the Westminster Confession of Faith." In *The Westminster Confession into the 21st Century*, edited by J. Ligon Duncan III, 1:57–99. Fearn, Scotland: Christian Focus, 2003.

Ryken, Leland. *Worldly Saints: The Puritans as They Really Were*. Grand Rapids: Zondervan, 1986.

Ryrie, Alec. *Being Protestant in Reformation Britain*. Oxford: Oxford University Press, 2015.

Schaff, Philip, and David S. Schaff, eds. *The Creeds of Christendom: With a History and Critical Notes*. Vols. 2 and 3. Grand Rapids: Baker Books, 2007.

Schreiner, Thomas R., and Ardel B. Caneday. *The Race Set before Us: A Biblical Theology of Perseverance and Assurance*. Downers Grove, Ill.: InterVarsity Press, 2001.

Schreiner, Thomas R., and Bruce A. Ware, eds. *Still Sovereign: Contemporary Perspectives on Election, Foreknowledge and Grace*. Grand Rapids: Baker Books, 2000.

Schwanda, Tom. *Soul Recreation: The Contemplative-Mystical Piety of Puritanism*. Eugene, Ore.: Pickwick, 2012.

Shaddix, Jim. *The Passion Driven Sermon: Changing the Way Pastors Preach and Congregations Listen*. Nashville: Broadman & Holman, 2003.

Thomas, John, Jr. "An Analysis of the Use of Application in the Preaching of John Flavel." PhD diss., New Orleans Baptist Theological Seminary, 2007.

Van Dixhoorn, Chad B. *Confessing the Faith: A Reader's Guide to the Westminster Confession of Faith*. Edinburgh: Banner of Truth Trust, 2016.

———, ed. *The Minutes and Papers of the Westminster Assembly, 1643–1653*. 5 vols. Oxford: Oxford University Press, 2012.

———. "Reforming the Reformation: Theological Debate at the Westminster Assembly, 1642–1652." PhD diss., University of Cambridge, 2004.

———. "Westminster Assembly." In *Oxford Dictionary of National Biography*. Oxford University Press, 2004.

Vickers, Douglas. Review of *The Works of John Flavel*, by John Flavel. *Westminster Theological Journal* 32 (November 1969–May 1970): 93.

Von Rohr, John R. "Covenant and Assurance in Early English Puritanism." *Church History* 34, no. 2 (June 1965): 195–203.

———. *The Covenant of Grace in Puritan Thought.* Studies in Religion/ American Academy of Religion 45. Atlanta: Scholars Press, 1986.

Wakefield, Gordon F. *Puritan Devotion: Its Place in the Development of Christian Piety.* London: Epworth, 1957.

Wallace, Dewey, Jr. "Flavel (Flavell), John (1627–1691)." In *Puritans and Puritanism in Europe and America: A Comprehensive Encyclopedia,* edited by Francis Bremer and Tom Webster, 98. Santa Barbara, Calif.: ABC-CLIO, 2006.

———. "Puritan Polemical Divinity and Doctrinal Controversy." In *The Cambridge Companion to Puritanism,* edited by John Coffey and Paul Lim, 206–22. Cambridge: Cambridge University Press, 2008.

———. *Puritans and Predestination: Grace in English Protestant Theology, 1525–1695.* Chapel Hill: University of North Carolina Press, 1982.

———. *Shapers of English Calvinism, 1660–1714.* Oxford: Oxford University Press, 2011.

———, ed. *The Spirituality of the Later English Puritans: An Anthology.* Macon, Ga.: Mercer University Press, 1987.

Walsham, Alexandra. *Charitable Hatred: Tolerance and Intolerance in England, 1500–1700.* Manchester, England: Manchester University Press, 2006.

———. *Providence in Early Modern England.* Oxford: Oxford University Press, 1999.

Webber, Richard. "Sanctifying the Inner Life." In *Aspects of Sanctification: The Westminster Conference 1981,* 41–61. Hertfordshire, England: Evangelical Press, 1982.

Whiting, C. E. *Studies in English Puritanism from the Restoration to the Revolution, 1660–1688.* New York: Macmillan, 1931.

Whitney, Donald S. *How Can I Be Sure I'm a Christian? The Satisfying Certainty of Eternal Life.* Colorado Springs: NavPress, 2019.

Williams, Jean Dorothy. "The Puritan Quest for the Enjoyment of God: An Analysis of the Theological and Devotional Writings of Puritans in Seventeenth Century England." PhD diss., University of Melbourne, 1997.

Winship, Michael P. *Hot Protestants: A History of Puritanism in England and America*. New Haven, Conn.: Yale University Press, 2018.

———. *Seers of God: Puritan Providentialism in the Restoration and Early Enlightenment*. Baltimore: Johns Hopkins University Press, 1996.

———. "Weak Christians, Backsliders, and Carnal Gospelers: Assurance of Salvation and the Pastoral Origins of Puritan Practical Divinity in the 1580s." *Church History* 70, no. 3 (2001): 462–81.

Yuille, J. Stephen. "Conversing with God's Word: Scripture Meditation in the Piety of George Swinnock." *Journal of Spiritual Formation & Soul Care* 5, no. 1 (2012): 35–55.

———. *Great Spoil: Thomas Manton's Spirituality of the Word*. Grand Rapids: Reformation Heritage Books, 2019.

———. *The Inner Sanctum of Puritan Piety: John Flavel's Doctrine of Mystical Union with Christ*. Grand Rapids: Reformation Heritage Books, 2007.

———. *Puritan Spirituality: The Fear of God in the Affective Theology of George Swinnock*. Eugene, Ore.: Wipf & Stock, 2008.

———. "A String of Pearls (Psalm 119): The Biblical Piety of Thomas Manton." In *Puritan Piety: Writings in Honor of Joel R. Beeke*, edited by Michael A. G. Haykin and Paul M. Smalley, 215–34. Fearn, Scotland: Christian Focus, 2018.